Certification Manual

LEAN SIX SIGMA YELLOW BELT

Collection: Gestiona
Publishing director: David Soler

Lean Six Sigma Yellow Belt. Certification Manual
1st Edition, 2021

© 2020, Luis Vicente Socconini Pérez Gómez
© of this Edition: ICG Marge, SL

Publisher: Marge Books
València, 558 – 08026 Barcelona
Tel. 931 429 486 – marge@margebooks.com
www.margebooks.com

Managing editor: Adrià Gibernau
Edition coordination: Karina Ahumada Serrano
Make-up editor: Mercedes Lara
Printed by: Safekat, SL (Madrid)

Paper Edition ISBN: 978-84-17903-60-2
Digital Edition ISBN: 978-84-17903-61-9
Legal Deposit: B 16131-2021

The paper used in this books has not been bleached with elemental chlorine (CI_2).

The author

ABOUT LUIS SOCCONINI

He holds a bachelor's degree in Industrial Engineering and a master's degree in Quality and Productivity from Monterrey Tec. He is also a Master Black Belt in Lean Six Sigma and a distinguished professor at several prestigious universities in Mexico.

Luis is certified in Strategic Management by Stanford University, in Leading Product Innovation by Harvard University, and in Industry 4.0 by MIT.

He has worked as a business consultant for the Wharton Business School in Pennsylvania, as a process engineer for Grolsch Brewery in the Netherlands, and as a manufacturing engineer at IBM.

As director of Lean Six Sigma Institute, Luis develops high-impact projects for companies such as Abbott Laboratories, Kraft Heinz, Coca-Cola, BMW, Bimbo, and Fender – to name a few. He has a broad base of experience and is continually developing productivity applications in diverse industries such as construction, mining, agriculture, government, energy, service, and more.

Luis is the author of **Lean Six Sigma Green Belt, Certification Manual, Lean Company, Lean Manufacturing, The Process of the 5's in Action,** as well as co-author of **Lean Six Sigma Management System** and **Lean Energy 4.0.**

SOCCONINI
www.socconini.com

Index

Introduction to Lean Six Sigma

- Canvas
- Lean Strategy: Hoshin Kanri
- Value Stream Structure
- Talent Development

Introduction to White Belt

- Problem Solving
- 5S Housekeeping
- Andon
- Standard Work Instructions

Introduction to Yellow Belt

Define

- 4-Quadrant Analysis
- Project Definition: A3

Measure and Map

- Data Collection
- Overall Equipment Effectiveness (OEE)
- Current State Value Stream Map (VSM)

Analyze

- Spaghetti Diagram
- Balance Chart
- Waste Analysis
- Failure Mode & Effects Analysis (FMEA)

Improve

- Kaizen
  - Continuous Flow
  - Quick Preparations (SMED)
  - Total Productive Maintenance (TPM)
  - Kanban
- Future Value Stream Map (VSM)

Control

- Standardized Work
- Poka Yoke
- Kata

Preface

Dear Reader,

I warmly welcome you on this journey to obtain the **Lean Six Sigma Yellow Belt Certification** and I wish to congratulate you because having this certification manual in your hands means that you seek to contribute to social development through the improvement of people, processes, and organizations – which ultimately leads to the well-being of our communities.

This certification manual is born from the need to share what we at Lean Six Sigma Institute (LSSI) teach people who participate in organizational processes – including managers, business owners, government officials, engineers, operators, and students. All of them receive training to transform today's key processes and design the organizations of the future.

At first, this manual was part of the material delivered to LSSI course participants across the world. Until one day, our regional Director in Spain suggested that our manuals could also be distributed in bookstores – allowing anyone to access the knowledge that is revolutionizing business thinking and the way organizations work today. We know that as long as people are trained and – above all – committed to a new spectrum of design and improvement possibilities, organizations will grow stronger as they face the new challenges posed by the ever-changing world we live in.

In this manual you will find a particularly useful toolbox that will help you successfully develop and continuously improve organizational activities. This toolbox is the result of decades of best practices proven to help organizations maximize value and achieve their goals.

You will find management tools that leaders must understand and implement in order to plan and execute strategies, analyze results, design organizational structures, nourish new talent, and develop a new financial thinking that accurately reflects real costs.

You will also find fundamental basic tools that every member of any organization must put into practice in order to establish a continuous improvement culture and system.

And finally, you will find tools and material to help you polish your processes and implement continuous improvements aimed at creating positive, significant impacts on results – including quality, cost, delivery cycle time, safety, and productivity.

The work philosophy, tools, and methodologies explained in this manual will allow you to easily understand how the organizations of the future should be run – and will therefore enable you to become an agent of change and to produce positive, impactful results.

The goal of this certification manual is to help you understand and implement simple yet practical tools that you can also teach your colleagues and use to develop new ways of working – thus continuously adapting to complex, changing business environments.

In this world, improvement is optional – but progress is up to you. I appreciate your trust and confidence in giving us the opportunity to provide you with high-quality, widely tested material and I thank you for granting us the responsibility to guide you on this continuous improvement journey that starts but never finishes.

Luis Socconini
Founder and Director of Lean Six Sigma Institute

Introduction to Lean Six Sigma

When the winds of change blow, some people build walls and others build windmills. Chinese Proverb

Learning objectives

1. Understand the fundamentals of Lean and Six Sigma.
2. Understand the importance of improving productivity by eliminating waste and variability.
3. Learn how to successfully implement and manage Lean Six Sigma philosophy, tools, and methodologies.
4. Develop a leadership mindset and become a change agent in establishing the structure needed to achieve impactful results.

Content

> Background
> Business Development Model
> What is Lean & Six Sigma?
> Benefits
> Implementation Process
> Change Management
> Structure and Roles
> Leadership

Background

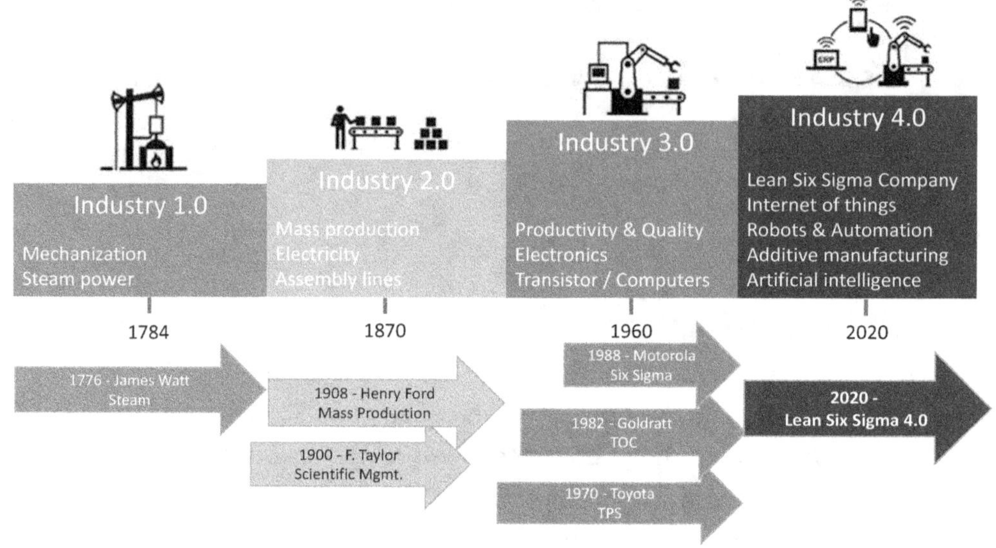

- Many companies continue to encounter:
  - Slow delivery of products or services
  - Constant customer complaints
  - Inconsistent quality
  - Poor customer service
  - High costs and prices
  - Poor internal communication

These companies are destined to vanish!

"It's not the big that eat the small...it's the fast that eat the slow."
Jason Jennins

Industry 4.0 elements

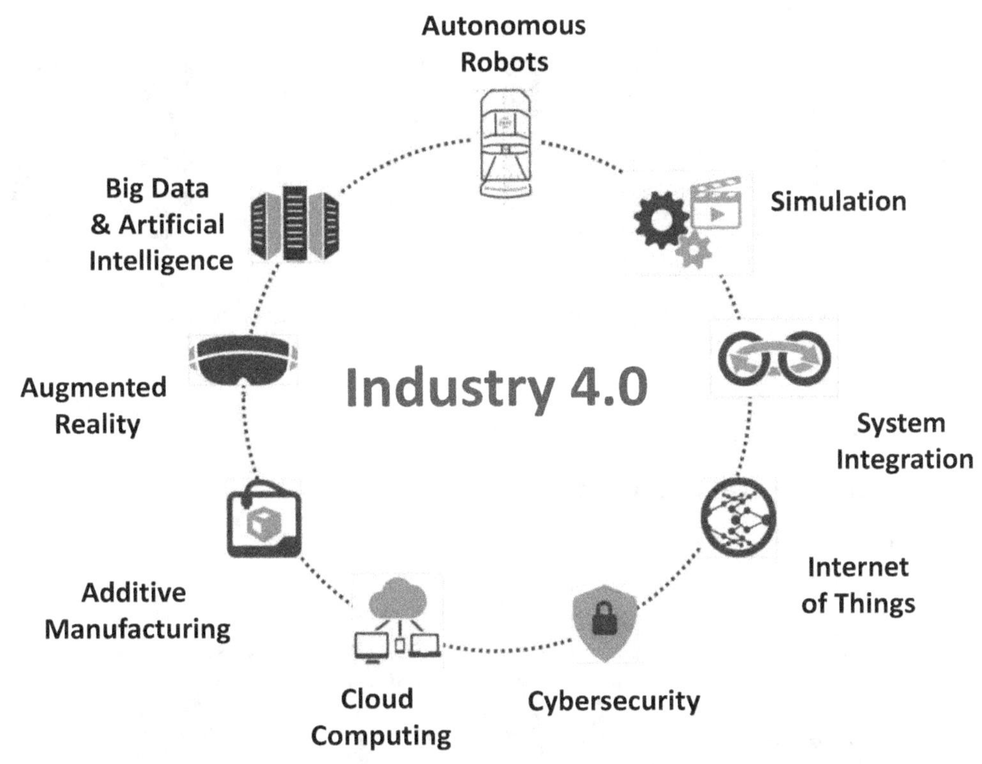

Which model represents your business?

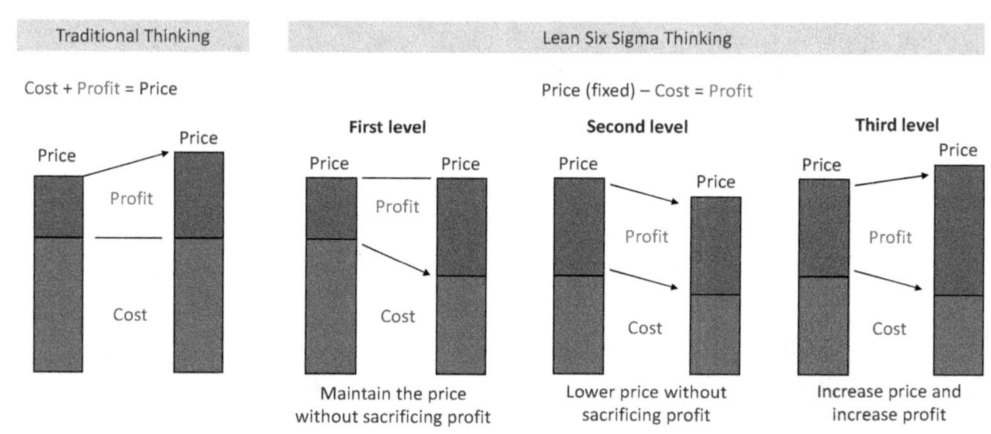

The key to increasing profits: *reduced costs & increased revenues*

Productivity and its limitations

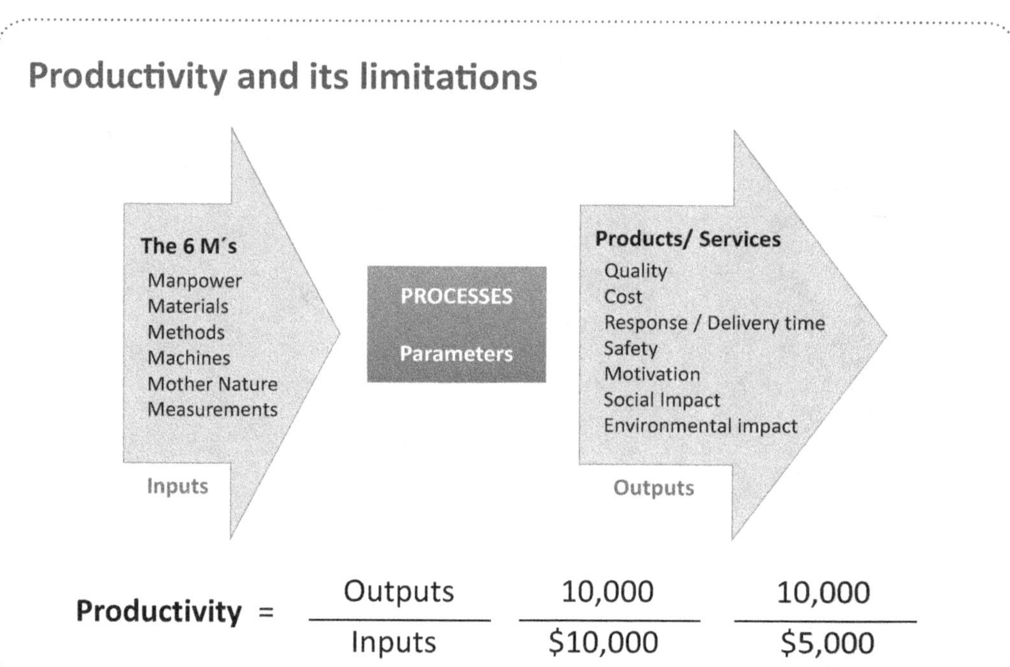

$$\text{Productivity} = \frac{\text{Outputs}}{\text{Inputs}} \qquad \frac{10{,}000}{\$10{,}000} \qquad \frac{10{,}000}{\$5{,}000}$$

Methods to increase productivity

How can we increase productivity?

- Quantitative approach
  - More people
  - More machines
  - Larger investment
- Qualitative approach
  - Work harder
  - Eliminate waste & simplify

Lean Six Sigma Approach

Let's work smart!

Limitations to Productivity

Muri Overburden	*Mura* Variability	*Muda* Waste
• Overbearing Tasks • Work related stress • High-Risk Tasks	**Total Variability** • The variation that results from all process inputs	• Overproduction • Excess inventory • Defects and Rework • Unnecessary movements • Overprocessing • Waiting and Searching • Transport • Waste of energy • Non-utilized talent • Contamination / Pollution

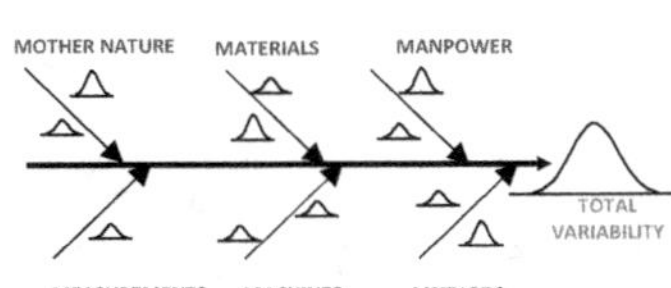

Lean Six Sigma reduces non-value adding time

Eliminate overload, variation, and waste

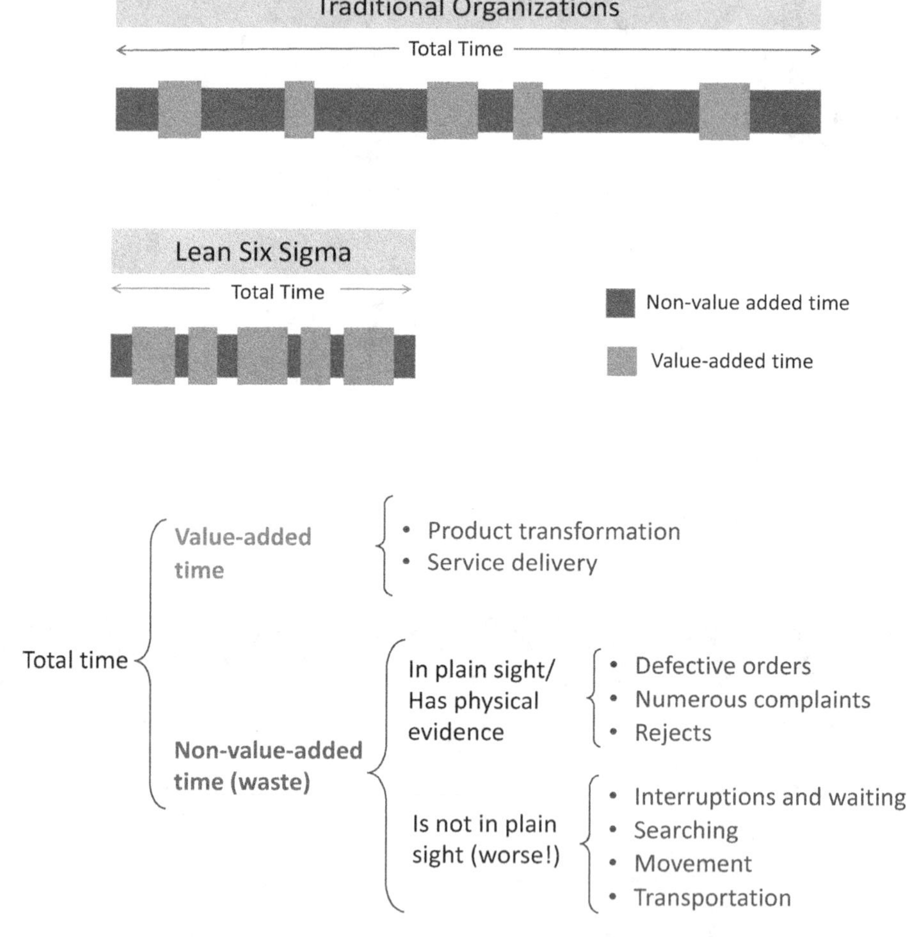

Reduce: Time, Costs, Defects, Inventory, Space, Waste.

Increase: Productivity, Customer Satisfaction, Quality, Cash Flow.

Business Development Model

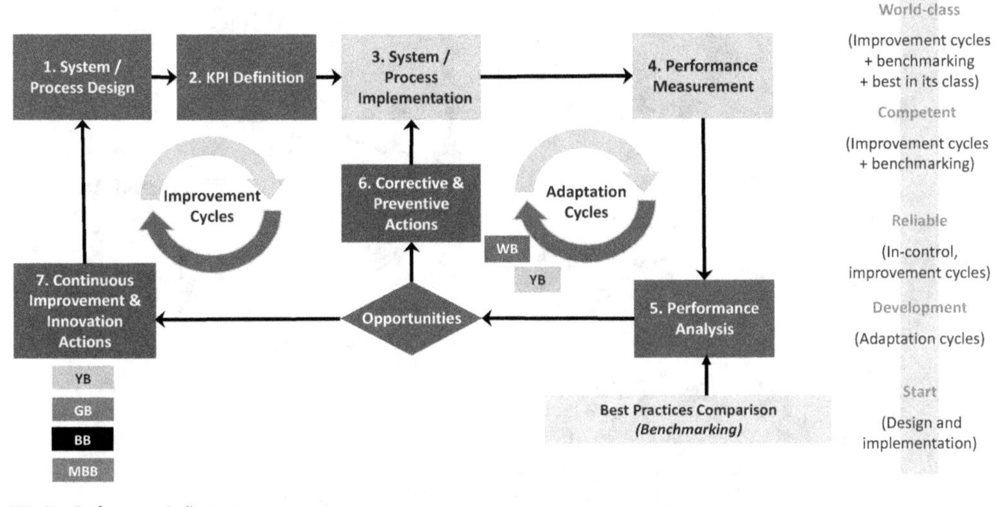

KPI - Key Performance Indicators

What is Lean & Six Sigma?

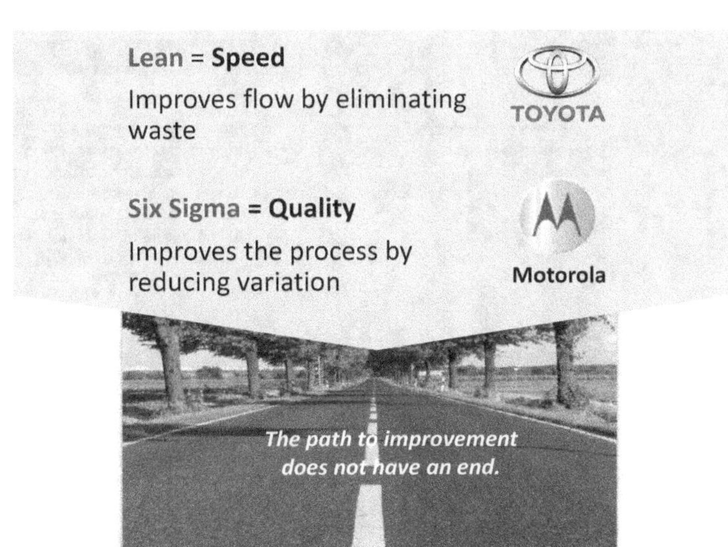

Lean Six Sigma Model

Goals:
Delight Customers, Sustain Profitability,
Company, Employee, and Societal Benefits

Speed

- Continuous Flow
- TPM
- Theory of Constraints
- Quick Preparations (SMED)
- Pull System

Motivated Team

Focus on the Constraint (TOC)

Quality

- Visual Management *(Andon)*
- Jidhoka
- Error-Proofing *(Poka- Yoke)*
- 6 Sigma
- FMEA
- Problem Solving

Stability: 5S Housekeeping, Visual Management, Standardization, etc.

Leadership: Strategy, Structure, Talent Development, VSM, etc.

Benefits

Hard Savings

- Reduce Cost
- Increase profit
- Increase demand
- Reduce inventory
- Timely response and delivery
- Increase productivity
- Improve cash flow
- Improve quality
- Reduce defects and rework
- Improve space utilization

Soft Savings

- Improve communication
- Improve customer satisfaction
- Improve customer and employee satisfaction
- Reduce employee turnover
- Improve safety / Reduce risks
- Build a culture of continuous improvement
- Improve decision making

**Lean Six Sigma =
Breakthrough Results**

LSSI
LEAN SIX SIGMA INSTITUTE

Lean Six Sigma is applied throughout the company

LEAN SIX SIGMA COMPANY

Upper Management	Human Resources	Research & Development	Sales & Marketing	Accounting & Finance	Procurement	Service	Manufacturing	Maintenance	Logistics	Quality	IT

Strategic Tools

All areas use management tools to define, execute and follow up on strategies.

Tactical Tools

All areas use basic tools to support identification, development and sustainment of improvements.

Upper Management	Human Resources	Research & Development	Sales & Marketing	Accounting & Finance	Procurement	Service	Manufacturing	Maintenance	Logistics	Quality	IT
Planning	Talent Attraction	Product Development	Mktg. Campaigns	Budget	Supplier Development	Lean Service	Lean Manufacturing	Autonomous	Incoming	Quality Deployment	Hardware
Strategic Mgmt.	Talent Development	Lean Startup	Surveys	Cost Acct.	Purchasing			Preventive	Warehouse	Quality System	Software
				Inventory				Predictive	Routing	Calibration	Communication
Decision Making		Design for Six Sigma	Pricing	Payroll	Warehouse			Energy	Loading		Help Desk
			Lean Retail	Invoicing					Transportation		
				Credit							
				Acct. Payable							
				Financial Statements							

STRATEGIC TOOLS

- Hoshin Kanri
- Value Stream Structure
- Value Stream Map
- Talent Development
- Agile Project Management
- Standard Work for Leaders
- Kata
- Gemba Walks

BASIC TOOLS

- 5S Housekeeping
- Visual Management (Andon)
- Standardize Work
- Personal (Self) Management

LEAN | **SIX SIGMA**

DMAIC

Tool Set

Lean Six Sigma applies to any industry

- Food & Beverage
- Electronics
- Services
- Automotive
- Government
- Agriculture
- Mining
- Packaging
- Airports
- Military

- Pharmaceutical
- Banking
- Insurance
- Hotels
- Restaurants
- Construction

- Healthcare
- Plastics
- Lubricants
- Logistics & Customs
- Education
- Cosmetics
- Footwear
- Textile
- Printing
- Foundry

LEAN MANAGEMENT	WHITE BELT	YELLOW BELT	GREEN BELT	BLACK BELT	MASTER BLACK BELT

Traditional vs. Lean Six Sigma

Traditional

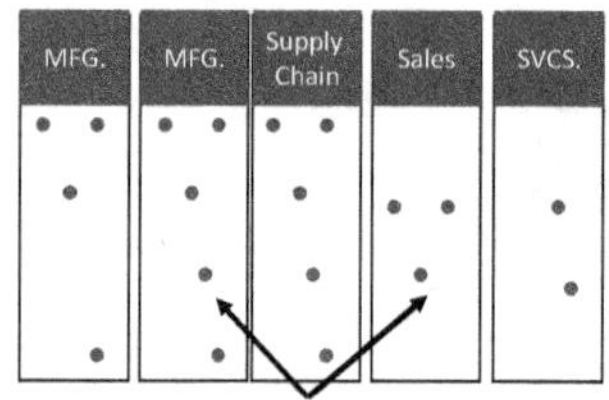

Isolated Projects by departments

Lean Six Sigma

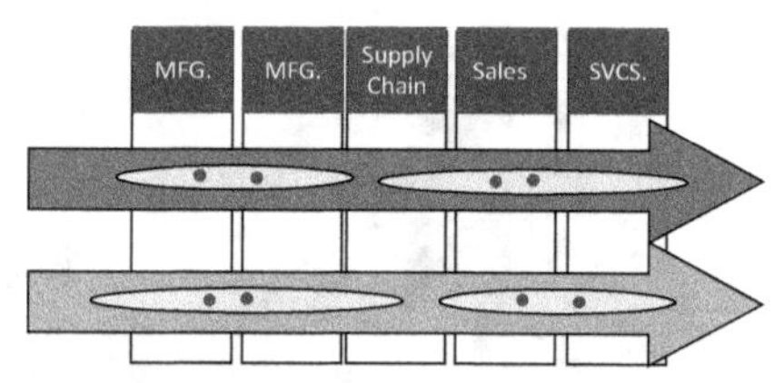

A few high-impact projects in the value stream or service family

*"If I could change the way we implemented it,
I would have started with Lean and then Six Sigma."*

Jack Welch, Ex-CEO GE

Benefits

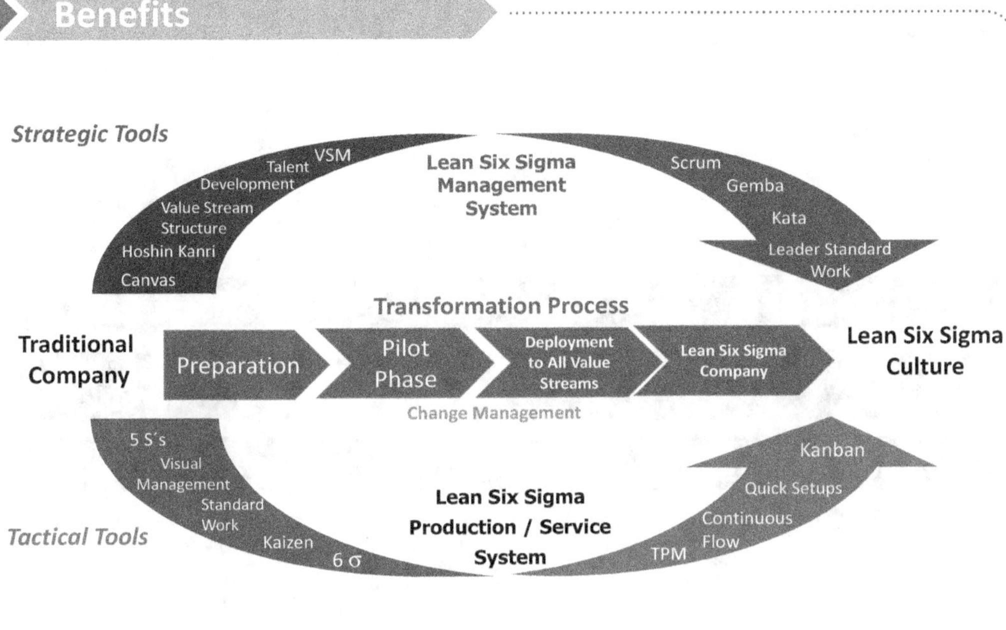

Implementation Process

1 -3 months	4 - 6 months	1 – 2 years	1 – 2 years and onward
Preparation	**Pilot**	**Deployment to All Value Streams**	**Lean Six Sigma Company**

Preparation

- Initial assessment
- Initial training
- Develop Hoshin Kanri
- Define team leader
- Define value stream / service family map
- Select pilot project
- Design initial plan
- Communicate plan
- Kick off

Pilot

Basic Tools
- 5 S Housekeeping, Visual Mgmt., Standard Work, etc.

Improvement and Problem-Solving Tools
- A3, FMEA, Continuous Flow, TPM, SMED, Kanban, Statistics, etc.

Certify
- White and Yellow Belts
- Pilot Process

Deployment to All Value Streams

- Design Value Stream
- Implement VS Office

Deploy to all processes
- Accounting
- Human Resources
- Sales & Marketing
- Logistics
- Service / Production
- IT
- Quality
- Maintenance

Certify
- Yellow, Green & Black Belts
- Value Stream

Lean Six Sigma Company

Certify
- Processes
- Value Streams
- Company / Organization

Change Management - John Kotter

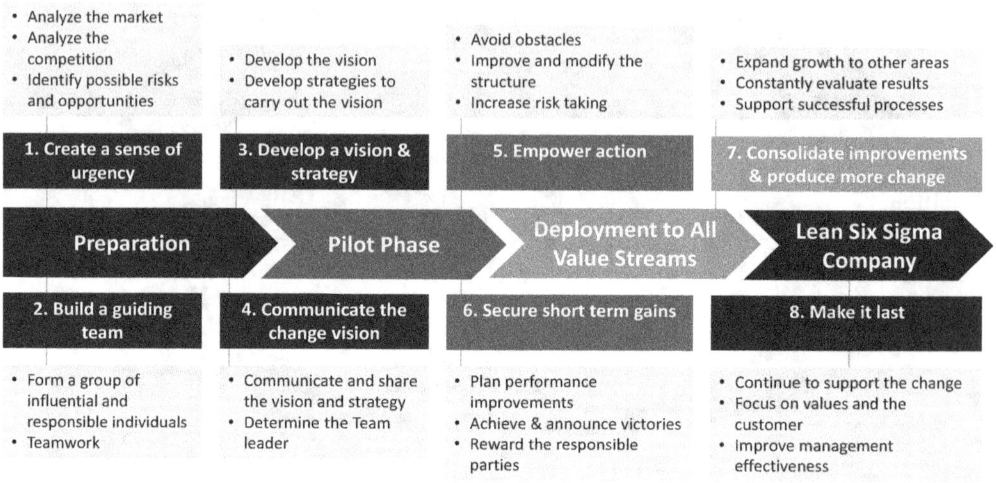

- Analyze the market
- Analyze the competition
- Identify possible risks and opportunities

- Develop the vision
- Develop strategies to carry out the vision

- Avoid obstacles
- Improve and modify the structure
- Increase risk taking

- Expand growth to other areas
- Constantly evaluate results
- Support successful processes

1. Create a sense of urgency

3. Develop a vision & strategy

5. Empower action

7. Consolidate improvements & produce more change

Preparation → **Pilot Phase** → **Deployment to All Value Streams** → **Lean Six Sigma Company**

2. Build a guiding team

4. Communicate the change vision

6. Secure short term gains

8. Make it last

- Form a group of influential and responsible individuals
- Teamwork

- Communicate and share the vision and strategy
- Determine the Team leader

- Plan performance improvements
- Achieve & announce victories
- Reward the responsible parties

- Continue to support the change
- Focus on values and the customer
- Improve management effectiveness

Resistance to change

It has been proven that when facing projects:

20 % +

- 20% of people tend to have a positive attitude towards change.

60 % Neutral

- 60% of people tend to be neutral.

20 % -

- 20% of people tend to have a negative attitude towards change.

If there is **good leadership**, many who are neutral or negative will become positive. Otherwise, the project may not evolve.

Why some companies can and others don't?

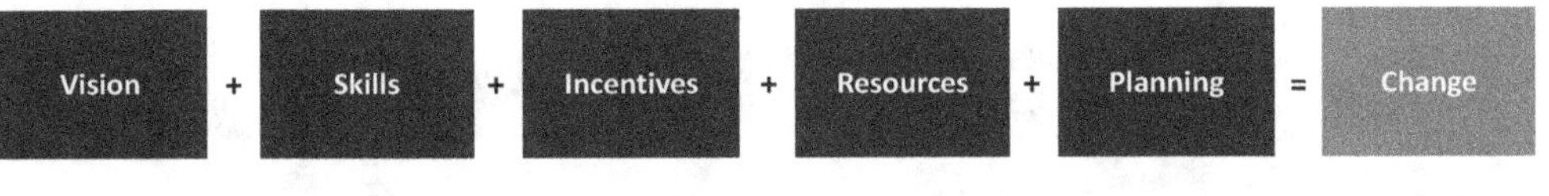

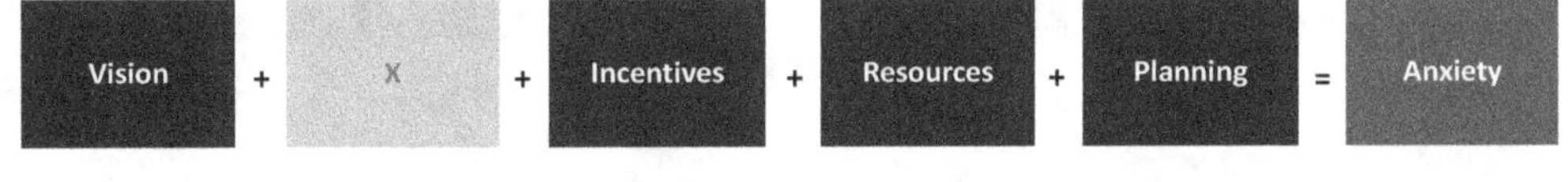

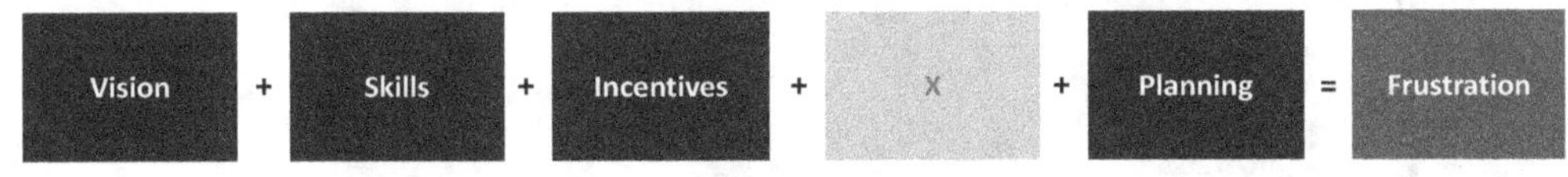

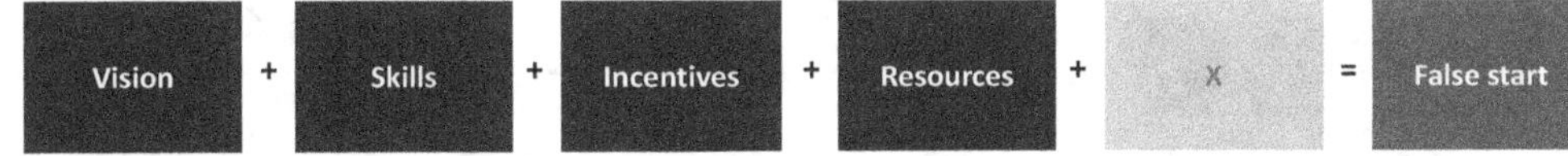

Structure and Roles

Lean Six Sigma certifications

There are four certification categories:

1. People Certification	2. Process Certification	3. Value Stream Certification	4. Company Certification
• Training and certification as: – White Belt – Yellow Belt – Green Belt – Black Belt – Master Black Belt	• Evaluate if the processes meet the requirements. • Make sure that the methods are supported and the tools work.	• All value stream processes have achieved a certain level of progress and people are exercising the correct habits.	• The company has a Lean / agile management culture and a leadership team that makes decisions based on facts and data.
2 Projects per year	2 Evaluations per year	2-4 Evaluations per year	2 Evaluations per year

Certification levels

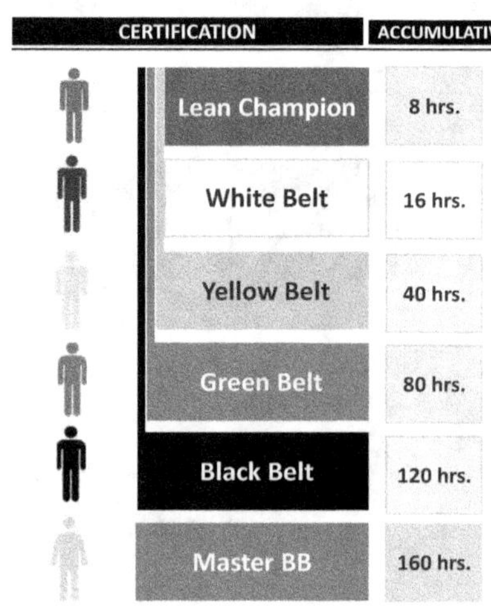

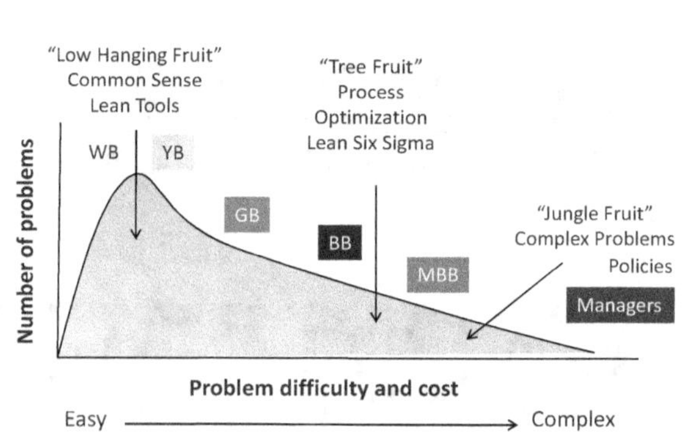

Roles

CHAMPION **LSS Management**	**WHITE BELT**	**YELLOW BELT**	**GREEN BELT**	**BLACK BELT**	**MASTER BLACK BELT**
Responsible for budget and resources	Project Team Member	Lean Practitioner	Small Project Leader who provides specific support	Project Leader & Coach	Experienced Implementation Expert and BB coach
Lean Six Sigma Project Sponsor	Practices the basic tools every day as part of his/her work	Ensures philosophy is sustained on a daily basis	Ensures sustainability in his / her area of responsibility	Ensures correct implementation for the value stream	Expert in practicing Lean Six Sigma throughout the company and supply chain
Leaders	100 %	20 % - 50 %	10 % - 20 %	1 % - 3 %	1 %

Structure

			Staff	Experts	Selected People
Corporate Office Region Country	**Executive Staff** 		 Corporate Champion	 Master BB  Black Belt	 Improvement Teams
Family of Products or Services	**Value Stream Teams** 	**Support Teams** 	 Value Stream Champion	 Black Belt Green Belt	 Improvement Teams
Productive Teams	**Products / Services** 	**Transactions** 	 Project Champion	 Green Belt  Yellow Belt	 Improvement Teams

> Leadership

Lean Six Sigma requires Leaders

Boss

- Manages employees
- Depends on authority
- Inspires fear
- Says, "I"
- Places blame for breakdowns
- Knows how it is done
- Uses people
- Takes credit
- Commands
- Says, "Go"

Leader

- Coaches employees
- Has goodwill
- Generates enthusiasm
- Says, "We"
- Fixes the breakdowns
- Shows how it is done
- Develops people's talent
- Gives credit
- Asks
- Says, "Let's go"

Conclusion

"No organization, large or small, local or global, is immune to change."

"To address new technological, competitive, and demographic forces, leaders from all sectors are trying to fundamentally alter the way their organizations do business."

John P. Kotter

LSSI
LEAN SIX SIGMA INSTITUTE

Canvas

Learning objectives

1. Understand the importance of business models in developing new ideas and in contributing new ways to develop business strategy.
2. Understand the elements that form part of it.
3. Identify opportunities for implementation.
4. Understand how it is developed.

Content

> Background
> What is Canvas?
> Who uses Canvas?
> Elements
> Examples
> Procedure
> Exercise

Background

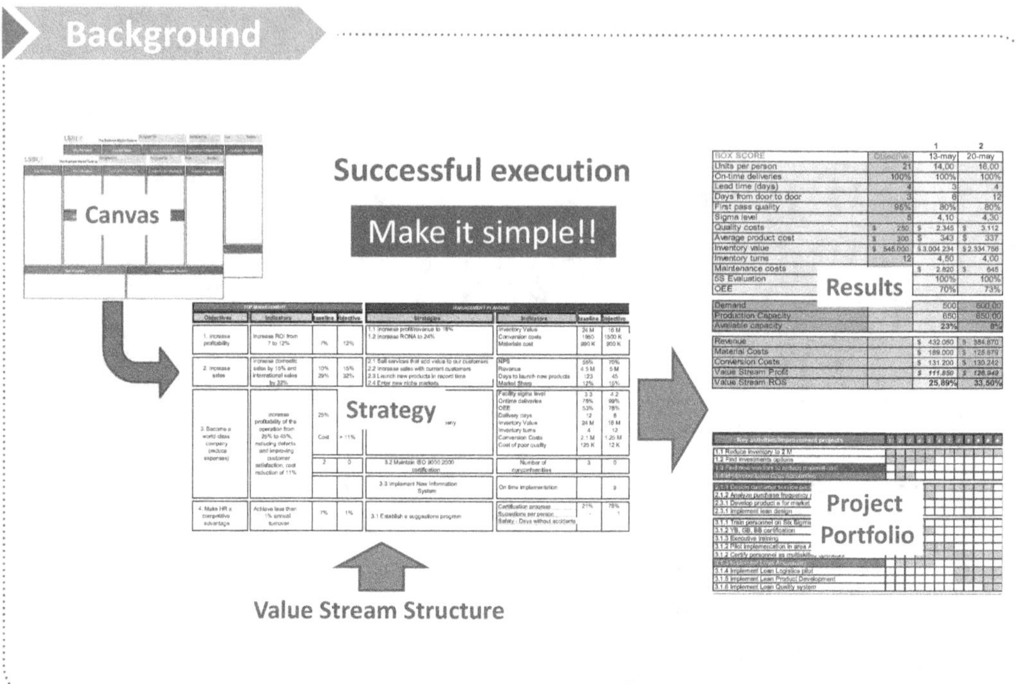

Origin

Alex Osterwalder

The Business Model Ontology – A Proposition in a Design Science Approach

January 2004

PhD Thesis, University of Lausanne, Switzerland

Is Canvas for you?

- Do you have an entrepreneurial spirit?
- Are you constantly thinking about how to create value and develop new business?
- Are you constantly thinking about how to improve or transform your organization?
- Are you looking for innovative ways to do business to replace old or obsolete ones?

Not everyone has a clear understanding of what a business model is.

Strategic conversations about business models are unproductive.

Typical conversation when there is no common language:

- Director: The world is changing ... we urgently need to reinvent our business model.
- Person 1: We should focus on services.
- Person 2: The numbers indicate that we should grow in emerging markets.
- Person 3: But, what about the new technology that we have been looking for?
- Director: In fact, I know the right person to acquire that technology.

3 hours later.....

- Person 2: bla bla bla bla.
- Person 4: bla bla bla bla.
- Person 1: bla bla bla bla.
- Person 3: bla bla bla bla.

What is Canvas?

It is a visual and practical business tool to describe, **test**, **implement**, and **manage** business models during their life cycle.

Who uses Canvas?

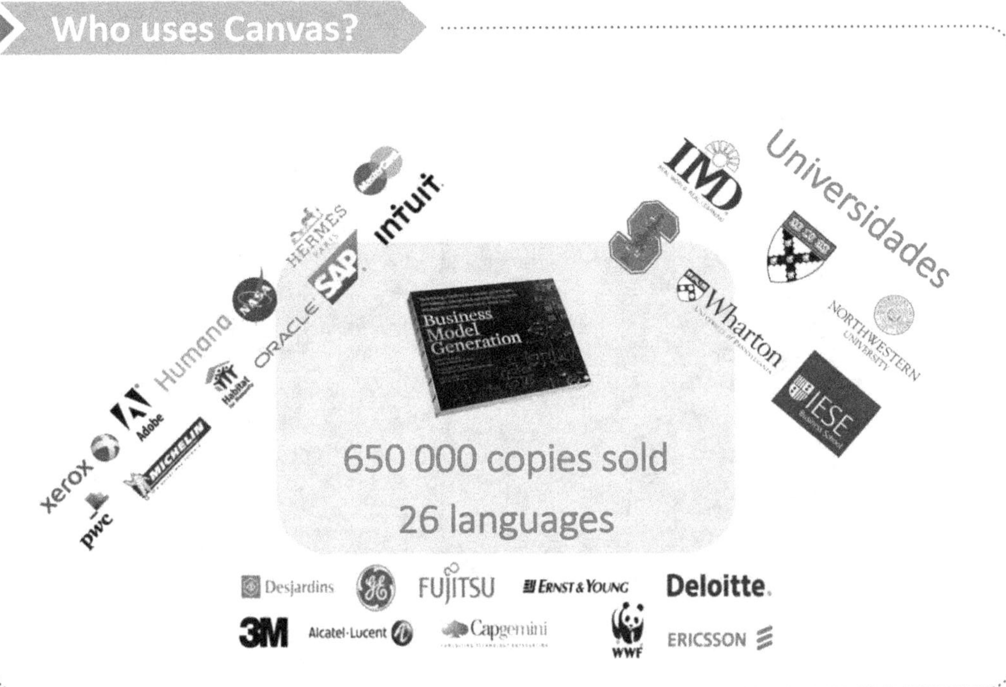

What types of professionals use Business Model Canvas?

- **Directors, Executives and Managers:** Manage business and organizations

- **Entrepreneurs:** Develop new business and organizations

- **Employees:** Sustain and improve business models

- **Consultants:** Help their clients

- **Designers:** Create high value products

- **Investors:** Evaluate business opportunities

Elements

Your business model on one page

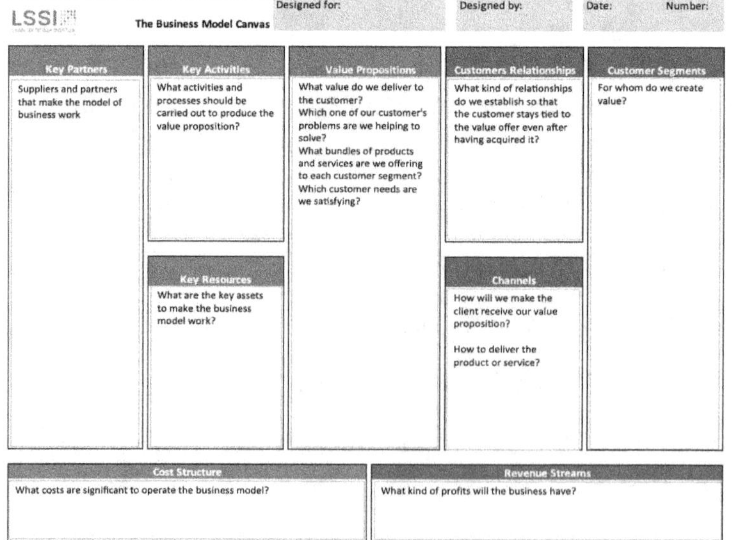

Business Model Canvas Template

Key Partners	Key Activities	Value Propositions	Customers Relationships	Customer Segments
Suppliers and partners that make the model of business work	What activities and processes should be carried out to produce the value proposition?	What value do we deliver to the customer? Which one of our customer's problems are we helping to solve? What bundles of products and services are we offering to each customer segment? Which customer needs are we satisfying?	What kind of relationships do we establish so that the customer stays tied to the value offer even after having acquired it?	For whom do we create value?

The Business Model Canvas — LSSI — Designed for: — Designed by: — Date: — Number:

Key Resources: What are the key assets to make the business model work?

Channels: How will we make the client receive our value proposition? How to deliver the product or service?

Cost Structure: What costs are significant to operate the business model?

Revenue Streams: What kind of profits will the business have?

Canvas is designed like the human brain

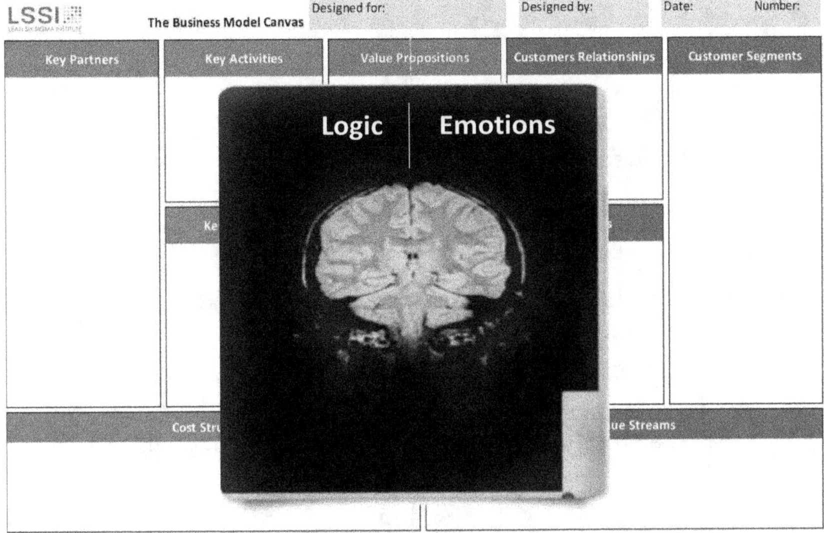

Another way to see it

Backstage	Frontstage

Why use Canvas?

- The best ideas are put on the table

- Create a common and shared language

- Improve teamwork with better conversations about strategies

- Promotes collaboration between areas

- Creates a structured and practical approach that helps to implement ideas for improvement

Google was founded in 1998

Revenue 2017 = $109.65 Billions US Dollars

- Larry Page and Sergey Brin
- They created the Google search engine
- It is free!
- So, how to make money from a free service?

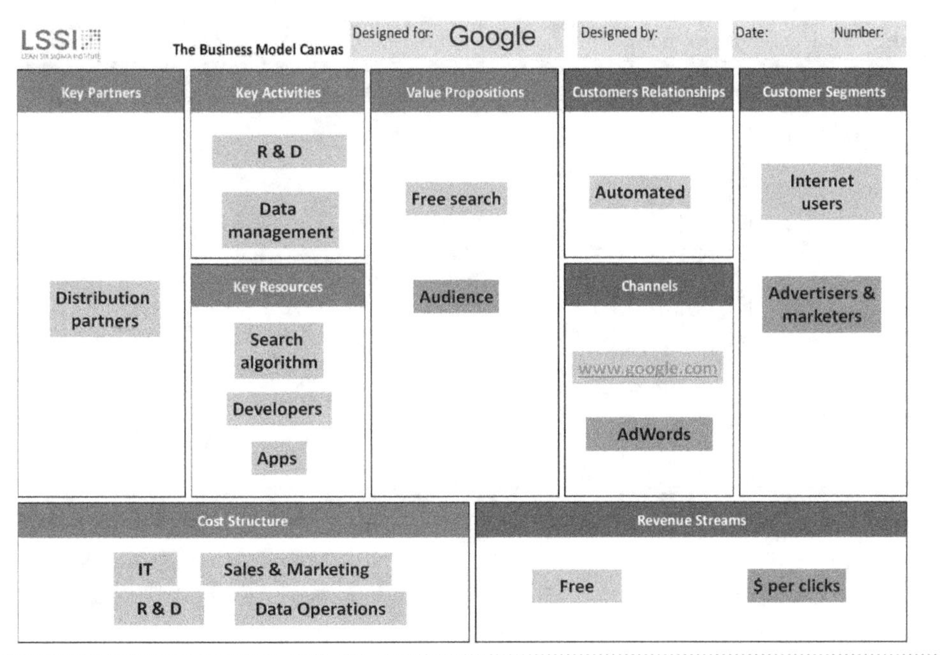

Xerox 1958

- They invented a machine that could photocopy 2000 copies a day when the competition could do 30 to 40 copies a day.
- The machine was 7 times more expensive.
- They did a market study and they found that no customer would buy such an expensive machine.

Great product! Wrong business model

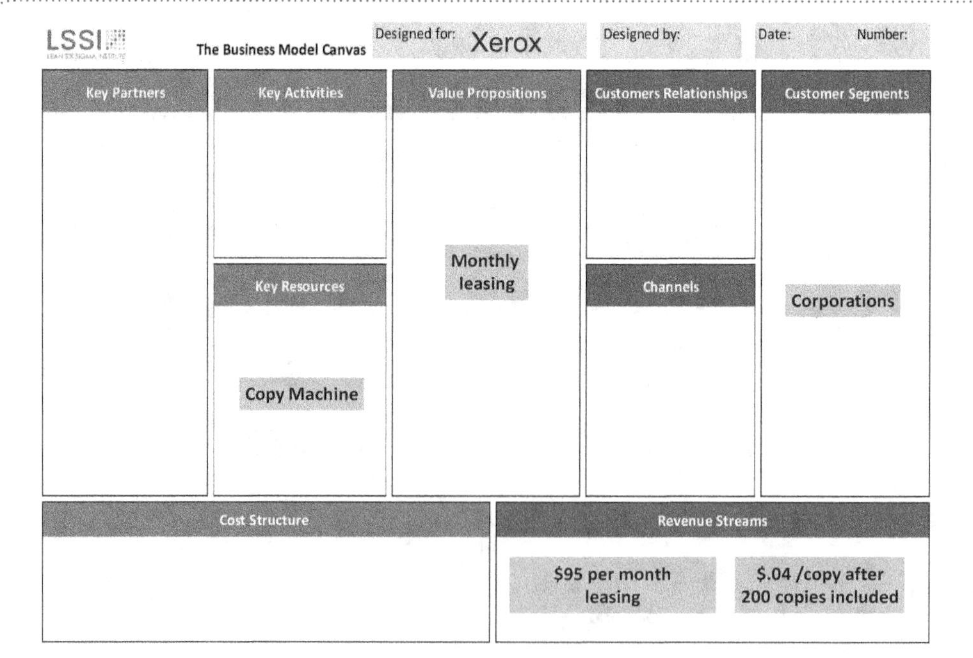

How is it develop?

- Choose a business product / service

- Teams of 5 people

- **Structure of the Canvas:**

1. Introduction to the methodology
2. Current Canvas
3. Research environment around the current canvas:
   - Market trends
   - Technology trends
   - Needs Trends
   - Strengths and weaknesses
4. Generate future canvas prototypes
5. Feedback
6. Define Canvas future and following

Implementation phases

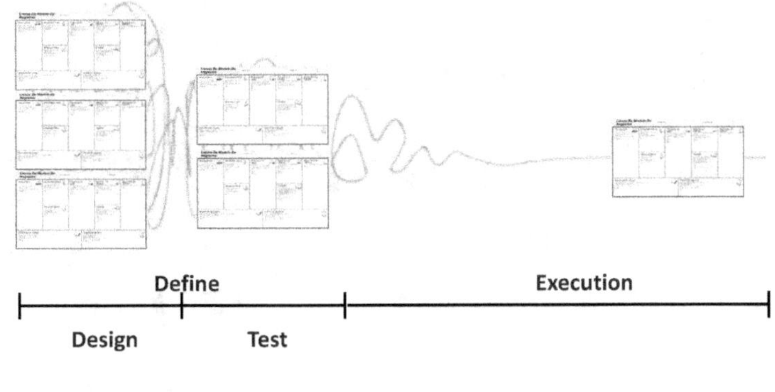

Define

Execution

Design

Test

Note

- Several business models can be generated for each line of business.
- To make it effective, only those that can be executed must be chosen. Generally, great enthusiasm is generated in the creation of the model.
- Make sure you keep that enthusiasm in the execution.

- Develop the Nespresso business model with the elements shown on the next slide.

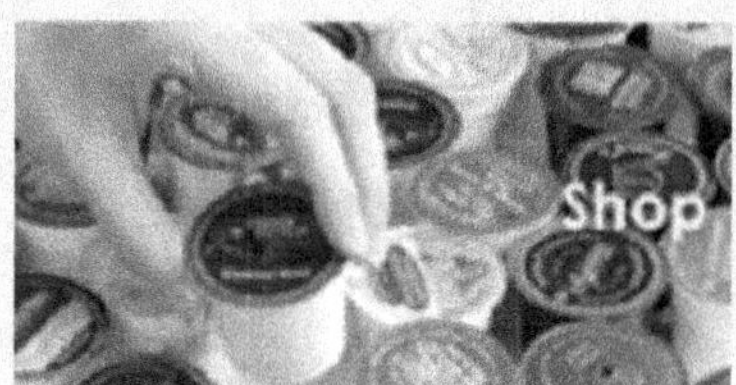

LSSI
LEAN SIX SIGMA INSTITUTE

The Business Model Canvas

Designed for: **Nespresso** Designed by: Date: Number:

Key Partners	Key Activities	Value Propositions	Customers Relationships	Customer Segments
	Key Resources		**Channels**	

Cost Structure	Revenue Streams

Lean Strategy:
Hoshin Kanri

Learning objectives

1. Understand the key elements of Strategic Planning.
2. Understand the Hoshin Kanri implementation process.
3. Start the Hoshin Kanri planning process in a company.

Content

> Background
> What is Hoshin Kanri?
> Benefits
> When is it used and how long does it take?
> Procedure
> Example

Background

- Only between 10% and 20% of companies in the world create a strategic plan.

- Only between 10% and 20% execute the plan successfully.

- 91% of executives qualify as "exceptional decision-makers".

Source: Harvard Business School.

Symptoms of companies in need of Hoshin Kanri planning

- No connection between strategy and continuous improvement

- Too many projects in process

- The plans from one year to the next never seem to connect

What is strategy?

Strategy

Strato = A group of people
E.g. Army

Agein = Guide
E.g. Direct

"Art of conducting military operations."

Strategy deployment

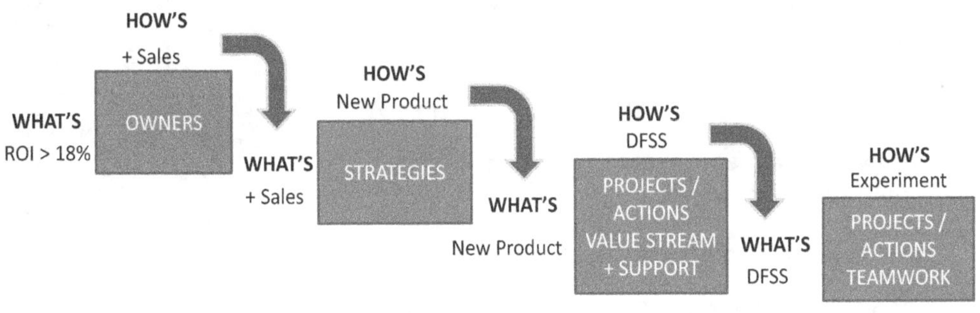

DFSS (Design for Six Sigma)

Example of strategy deployment

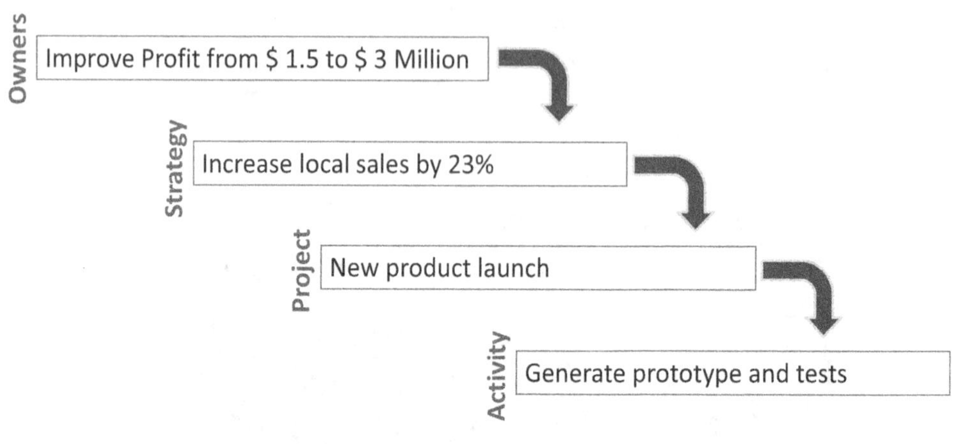

What is Hoshin Kanri?

Hoshin is a management tool to address 4 fundamental questions:

- **What is it about?** - vision and key results areas.

- **How will we measure our performance?** - key metrics and objectives.

- **What are we going to do?** - strategies, action plans.

- **How will we behave?** - core values.

Meaning of hoshin kanri

Hoshin kanri

ho = Direction

shin = Needle

hoshin = Direction of needle or compass

方針

kan = Control

ri = Reason or logic

kanri = Administration control

管理

Hoshin kanri means management and control of an organization's direction or focus.

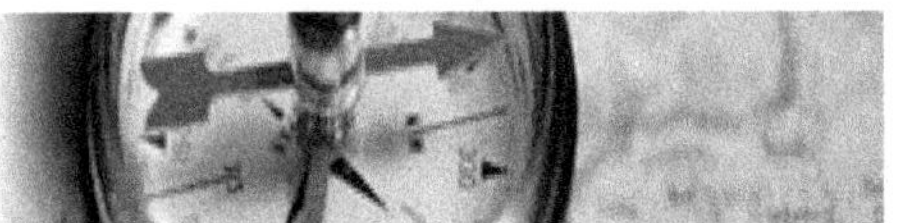

Hoshin Kanri model

Year: 2019-2022   Company Name:

Philosophy

Vision: Achieve the best market value by offering the best quality at the lowest

Mission: To develop, produce, and distribute high-quality products and services.

Values: Customer Commitment, Quality, Respect for people, Integrity, Teamwork.

Strategic Plan: HOSHIN KANRI

Date Prepared: Date Revised:

LSSI
LEAN SIX SIGMA INSTITUTE

1. Guidelines (What's)

4. Indicators (How much)

2: Strategies (How's)

4. Indicators (How much)

3. Projects (How's of strategies)

5. Resources (Who)

Other terms used for Hoshin Kanri

- Hoshin Planning (Hewlett-Packard)

- Policy Deployment (AT&T, Infineon Technologies)

- Policy Management (Texas Instruments)

- Management by Results (Xerox)

- Priority Management

- Goals Deployment

- "Catch-ball" Process

Benefits

- **Focuses** the whole company on a few **vital goals**, instead of the many trivial ones.

- Creates **alignment** towards objectives through the **participation** of the entire management team in the planning process.

- **Leadership** at **all** levels.

- **Communicates** key goals to all managers and staff.

- **Integrates and encourages** inter-functional cooperation to achieve significant progress. A review process that holds participants accountable for achieving their part of the plan.

When is it used and how much time does it require?

- **Start of operations:** fundamental plan (Hoshin Kanri and Box score).
  - Realization time: **1 week**
- **Annually:** update of the fundamental plan (Hoshin Kanri).
  - Realization time: **2-4 days**
- **Monthly:** evaluation of global progress (balanced scorecard).
  - Realization time: **1 hour**
- **Weekly:** evaluation of value streams (box score).
  - Realization time: **30 minutes**
- **Daily:** evaluation of progress per hour (process board).
  - Realization time: **5 minutes**

Procedure

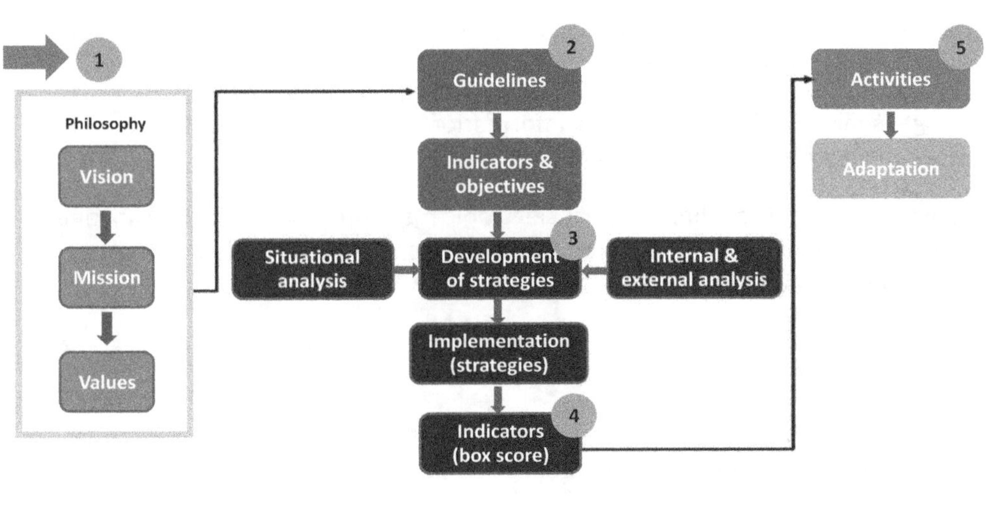

1. Establish the philosophy of the company

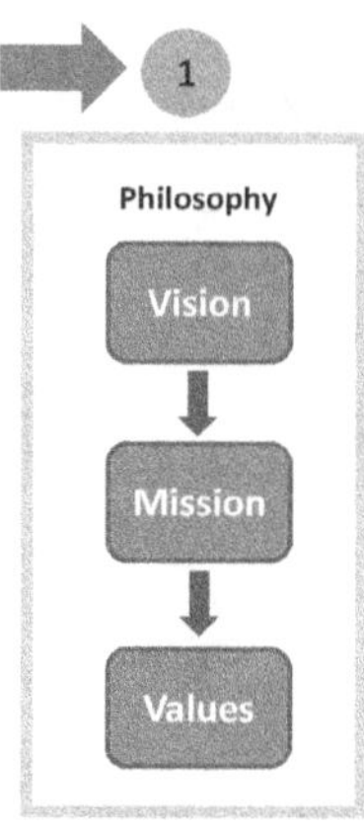

VISION
What do we want to be?

MISSION
What is our business?
Why do we exist?

VALUES
What do we believe in and how do we behave?

Examples of vision / mission

Disney's mission: "We create happiness by providing the finest entertainment for people of all ages, anywhere."

Google's mission: "Organize world information so that it is universally accessible and useful."

eBay's mission: "Providing a global electronic market in which virtually anyone can trade with almost any product, thus creating economic opportunities throughout the world."

Apple's vision: "We believe that we are on the face of the earth to make great products and that's not changing ."

Nike's vision: "Bring inspiration and innovation to every athlete in the world. If you have a body, you are an athlete."

Example of philosophy

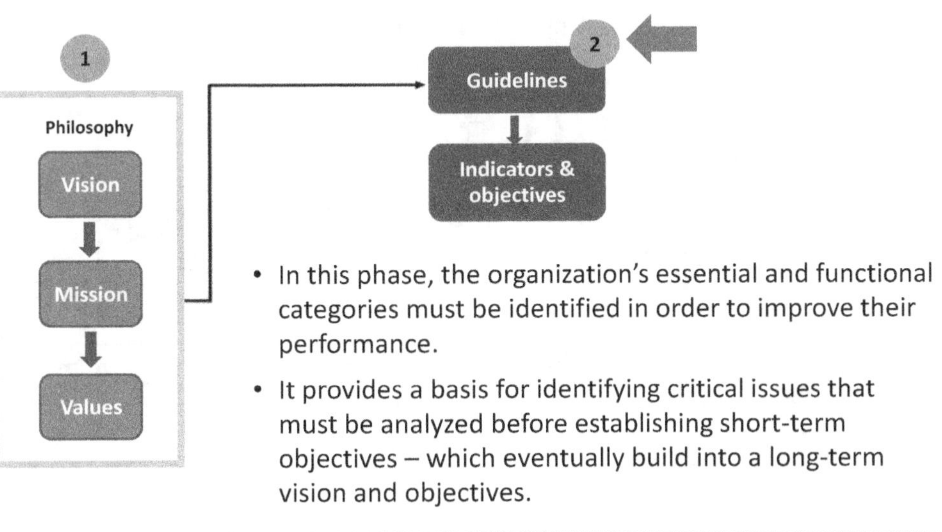

2. Establish objectives (what's)

- In this phase, the organization's essential and functional categories must be identified in order to improve their performance.

- It provides a basis for identifying critical issues that must be analyzed before establishing short-term objectives – which eventually build into a long-term vision and objectives.

Establish objectives (what's)

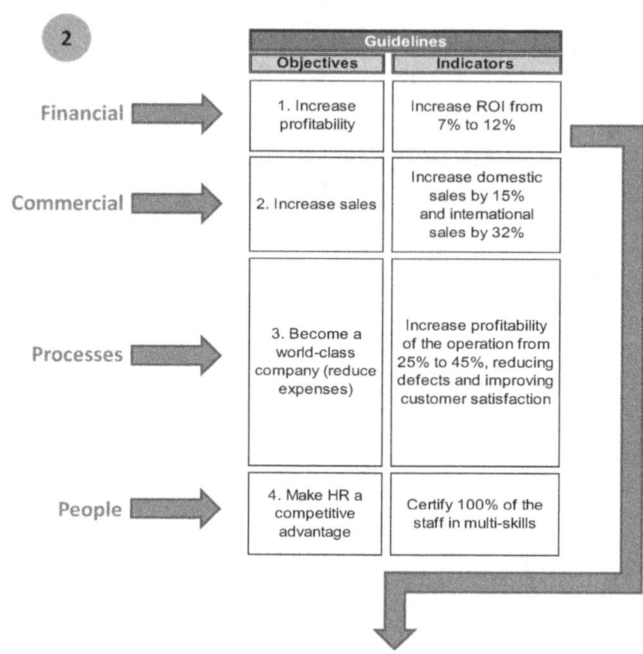

Example: DuPont Model

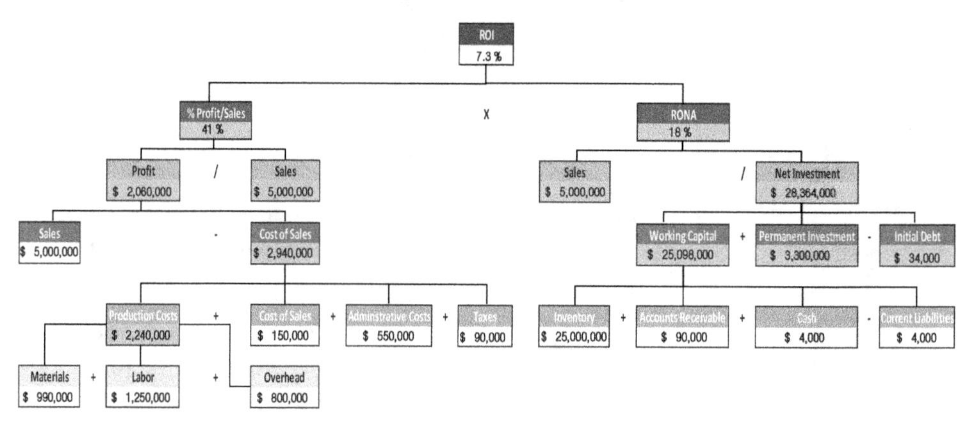

Indicators and objectives of the guidelines

Balanced Scorecard

Monthly Executive Indicator

Guidelines	Objectives	Goal	(YTD)	January	February	Ma…
Financial	Economic Value Added	4%				
	ROI	12%				
	RONA	18%				
	$ Backlog	$100,000				
	Throughput	$4,010,000				
	Cash Flow	$800,000				
Commercial	Profit / Loss	$2,060,000				
	Revenue	$5,000,000				
	Net Promoter Score	78%				
	Market Share	22%				
Processes	Conversion Costs	$1,250,000				
	Direct Cost	$990,000				
	Inventory Value	$650,000				
	Total Investment	$27,364,000				
People	Internal NPS	90%				
	Employee engagement	90%				
	Turnover	1%				
	Talent Development	85%				

3. Development of strategies

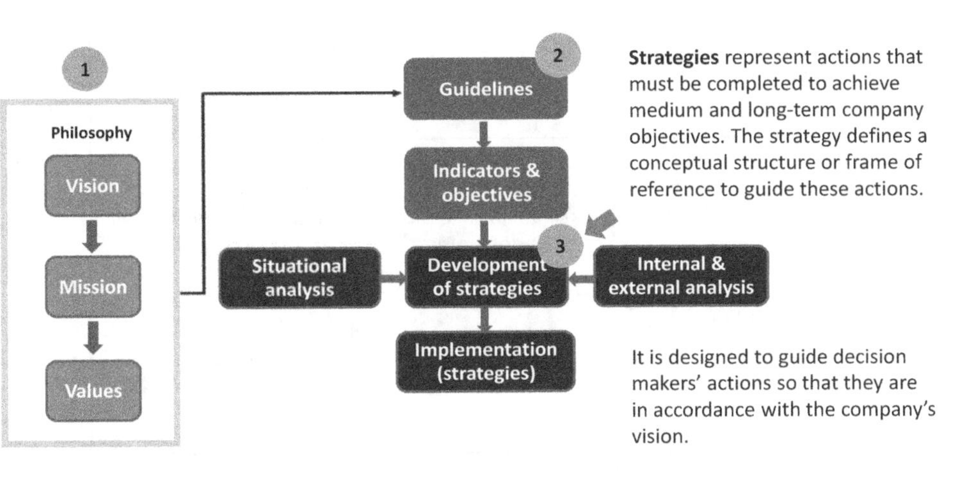

Strategies represent actions that must be completed to achieve medium and long-term company objectives. The strategy defines a conceptual structure or frame of reference to guide these actions.

It is designed to guide decision makers' actions so that they are in accordance with the company's vision.

Example of development of strategies

GUIDELINES		MANAGEMENT PLANNING		
Objectives	Indicators	Strategies	Indicators	Person Responsible
1. Increase profitability	Increase ROI from 7% to 12%	1.1 Increase profit / sales to 18% 1.2 Increase sales to 24%	Profits / sales Sales / investments	VT, MK, DG VT, MK, DG VT, MK, IN
2. Increase sales	Increase domestic sales by 15% and international sales by 32%	2.1 Sell services that add value to our customers 2.2 Increase sales with current customers 2.3 Launch products in record time 2.4 Enter new niche markets	Sales in $ NPS Days to launch Targeted segments	VT, MK, DG VT, MK, DG VT, MK, IN
3. Become a world-class company (reduce expenses)	Increase profitability of the operation from 25% to 45%, reducing defects and improving customer satisfaction	3.1 Implement Lean Company	Facility sigma level Level of customer satisfaction OEE Delivery days Inventory turns Operation expenses % scrap	IN, CA, DG, RH IN, CA, DG, RH IN, CA, DG, RH IN, CA, DG, RH IN, CA, DG, RH IN, CA, DG, RH IN, CA, DG, RH
		3.2 Maintain ISO 9000:2000 certification	Number of nonconformities	CA All
		3.3 Implement lean logistics	On-time deliveries (punctuality)	CA, SE, DG All IN, CAL
4. Make HR a competitive advantage	Certify 100% of the staff in multi-skills	4.1 Establish talent development program	% progress of the program % of certified personnel	HR

3

Strategies "HOW'S"

SWOT Matrix

	Strengths	Weaknesses
Method: **SWOT Matrix**	1. 2. 3.	1. 2. 3.
Opportunities 1. 2. 3.	Use the strengths to take advantage of the opportunities	Overcome weaknesses while taking advantage of opportunities
Threats 1. 2. 3.	Use the strengths to avoid threats	Minimize weaknesses and avoid threats

4. Indicators

Balanced Scorecard: monthly Indicator

Tracking the Value in the floor:
Day-by-the-hour board

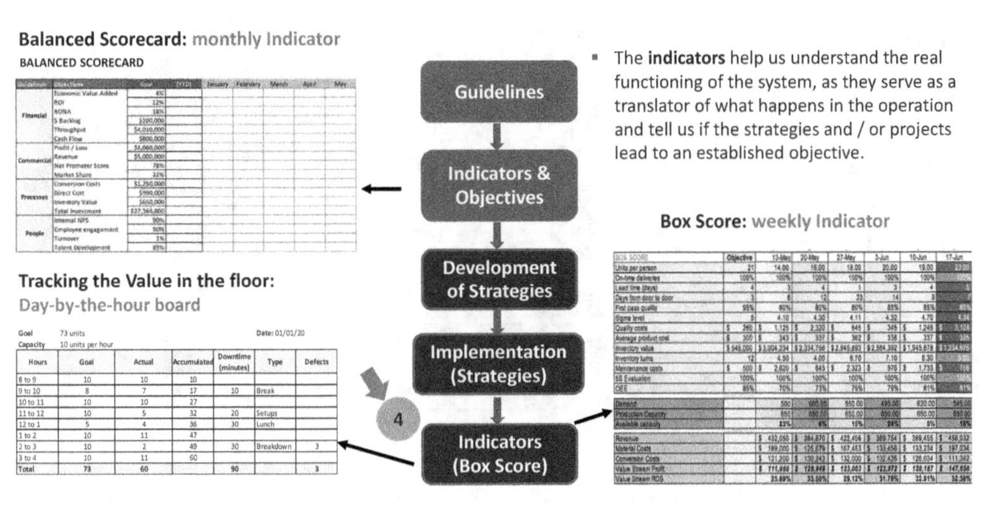

- The **indicators** help us understand the real functioning of the system, as they serve as a translator of what happens in the operation and tell us if the strategies and / or projects lead to an established objective.

Integration of indicators

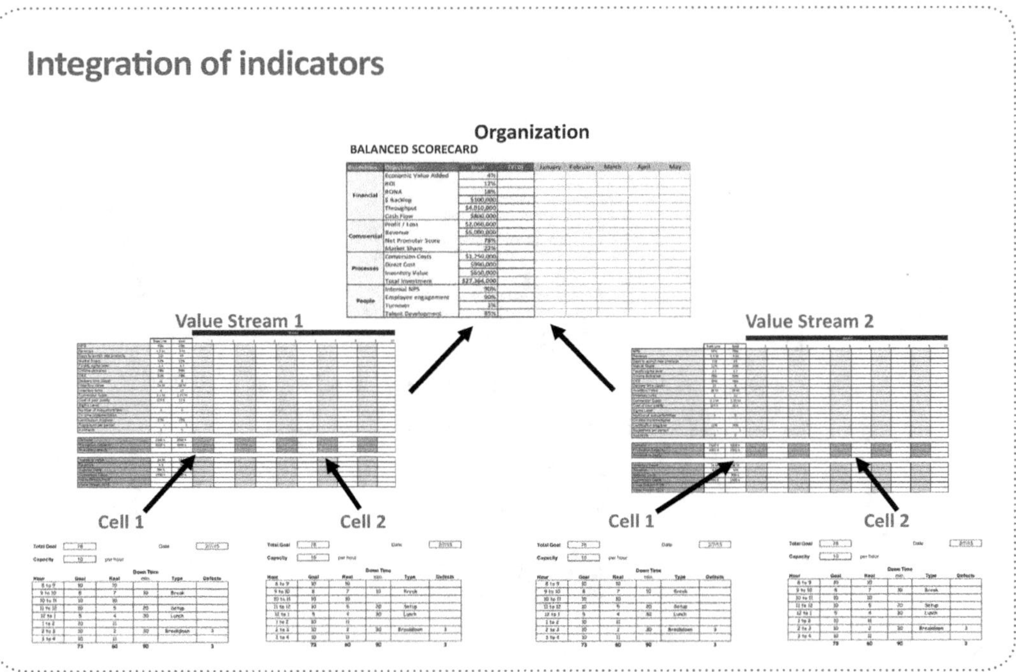

Box Score – weekly indicators

BOX SCORE	Objective	1 13-May	2 20-May	3 27-May	4 3-Jun	5 10-Jun	6 17-Jun
Units per person	21	14.00	16.00	18.00	20.00	19.00	23.00
On-time deliveries	100%	100%	100%	100%	100%	100%	100%
Lead time (days)	4	3	4	1	3	4	5
Days from door to door	3	6	12	23	14	9	7
First pass quality	95%	80%	80%	80%	85%	85%	85%
Sigma level	5	4.10	4.30	4.11	4.32	4.70	4.34
Quality costs	$ 250	$ 1,125	$ 2,320	$ 645	$ 345	$ 1,245	$ 3,124
Average product cost	$ 300	$ 343	$ 337	$ 362	$ 338	$ 337	$ 325
Inventory value	$ 545,000	$ 3,004,234	$ 2,334,756	$ 2,945,893	$ 2,564,392	$ 1,945,678	$ 1,234,975
Inventory turns	12	4.50	4.00	6.70	7.10	8.30	9.00
Maintenance costs	$ 500	$ 2,820	$ 645	$ 2,323	$ 976	$ 1,733	$ 756
5S Evaluation	100%	100%	100%	100%	100%	100%	100%
OEE	85%	70%	73%	75%	79%	81%	81%
Demand		500	600.00	550.00	495.00	620.00	545.00
Production Capacity		650	650.00	650.00	650.00	650.00	650.00
Available capacity		23%	8%	15%	24%	5%	16%
Revenue		$ 432,050	$ 384,870	$ 422,456	$ 389,754	$ 389,455	$ 456,032
Material Costs		$ 189,000	$ 125,679	$ 167,453	$ 133,456	$ 133,234	$ 197,034
Conversion Costs		$ 131,200	$ 130,242	$ 132,000	$ 132,426	$ 128,034	$ 111,342
Value Stream Profit		$ 111,850	$ 128,949	$ 123,003	$ 123,872	$ 128,187	$ 147,656
Value Stream ROS		25.89%	33.50%	29.12%	31.78%	32.91%	32.38%

Color codes

Prompt attention	
Good	
Alert	

- The results of quality, delivery, and costs are analyzed weekly to ensure that they are studied and decisions can be made weekly.
- Now there are **52 opportunities** to make good decisions, contrary to only 12 when it is done monthly.

5. Development of tactics

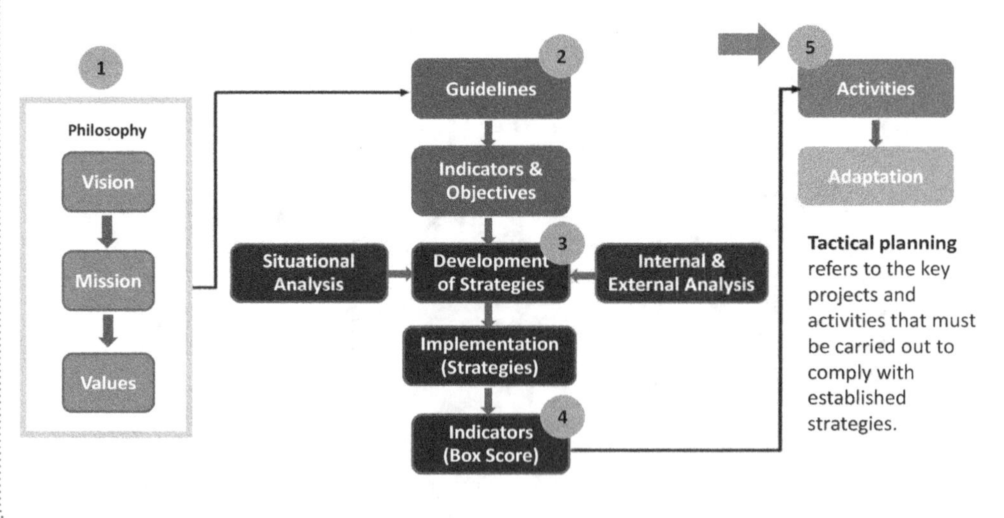

Tactical planning refers to the key projects and activities that must be carried out to comply with established strategies.

Example of development of tactics

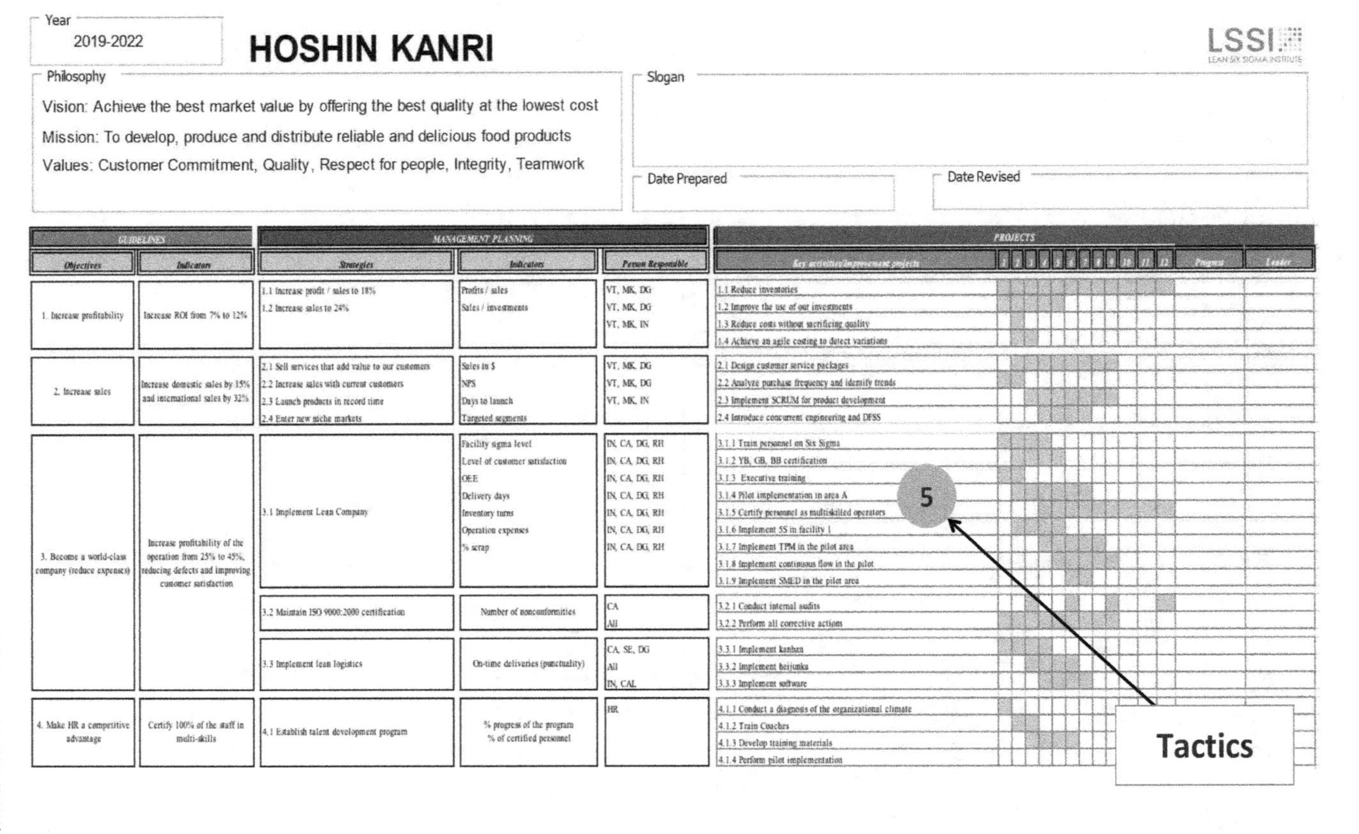

GUIDELINES		MANAGEMENT PLANNING			PROJECTS		
Objectives	Indicators	Strategies	Indicators	Person Responsible	Key activities/improvement projects	1 2 3 4 5 6 7 8 9 10 11 12 / Progress	Leader
1. Increase profitability	Increase ROI from 7% to 12%	1.1 Increase profit / sales to 18% 1.2 Increase sales to 24%	Profits / sales Sales / investments	VT, MK, DG VT, MK, DG VT, MK, IN	1.1 Reduce inventories 1.2 Improve the use of our investments 1.3 Reduce costs without sacrificing quality 1.4 Achieve an agile costing to detect variations		
2. Increase sales	Increase domestic sales by 15% and international sales by 32%	2.1 Sell services that add value to our customers 2.2 Increase sales with current customers 2.3 Launch products in record time 2.4 Enter new niche markets	Sales in $ NPS Days to launch Targeted segments	VT, MK, DG VT, MK, DG VT, MK, IN	2.1 Design customer service packages 2.2 Analyze purchase frequency and identify trends 2.3 Implement SCRUM for product development 2.4 Introduce concurrent engineering and DFSS		
3. Become a world-class company (reduce expenses)	Increase profitability of the operation from 25% to 45%, reducing defects and improving customer satisfaction	3.1 Implement Lean Company	Facility sigma level Level of customer satisfaction OEE Delivery days Inventory turns Operation expenses % scrap	IN, CA, DG, RH IN, CA, DG, RH IN, CA, DG, RH IN, CA, DG, RH IN, CA, DG, RH IN, CA, DG, RH IN, CA, DG, RH	3.1.1 Train personnel on Six Sigma 3.1.2 YB, GB, BB certification 3.1.3 Executive training 3.1.4 Pilot implementation in area A 3.1.5 Certify personnel as multiskilled operators 3.1.6 Implement 5S in facility 1 3.1.7 Implement TPM in the pilot area 3.1.8 Implement continuous flow in the pilot 3.1.9 Implement SMED in the pilot area		
		3.2 Maintain ISO 9000:2000 certification	Number of nonconformities	CA All	3.2.1 Conduct internal audits 3.2.2 Perform all corrective actions		
		3.3 Implement lean logistics	On-time deliveries (punctuality)	CA, SE, DG All IN, CAL	3.3.1 Implement kanban 3.3.2 Implement heijunka 3.3.3 Implement software		
4. Make HR a competitive advantage	Certify 100% of the staff in multi-skills	4.1 Establish talent development program	% progress of the program % of certified personnel	HR	4.1.1 Conduct a diagnosis of the organizational climate 4.1.2 Train Coaches 4.1.3 Develop training materials 4.1.4 Perform pilot implementation		

Example of development of tactics

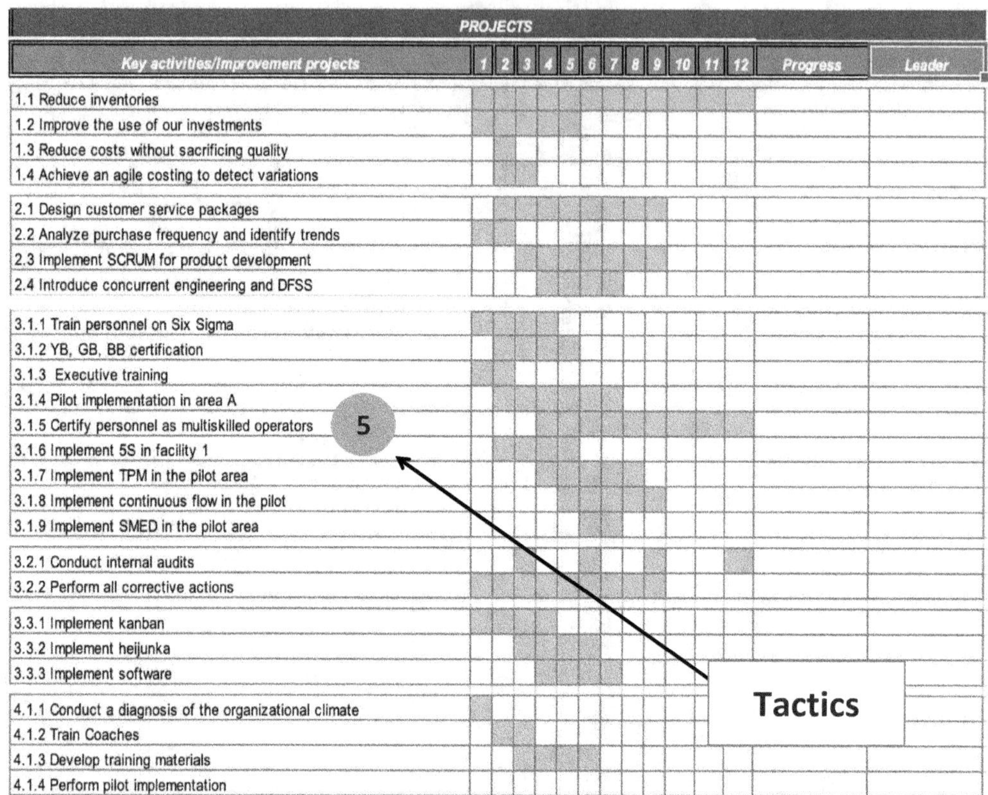

- Once the tactical planning has been defined, work on the development of the projects can begin.

- To ensure that the strategy is executed, these projects must be successfully carried out through an agile management system called **SCRUM.**

Note: Scrum is a tool that will be reviewed during the Black Belt certification

Value Stream Structure

Teamwork is possible if the structure is right

Learning objectives

1. Understand how companies of the future will be designed by value streams.
2. Show how self-managed teams can perform.
3. Understand the basic concepts of Lean Accounting in value streams.

Content

> Background
> What is value stream structure?
> Why implement value streams?
> Who participates?
> Procedure
> Example

Background

A company that has decided to be agile in response to the client's needs, and is sufficiently productive to stay in the market, should consider:

- Direct and effective communication
- A flat and agile organization
- Teamwork

A good strategic plan is not enough

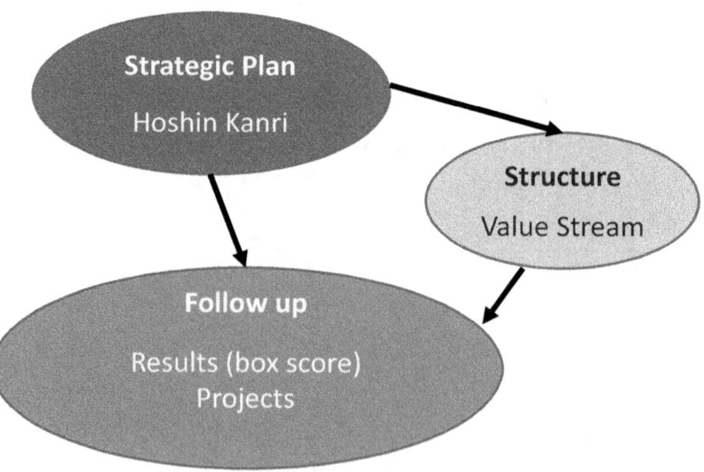

LSSI
LEAN SIX SIGMA INSTITUTE

Traditional organization structure

- Companies are traditionally organized by departments and use structures similar to family trees.

- Currently many companies are still organized in this way.

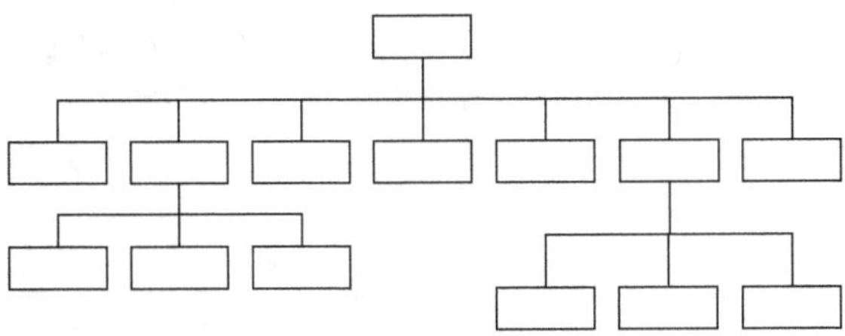

- These systems work relatively well in high-volume, low-mix product or service environments.

Example of traditional structure

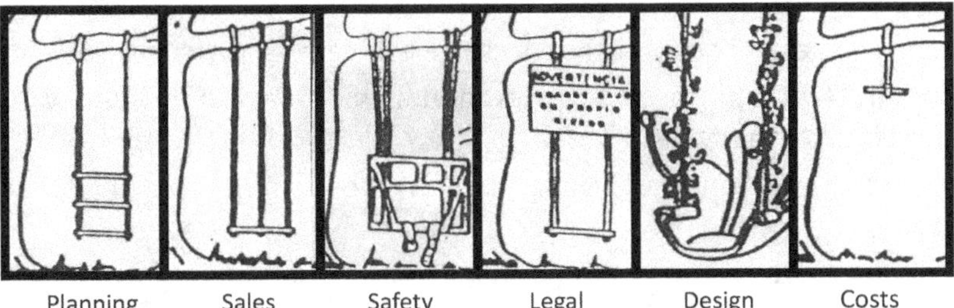

Planning　　Sales　　Safety　　Legal　　Design　　Costs

Engineering　　Manufacturing　　Packaging　　Marketing　　Service　　Client needs

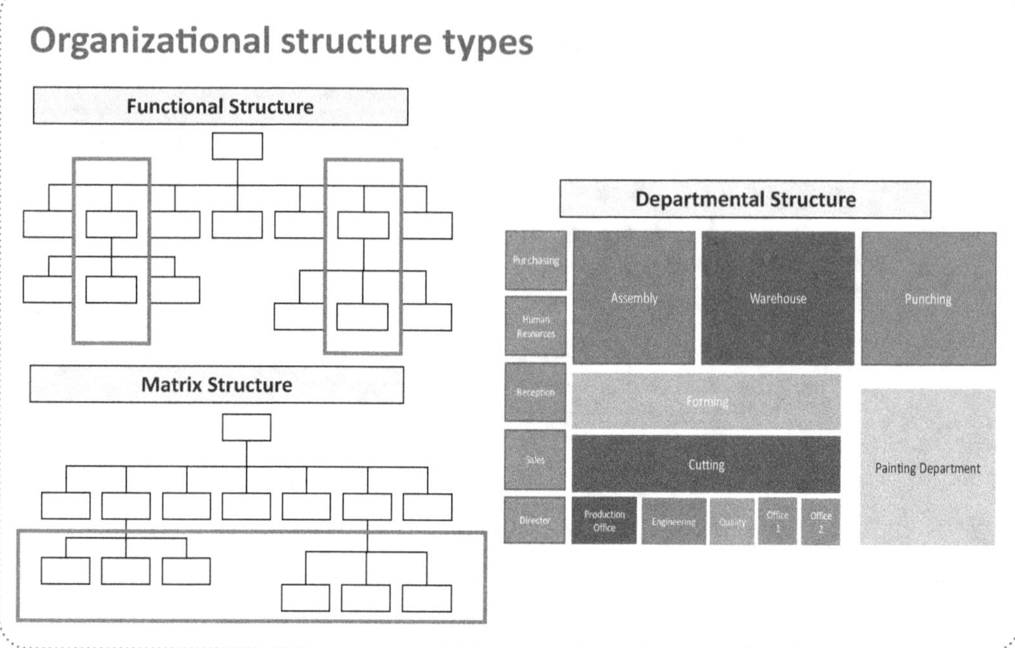

Conclusions

▸ Managers delegated poorly or tried to solve problems at all levels.

▸ Lower-level staff simply received orders and didn't always understand why they were doing certain activities.

▸ It was rare that everyone involved in the processes could answer the following questions:

- At what speed the customer is willing to buy? (Takt-time)
- What is the companies' capacity?
- Where is the main constraint?
- Are we delivering our products or services on time?
- Do you really know what the customer thinks about your products?
- Are you reaching the costs goals and are you making money?
- Does everybody knows the same?

What is value stream structure?

A value stream structure is a business unit that:

- Is composed of all those directly responsible for the activities of a family of products or services.
- Is comprised of cross functional teams that continually analyze available information and execute any necessary changes.

Each value stream will be analyzed through a map (VSM), where you will see the process flow of information, activities and materials.

"The way companies of the future are being designed."

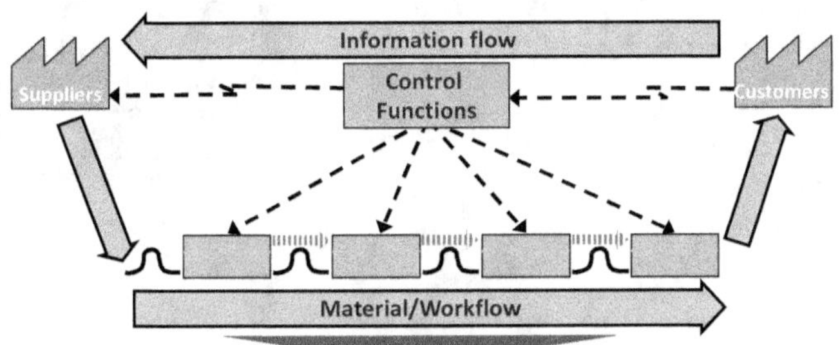

Value stream structure

Each value stream represents a product or service family.

Why implement value streams?

- To eliminate all the bureaucracy that prevents to develop successful businesses.

- It gives management time to plan, analyze the future of the business, and devote more energy to future development.

- It allows strategies such as Lean Six Sigma to be successful.

Who participates?

Level 3: **Owners and Directors**

Level 2: **Value Stream Teams and Support**

Level 1: **Production or Service Teams**

LSSI
LEAN SIX SIGMA INSTITUTE

1. Define **level 1** staff and train them on their roles (standardized work).

2. Define **level 2** staff and train them on their roles (leader standard work).

3. Design the value office and boards for the reviews of each level (Andon, Leader Standard Work, etc.)

4. Analyze the performance of the value stream:

    A. Update the box score and floorboards

    B. Value stream cost analysis

5. Design how the **level 3** (management team) will work, if the pilot was successful in the deployment phase.

1. Define level 1 staff and train them on their roles

Level 1 responsibilities

> **Leaders, operators, material handlers, and technicians**

- Conduct meetings at the beginning and end of a shift
- Daily planning and hourly analysis of progress
- Team-based decision making
- Analyze their own results
- Solve problems

Update the day by-the-hour board

Goal 73 units   **Date:** 01/01/20
Capacity 10 units per hour

Hours	Goal	Actual	Accumulated	Downtime (minutes)	Type	Defects
8 to 9	10	10	10			
9 to 10	8	7	17	10	Break	
10 to 11	10	10	27			
11 to 12	10	5	32	20	Setups	
12 to 1	5	4	36	30	Lunch	
1 to 2	10	11	47			
2 to 3	10	2	49	30	Breakdown	3
3 to 4	10	11	60			
Total	**73**	**60**		**90**		**3**

2. Define level 2 staff and train them on their roles

Level 2 responsibilities

> **Value stream manager, financial analyst, customer service representative, sales associate, scheduler, manufacturing engineer, quality analyst, etc.**

- Work in the "value office"
- Weekly planning and review of box score
- Daily analysis of obligations, profitability, potential problems and requirements
- Daily analysis of results
- Take action
- Solve level 2 problems
- Support level 1

> **Support areas: HR, Maintenance, IT, etc.**

- They work in their processes as internal service providers
- Weekly planning
- Daily analysis of box score results, responsibilities, profitability, and potential problems
- Take action
- Solve level 2 problems

Value stream board

Value stream board: name

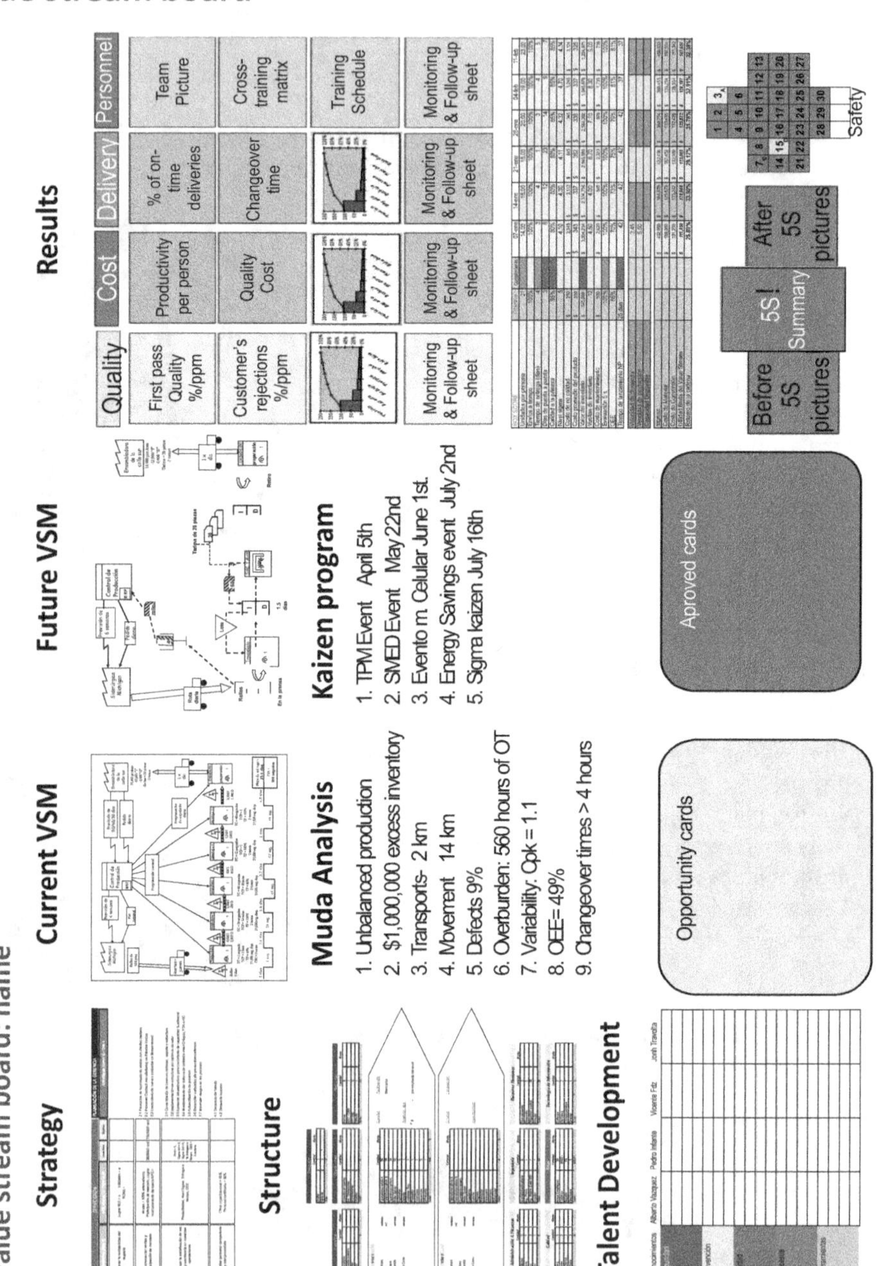

3. Value office design

You must select an area in which the value stream team members will work.

The room must have:
- Visibility to areas that generate value
- A strategic location
- Proper lighting
- Work stations for each member
- A meeting table at the center of the room
- A projector and screen
- Writing board

People responsible for the value stream work full-time in the value office. They have scheduled meetings to review and analyze results, and make decisions.

- Value stream Manager
- Sales
- Planner/Buyer
- Finance
- Process Engineer
- Quality Engineer
- Equipment Engineer

4. Analyze the performance of the value stream

A. Update the Box Score

The **Box Score** provides:

- Lean measurements that replace traditional ones

- Methods to identify the financial impact of Lean improvements

- An improved way to understand the cost of products and the cost of value streams

- New ways to make decisions related to price and profitability

- Better ways to decide between buying or producing

- A way to focus the business around the value created by customers

BOX SCORE	Objective	Progress	7-Jan	14-Jan	21-Jan	28-Jan	4-Feb	11-Feb
Units/person	21		14	16	18	20	19	23
On-time deliveries	100%		100%	100%	100%	100%	100%	100%
Lead time (days)	4		3	4	1	3	4	5
Days from door-to-door	3		6	12	23	14	9	7
First pass yield	95%		80%	80%	80%	85%	85%	85%
Sigma level	5		4.10	4.30	4.11	4.32	4.70	4.34
No quality cost	$ 250		$ 2,345.00	$ 3,112.00	$ 645.00	$ 345.00	$ 1,245.00	$ 3,124.00
Average product cost	$ 300		$ 343.00	$ 337.00	$ 362.00	$ 338.00	$ 337.00	$ 325.00
Inventory value	$ 545,000		$ 3,004.23	$ 2,334.76	$ 2,945.89	$ 2,564.39	$ 1,945.68	$ 1,234.98
Inventory turns	12		4.5	4	6.7	7.1	8.3	9
Maintenance cost	$ 500		$ 2,820.00	$ 645.00	$ 2,323.00	$ 976.00	$ 1,733.00	$ 756.00
5S evaluation	100%		100%	100%	100%	100%	100%	100%
OEE	85%		70%	73%	75%	79%	81%	81%
Launch time (days)	25		42	42	42	42	37	37

	Objective	Progress	7-Jan	14-Jan	21-Jan	28-Jan	4-Feb	11-Feb
Demand			100					
Production capacity			200					
Available capacity			50%					

	Objective	Progress	7-Jan	14-Jan	21-Jan	28-Jan	4-Feb	11-Feb
Revenue			$ 432,050	$ 384,870	$ 422,456	$ 389,754	$ 389,455	$ 456,032
Material cost			$ 189,000	$ 125,679	$ 167,453	$ 133,456	$ 133,234	$ 197,034
Conversion cost			$ 131,200	$ 130,242	$ 132,000	$ 132,426	$ 128,034	$ 111,342
Value Stream Net Profit			$ 111,850	$ 128,949	$ 123,003	$ 123,872	$ 128,187	$ 147,650
Return			25.89%	33.50%	29.12%	31.78%	32.91%	32.38%

- Every week the **box score** is updated to identify opportunities and to know if the established goals have been reached.

- The **box score** meeting is held every week with all members of the value stream.

B. Value stream cost analysis

Traditional cost method

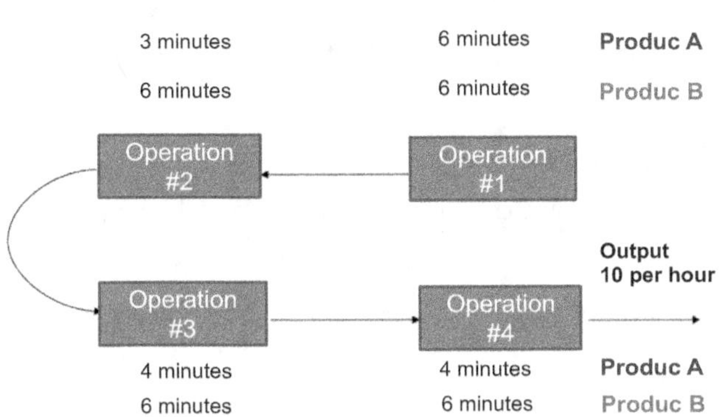

Product / Service A

Labor   = 17 minutes
Labor rate: $24.23 per hour
Overhead rate: 600%

Labor   = $6.87
Overhead = $41.19
Material = $42
Total Cost = $90.06

Product / Service B

Labor   = 24 minutes
Labor rate: $24.23 per hour
Overhead rate: 600%

Labor   = $9.69
Overhead = $58.15
Material = $42
Total Cost = $109.84

Lean Accounting

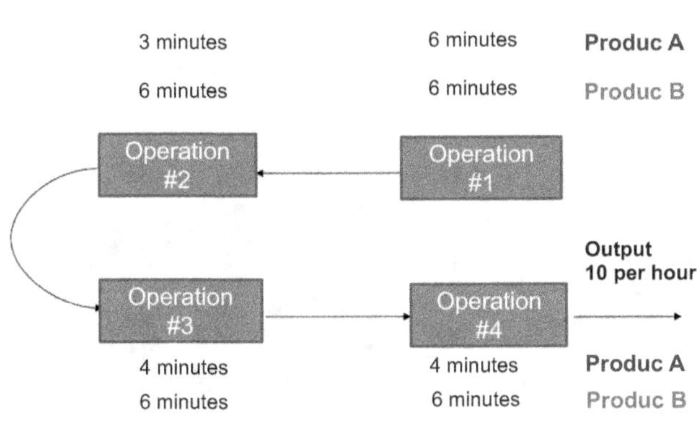

Product / Service A

Conversion cost = $580 per hour
Units produced = 10 per hour

Per unit
Conversion cost = $58
Material Cost = $42
Total Cost = $100 (REAL COST)

Product / Service B

Conversion cost = $580 per hour
Units produced = 10 per hour

Per unit
Conversion cost = $58
Material Cost = $42
Total Cost = $100 (REAL COST)

Lean Accounting benefits

- Eliminate waste from administrative and accounting processes
- Internal understanding of the real costs of a company's products and/or services
- Better marketing and sales strategies
- Members of the value stream share a common objective
- Guides decision-making in relation to the value created for customers and the business
- Financial statements delivered every week
- Eliminate bureaucracy that prevents better communication and therefore better results
- Calculate and evaluate the benefits of a Lean implementation

5. Design how level 3 (management team) will work, if the pilot was successful in the deployment phase

Level 3 responsibilities

▸ **Managers, directors, and chief executives**

- Strategic planning and monitoring
- Monthly review of results and annual strategic planning
- If necessary, weekly meetings for decision making
- Look for new business opportunities
- Solve level 3 problems
- Support level 2
- Conduct "Gemba Walks" frequently

Balanced Scorecard

Guidelines	Objectives	Goal	(YTD)	January	February	March	April	May
Financial	Economic Value Added	4%						
	ROI	12%						
	RONA	18%						
	$ Backlog	$100,000						
	Throughput	$4,010,000						
	Cash Flow	$800,000						
Commercial	Profit / Loss	$2,060,000						
	Revenue	$5,000,000						
	Net Promoter Score	78%						
	Market Share	22%						
Processes	Conversion Costs	$1,250,000						
	Direct Cost	$990,000						
	Inventory Value	$650,000						
	Total Investment	$27,364,000						
People	Internal NPS	90%						
	Employee engagement	90%						
	Turnover	1%						
	Talent Development	85%						

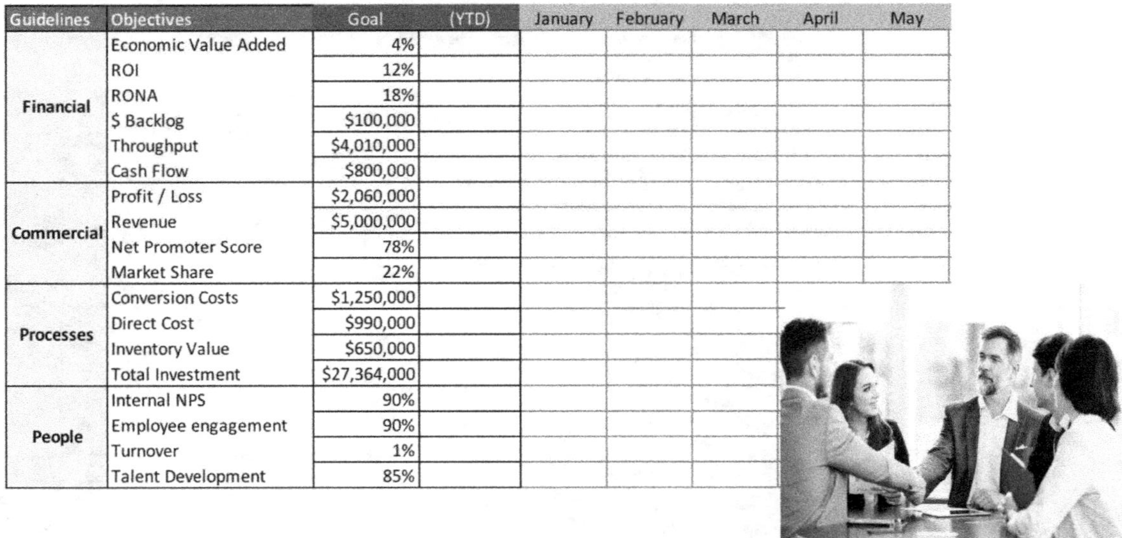

Example: initial situation

Individual work centers

The ACME company had a departmental work structure and separate offices in which people only worked in groups when they met in the meeting room.

Departmental structure

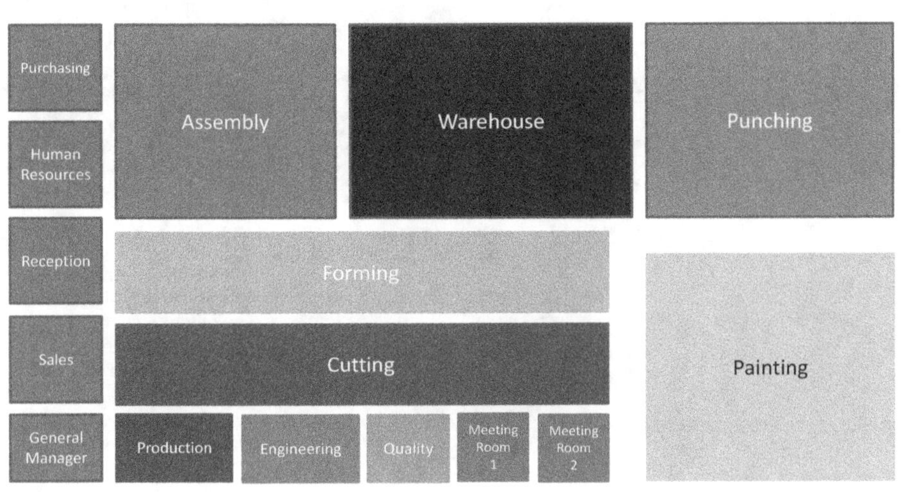

Define the pilot value stream

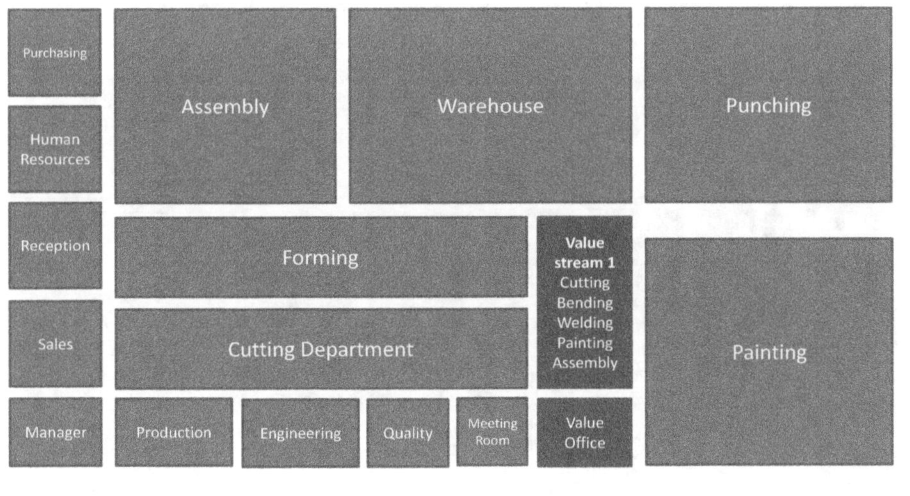

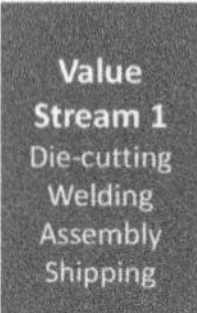

Value Stream 1
Die-cutting
Welding
Assembly
Shipping

Value Office

Members:
Value Stream Manager
Equipment Engineer
Materials Engineer
Process Engineer
Coach
Cost Engineer
Planner-Buyer

Deployment of all value streams

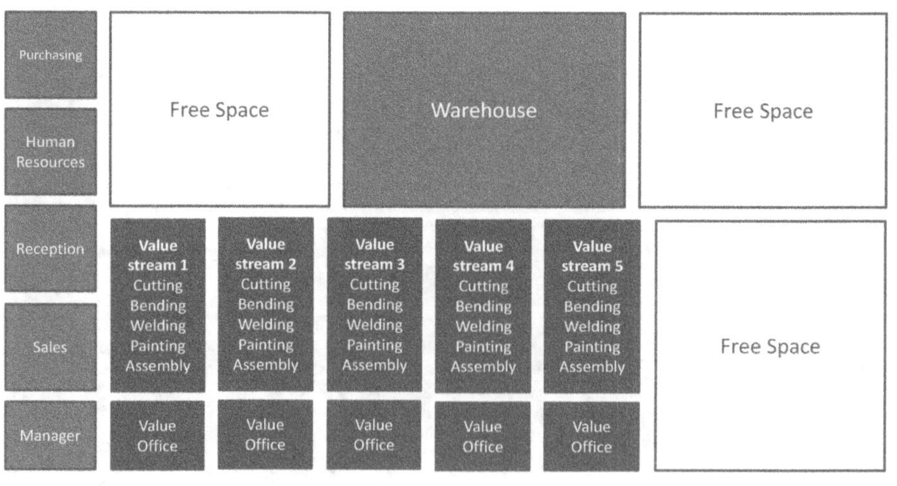

LSSI
LEAN SIX SIGMA INSTITUTE

Talent Development

Learning objectives

1. Understand the importance of talent development in an organization.
2. Understand the process to implement talent development as a competitive advantage.
3. Apply a creative and effective method to transfer knowledge.

Content

> Introduction
> Background
> What is talent development?
> Key elements
> When should an organization implement it?
> Talent development procedure
> Benefits
> Exercise

Introduction

- Many issues in **quality**, **communication**, and **productivity** are not caused by a lack of technology or special resources.

- What is really needed is sufficient time dedicated to **teaching**, **learning**, and **practicing**.

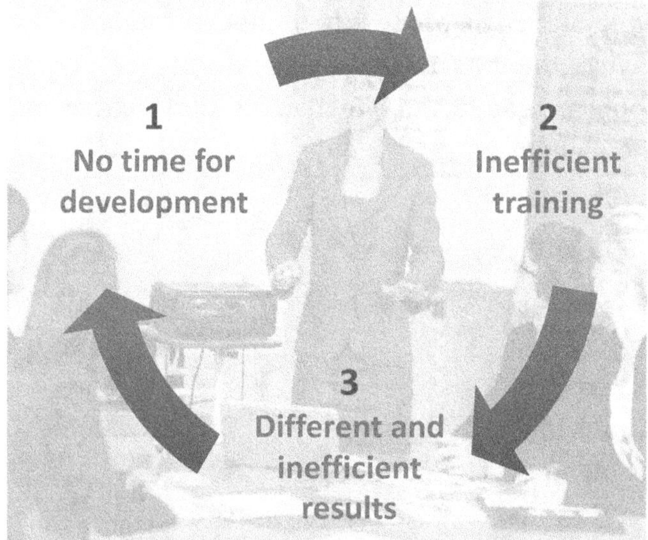

Background

- When the United States entered WWII, they began to deploy young working men to the war. However, the country still had to produce day-to-day products required by the country and its people.

- The new labor force was made up of older men and women, who were not necessarily prepared to take over those jobs.

- The US government decided to develop the **Training Within Industry (TWI)** method to train the employees who would be replacing the workers going to war.

- The program would prepare trainers in any industry who are capable of teaching employees key skills, in order to help them perform their jobs effectively (i.e., leadership skills, teaching skills, improvement skills, etc.)

- The program was aimed for: managers, supervisors and team leaders.

- The training program included 3 courses:
  - Job Instruction (JI)
  - Job Methods (JM)
  - Job Relations (JR)

TWI: A forgotten program

- At the end of World War II, the United States stopped the TWI program.

- The teaching system is not encouraged or promoted among U.S companies.

Toyota brings it back

- Toyota reinvented the TWI program.

- Toyota produces cars and also talented people.

- Processes are designed to be analyzed and taught by leaders, who will then challenge the system continuously.

What is talent development?

- Talent development is a methodology used to develop a learning culture by **attracting, training, and retaining employees**.

- It includes accompanying each person on their journey to help them reach their full potential.

Key elements

TWI Components

Charles Allen 4-step Learning Process	TWI			PDCA Cycle	Scientific Method
	Job Instructions	Job Methods	Job Relations		
Preparation	Prepare the Worker	Breakdown the job	Get the facts	**Plan** - Observe data and reality; decide on a problem; define it	Observation & Description
Presentation	Present the Operation	Question every detail	Weigh & decide	**Do** - Analyze the problem; propose a countermeasure	Formulation of an hypothesis
Application	Try Out Performance	Develop new method	Take action	**Check** - Try the countermeasure; check the results	Use the hypothesis to make predictions
Testing	Follow Up	Apply new method	Check results	**Act** - If successful, standardize the change; if not, start the cycle over	Test the predictions through experiments

When should an organization implement it?

- As soon as an organization is established

- Any time where lack of knowledge is generating problems. Example: quality, speed, cost, sales, etc.

Talent development procedure

1. Prepare the organization to develop exceptional people.

2. Identify critical knowledge.

3. Transfer knowledge to others.

4. Verify the learning process and success of the program.

1. Prepare the organization

Assess the needs

- Develop the strategy (Hoshin Kanri) to focus on critical knowledge

- According with box score results, define where training is required

- Results determine the areas of focus for Talent Development

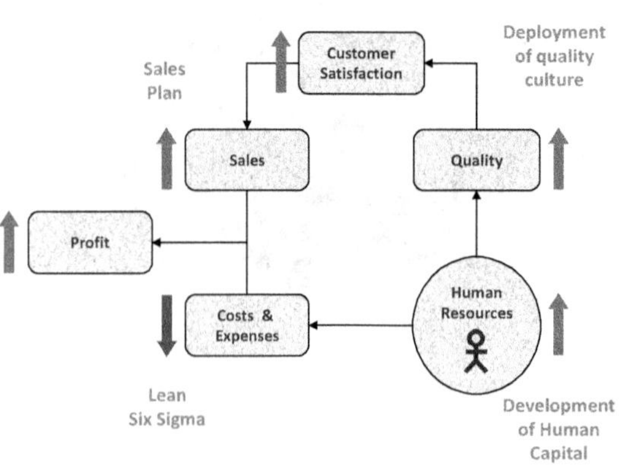

BOX SCORE	Objective	13-May	20-May	27-May	3-Jun	10-Jun	17-Jun
Units per person	21	14.00	16.00	18.00	20.00	19.00	23.00
On-time deliveries	100%	100%	100%	100%	100%	100%	100%
Lead time (days)	4	3	4	1	3	4	5
Days from door to door	3	8	12	23	14	9	7
First pass quality	95%	80%	80%	80%	85%	85%	85%
Sigma level	5	4.10	4.30	4.11	4.32	4.70	4.34
Quality costs	$ 250	$ 1,125	$ 2,320	$ 645	$ 345	$ 1,245	$ 3,124
Average product cost	$ 300	$ 343	$ 337	$ 362	$ 338	$ 337	$ 325
Inventory value	$ 545,000	$ 3,004,234	$ 2,334,756	$ 2,945,893	$ 2,584,392	$ 1,945,878	$ 1,234,975
Inventory turns	12	4.50	4.00	6.70	7.10	8.30	9.00
Maintenance costs	$ 500	$ 2,820	$ 645	$ 2,323	$ 976	$ 1,733	$ 756
5S Evaluation	100%	100%	100%	100%	100%	100%	100%
OEE	85%	70%	73%	75%	79%	61%	81%
Demand		500	600.00	550.00	485.00	620.00	545.00
Production Capacity		650	650.00	650.00	650.00	650.00	650.00
Available capacity		23%	8%	15%	24%	5%	16%
Revenue		$ 432,050	$ 384,870	$ 422,456	$ 389,754	$ 389,455	$ 456,032
Material Costs		$ 189,000	$ 125,879	$ 167,453	$ 133,456	$ 133,234	$ 197,034
Conversion Costs		$ 131,200	$ 130,242	$ 132,000	$ 132,426	$ 126,034	$ 111,342
Value Stream Profit		$ 111,850	$ 128,949	$ 123,003	$ 123,872	$ 128,187	$ 147,656
Value Stream ROS		25.89%	33.50%	29.12%	31.78%	32.91%	32.38%

2. Identify critical knowledge

Break down the job into steps for teaching

Only 20% of knowledge is critical and contributes 80% of the results.

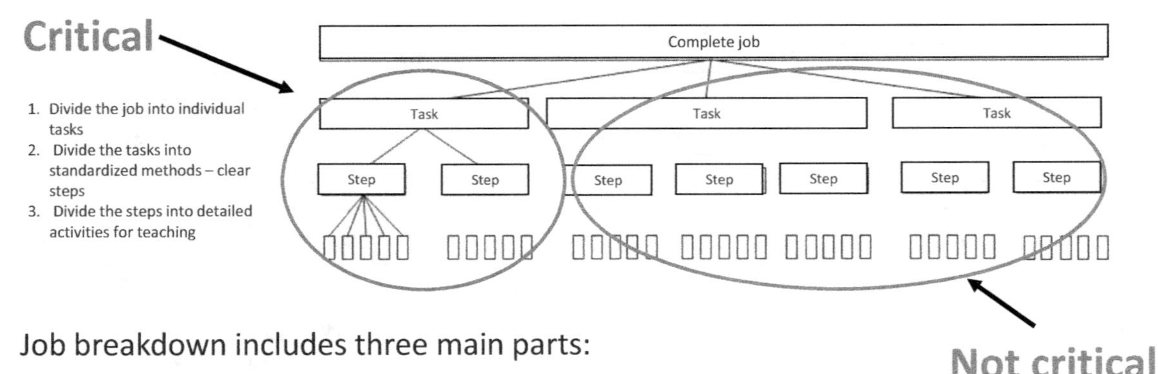

Job breakdown includes three main parts:

1. Identify key steps in the work task
2. Identify important information within the steps (key points)
3. Why are the key points important?

Identify critical knowledge

Critical knowledge must be documented in a work instruction format.

APOLLO SPRAYERS - WORK INSTRUCTIONS		Team leader
Area: Subassembly	Item: T100 Cord	Supervisor Created by Rodrigo Diaz Date 3/20/2012
KEY STEPS	**KEY POINTS** Safety Quality Technique Time	**REASON FOR KEY POINTS**
Step # 1	1. Insert thinner edge first	Right dimension to fit T100 and reach the switch
Insert strain relief	2. Strain relief must be 13" from the start of the cord	
Step # 2 Peel wire terminals	1. Make sure no copper wire is showing on the inside of the connector	
Step # 3	1. Twist wires before crimping	
Crimp wire terminals	2. Make sure to crimp connectors with the inside of the crimping tool 3. Make sure no copper wire is showing on the inside of the connector	
Step # 4 Check if wire terminals are loose	1. If yes, back to step 3	Could lead to problems during testing and final assembly

LSSI
LEAN SIX SIGMA INSTITUTE

3. Transfer the knowledge

Job Instruction
Prepare the Worker
Present the Operation
Try Out Performance
Follow Up

Present the Operation

Step 1: Trainer performs the task (without speaking).

Step 2: Trainer mentions the steps as he/she performs the task.

Step 3: Trainer mentions the steps, as well as the key points, as he/she performs the task.

Step 4: Trainer mentions the steps and key points and explains why the key points are important, as he/she performs the task.

4. Verify the learning process and success of the program

- Continuous monitoring and review of tasks

- Guide the student towards independence

- The team leader trains each member of the team

- Success is shown through results, not only actions

"For the things we have to learn before we can do them, we learn by doing them." Aristoteles

Evaluate knowledge and performance

Multi-skills Matrix

Each task has to be learned at the highest level of detail and must be evaluated according to the skills shown during practice.

Name	Register	Get info.	Diagnose	Fix	Testing	Invoice	Check out	Total	Ranking
John Smith	1	3	4	0	2	1	1	12	C
Bob Hope	5	5	5	5	5	5	5	35	G
Robert Mills	3	4	2	1	5	4	2	21	E
Dave Jones	1	0	4	4	2	2	1	14	C

Description	Values
Beginner (No experience)	1
Learning (Has a notion about the process)	2
Good (works well, with good quality & speed)	3
Expert (mastered the operation)	4
Trainer (can train others)	5

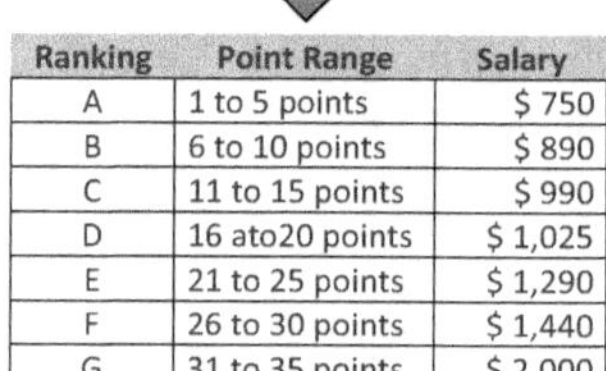

Ranking	Point Range	Salary
A	1 to 5 points	$ 750
B	6 to 10 points	$ 890
C	11 to 15 points	$ 990
D	16 ato20 points	$ 1,025
E	21 to 25 points	$ 1,290
F	26 to 30 points	$ 1,440
G	31 to 35 points	$ 2,000

Benefits

- A more stable workforce
- Reduces accidents
- Documented knowledge of critical processes
- People who are willing and motivated to learn
- People who are willing and motivated to teach
- Creates quality excellence
- Greater job satisfaction
- Minimal costs arising from poor quality
- High employee retention rates

Companies that have implemented TWI have reported improvements of at least 25% in their productivity.

- Establish the critical processes in your organization
- Choose one of them
- Identify critical knowledge
- Document the process in a work instruction format
- Prepare a trainer
- Teach the operation using the 4 steps method
- Evaluate knowledge and performance and discuss the benefits

Introduction to White Belt

Learning objectives

1. Understand the basic concepts and principles of Lean Six Sigma.
2. Understand the responsibilities associated with White Belts.
3. Learn how teamwork affects the Lean Six Sigma philosophy.
4. Understand Time Management techniques.

Content

> Background
> White Belt responsibilities
> Limitations to productivity
> Teamwork
> Time management

Background

Evolution

Total Quality Control

Quality Circle

Just in time (JIT)

Supplier Development

Total Productive Maintenance (TPM)

Theory of Constraints (TOC)

Six Sigma

All Processes

Automation, Human Approach, and Sustainability

TQM · World Class · Lean Six Sigma Operation System · Lean Six Sigma Company · Lean Six Sigma 4.0

40s 50s 60s 70s 80s 90s 2010s 2020s

Time dedication

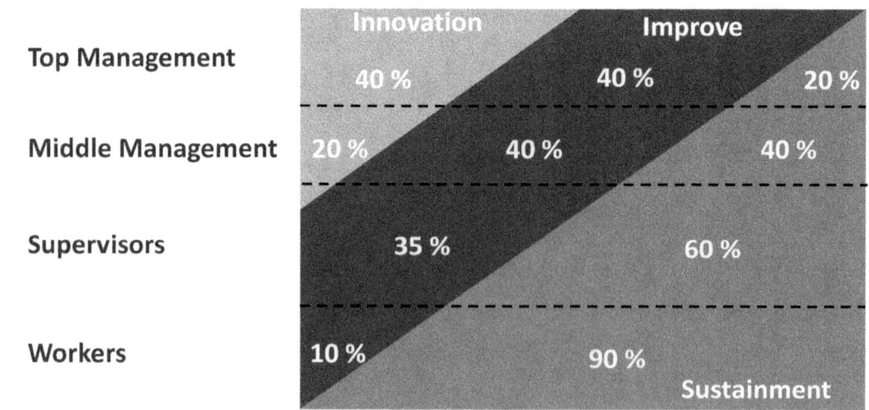

Lean Six Sigma tools

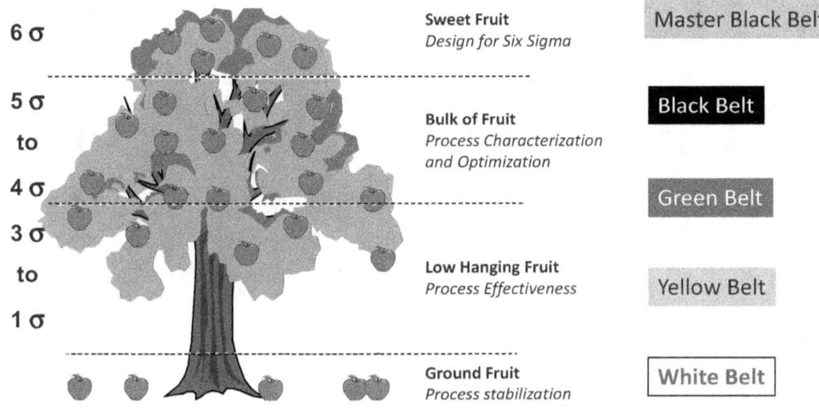

White Belts responsibilities

Personally

- Keep their area clean and tidy.
- Manage their time correctly.
- Work with quality and on time.

Teamwork

- Identifies opportunities for continuous improvement.
- Participates in solving simple problems.
- Participates in improvement projects frequently.

Knowledge

- Lean Six Sigma Philosophy.
- Essential Tools.

Limitations to productivity

無理

無駄

1. *Muri* = Overburden

2. *Mura* = Variability

3. *Muda* = Waste

Types of waste = Muda

Excess inventory = waste

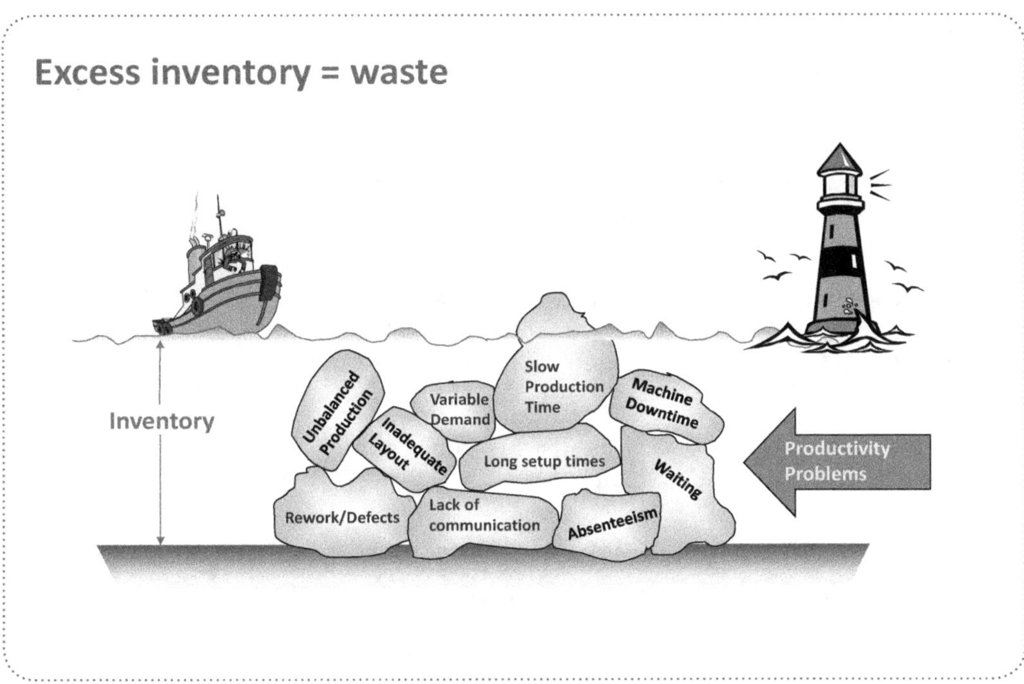

What is a team?

- A team is a group of people who perform interdependent tasks to work toward a common mission.

- **White Belts** are individuals that participate in teams and contribute ideas and actions to solve many problems with simple tools based on their individual job experience.

Types of teams

- **Process improvement teams** are project teams that focus on improving or developing specific business processes.

- **Work groups**, sometimes called "natural teams", have responsibility for a particular process (e.g., a department, a product line or a stage of a business process) and work together in a participative environment.

- **Self-managed teams** directly manage the day-to-day operation of their particular process or department.

White Belts **participate in every type of team and understand the team dynamics and the tools in order to maximize the results.**

Stages of team development

| Forming | Storming | Norming | Performing |

- Lack of integration or group maturity

- Effort to be pleasant among team members (complacent)

- Little progress in terms of work completed

- Roles and responsibilities are clarified and understood

- "Honeymoon" phase

- Team members start to voice their opinions

- The understanding of roles and responsibilities is questioned

- Conflict arises due to different ideas and conclusions

- Lack of agreement delays the team's work

- Team members resolve their conflicts

- The team reaches an understanding through mutually accepted ideas

- Some work is completed (team progress)

- Team members start to work as a team

- Trust is developed and more ideas are shared

- Synergy is created

- Interdependence is evident and accepted

- Team-based problem solving skills are developed

- Agreements are achieved

- Significant and noticeable progress in terms of work completed

Adapted from Bruce W. Tuckman.

Time management

- One of the most important causes of low team performance is a **lack of time management skills.**

- Time is one of the **most valuable resources.**

- By analyzing how we use our time, we will realize how we are wasting it and how we can find better ways to use it.

Parkinson's Law

It was first articulated by Cyril Parkinson in 1957 as a result of his research in the British Civil Service.

Examples:

- **Time**: work expands so as to fill the time available for its completion.
- **Income**: expenditures rise to meet income.
- **Space**: storage resources tend to increase (racks, drawers, etc.) to meet storage capacity.

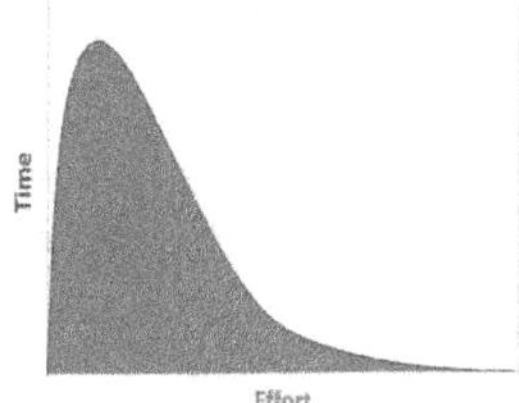

For many people, the more time they have to complete a task, the more their minds will wander, which can create problems.

Time management best practices

1. Plan your day.

2. Use the Pomodoro Technique.

3. Use your email effectively.

4. Conduct effective meetings.

5. Make effective phone calls.

1. Plan your day

- Spend at least 15 minutes to plan your day.
- Schedule the activities in the medium to long-term.
- Plan daily life activities (exercise, food, transportation).
- Classify activities as A, B or C.
    - A: Important and urgent
    - B: Important and not urgent
    - C: Less important and not urgent
- When taking notes, define your tasks and schedule.
- Before you start your day, picture what your day will look like.

Daily planning example

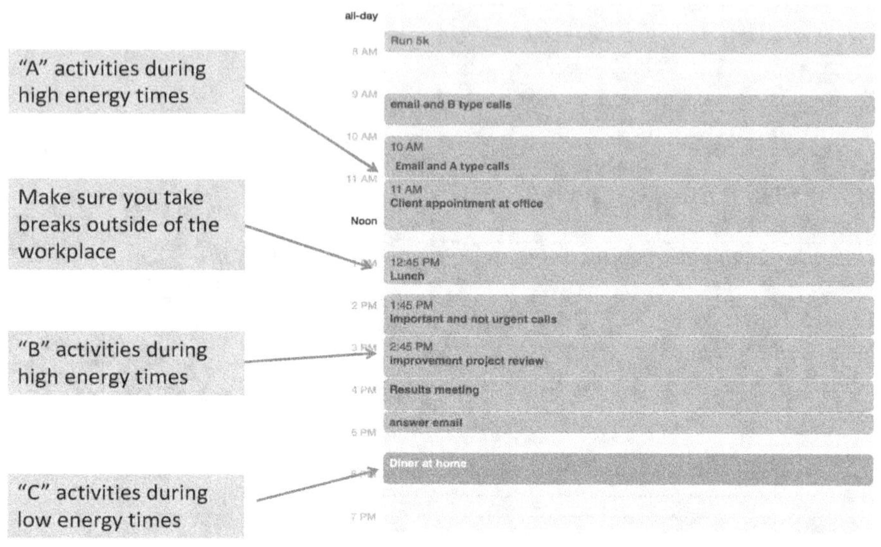

"A" activities during high energy times

Make sure you take breaks outside of the workplace

"B" activities during high energy times

"C" activities during low energy times

2. Use the Pomodoro technique

- The **Pomodoro Technique** is a time management method developed by Francesco Cirillo in the late 1980s.

- The technique uses a clock to divide the time spent on a job in 25-minute intervals - called "Pomodoros" - and separates them into short pauses.

A key objective of the technique is to eliminate (internal and external) interruptions.

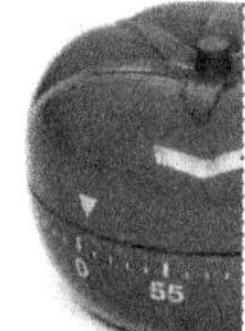

1. Pick the task.
2. Set the Pomodoro (watch or clock) to 25 minutes.
3. Work on the task until the clock rings and record it with an X.
4. Take a short break (5 minutes).
5. After 4 "Pomodoro", take a longer break (15-20 minutes).

3. Use your email effectively

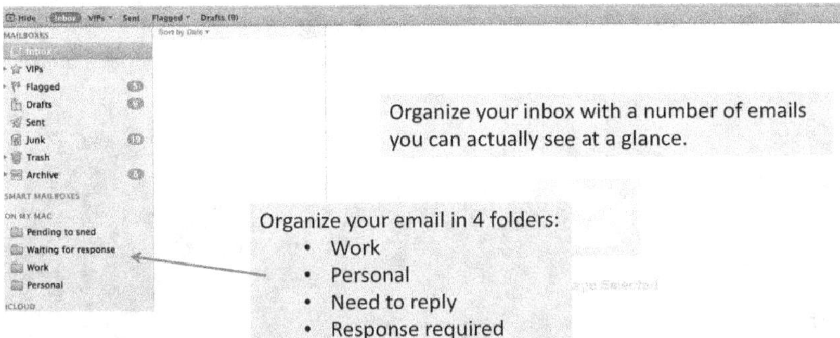

1. Answer only the emails you can complete in 2 minutes or less.
2. Eliminate the emails you don't need.
3. Archive the emails you need to keep.
4. Flag the emails you still need to reply to.

4. Conduct effective meetings

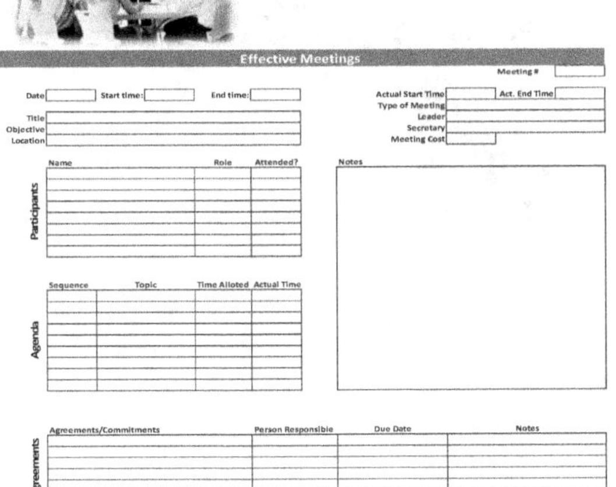

1. Plan the meeting
2. Send invitations
3. Confirm the logistics
4. Use an attendance sheet
5. Explain the objective of the meeting
6. Assign specific times during the meeting and follow them
7. Take notes
8. Write down the tasks to be completed and the person responsible
9. Summarize the meeting (confirm the objective)
10. Send a "meeting report" to all participants
11. Follow-up on the activities
12. Evaluate the meeting

5. Make effective phone calls

1. Prepare for the conversation as if it was a meeting.

2. Group phone calls together so that you can continue with other calls if one number is busy.

3. Prioritize your calls.

4. Use the speakerphone or headset so you can continue with other activities (only type C calls).

5. Schedule your phone calls.

The ABCs for teamwork

- **A**chievement

- **B**elonging

- **C**ontribution

LSSI
LEAN SIX SIGMA INSTITUTE

Problem Solving

Learning objectives

1. Apply a practical and simple method for defining problems.
2. Use a structured approach to understand the root cause of a problem.
3. Solve problems using a practical and simple methodology.

Content

> Background
> What is problem solving?
> Benefits
> When do we use the problem solving methodology?
> Methodology and example

Background

- Everyone faces different types of problems at work and personally.

- When trying to solve problems, most of the time we attack **symptoms** and **NOT causes**.

- How many of us know and apply a problem-solving methodology?

How do we normally solve problems?

The general tendency is:

How are we going to solve the problems now?

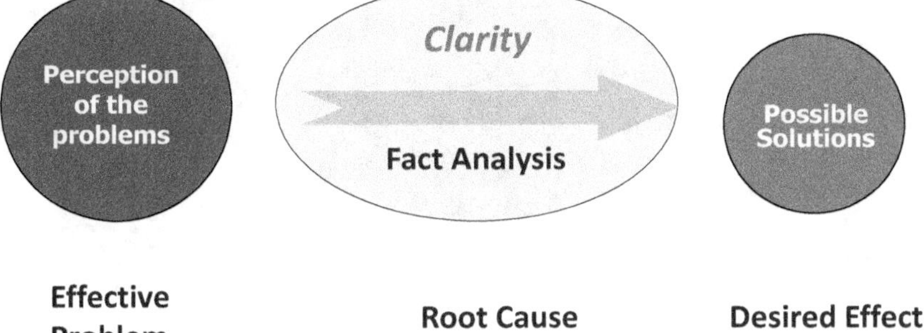

Effective Problem Definition

Root Cause Analysis

Desired Effect

What is problem solving?

A methodology to solve problems based on the root cause.

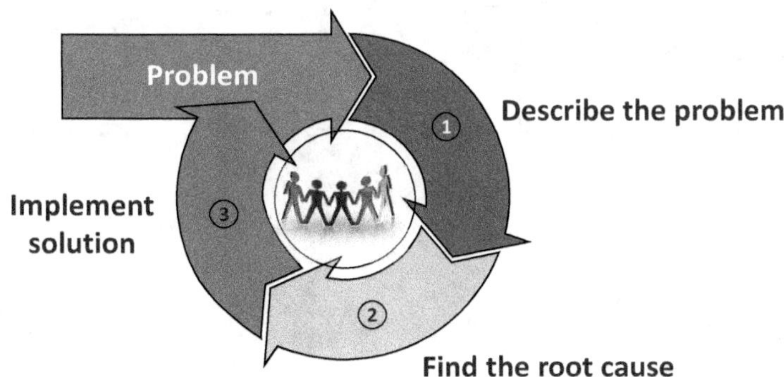

Benefits

- It provides the team with an approach to define causes of the problem

- Prevents recurrence

- Create better standards

- Motivate teamwork

- It helps solve the problems permanently

«Working as a team ensures success.» Henry Ford

When do we use the problem solving methodology?

- The problem has been defined and quantified.
- The gap between a desired state and the current state justifies the use of a problem solving methodology.
- The root cause is not know.
- The need to act decisively and with urgency to resolve a problem.
- During the adaptation cycles to further enhance process control.

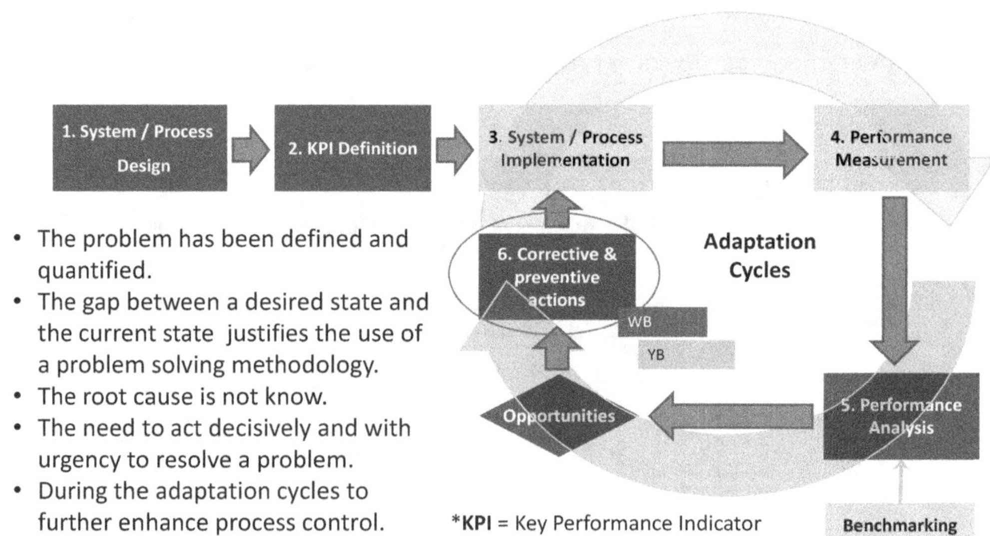

*KPI = Key Performance Indicator

How does it work?

Problem

Cause

Solution

STEP 1. DESCRIBE THE PROBLEM

STEP 2. FIND THE CAUSE

STEP 3. IMPLEMENT SOLUTION

PDCA - Share learning

Problem

- Define the problem as accurately as possible
- The problem is defined in the present tense

It should be written as a simple and concise statement that identifies the problem's subject using a present tense verb , along with the respective defect / situation.

Define the Problem

Find the Cause

Solution

Subject **+ present tense verb +** (defect/situation)

Defect / situation is an undesirable characteristic, present in a product or process. **Subject** is the name given to a specific product or process containing the defect.

e.g. The pizza is **delivered late.**

The problem statement should comply with the following

1. **Be specific:** problems are usually stated vaguely:

    "The water is too hot."

2. **Describe the problem, not its symptoms:**

    "The morale of the department is low."

3. **Avoid causes and solutions:**

    "The response time for providing the service is the cause of the customer's dissatisfaction, which indicates a potential problem"

Use the brainstorming process to define the problem

- **Objective**: to express without bias all the opinions of the group.

- To achieve this goal, all participants should be asked to write on a small paper (post-its) all the ideas generated from the question:

    What do you think is the problem?

- The facilitator gathers and classifies all the ideas and presents them in an un-biased way.

SOS Example

Brainstorming

What is the problem?

2 Cause

Define the problem

Find the Cause

Solution

- Observe and answer **"Why does this happen?"**

- If you cannot answer the previous question: Use some of the basic tools for problem solving (fish diagram, 5 whys, current reality tree, etc.)

- Prioritize if there is more than one cause (use FACTS)

What is the cause?

Basic Tools

Fishbone Diagram (Ishikawa)

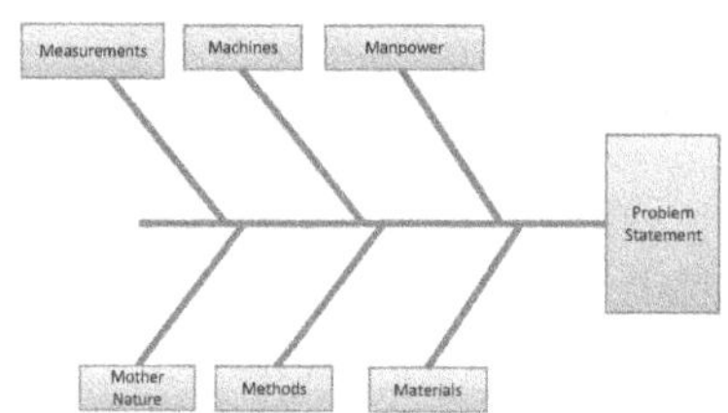

5 Whys

Current Reality Tree

LSSI
LEAN SIX SIGMA INSTITUTE

Fishbone Diagram / Ishikawa

Is a graphical tool that results from a brainstorming session in which all potential causes for a particular effect are listed and organized into categories. This makes it easier to separate problems and possible improvements.

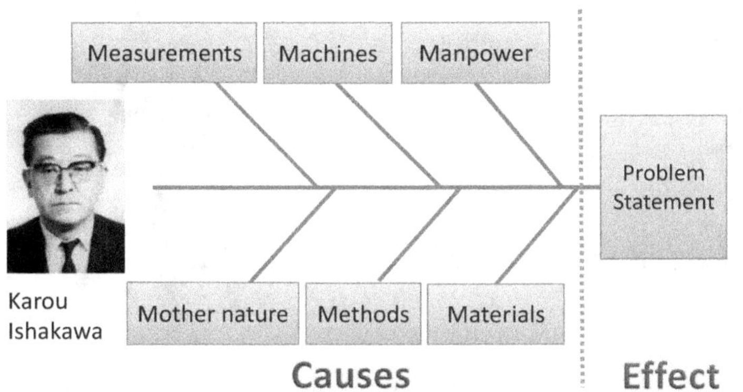

PROCEDIMIENTO

1. Define the problem.
2. Define categories.
3. Brainstorm in each category.
4. Verify ideas at the scene.
5. Mark the root causes in red.

Example S.O.S

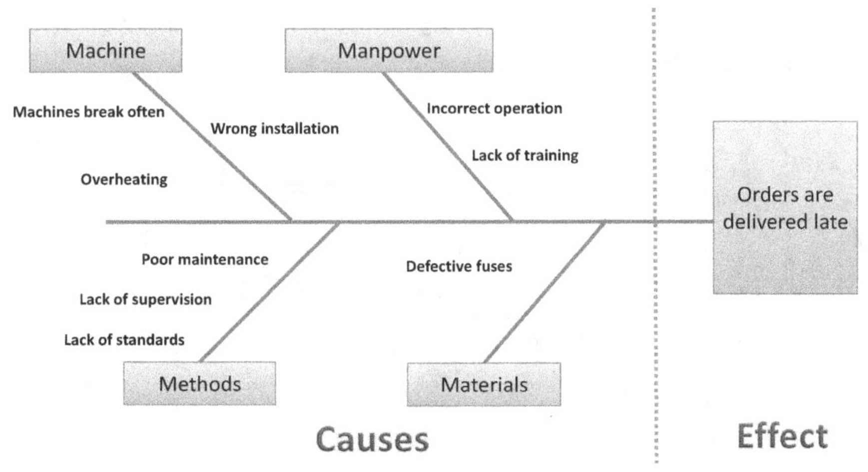

5 Whys

Define the problem:

Orders are delivered late to customers.

1. **Why?**
   - Because the machines are broken down
2. **Why?**
   - Because the fuses are melted
3. **Why?**
   - Because the machines are overheating
4. **Why?**
   - Because the oil changes are not made in time
5. **Why?**
   - Because there is no formal maintenance program

Current Reality Tree

A diagram that shows the **cause and effect relationships**, while taking into consideration all variables that influence a problem or a given situation. It includes circumstances, causes, effects, that pertain to the problem.

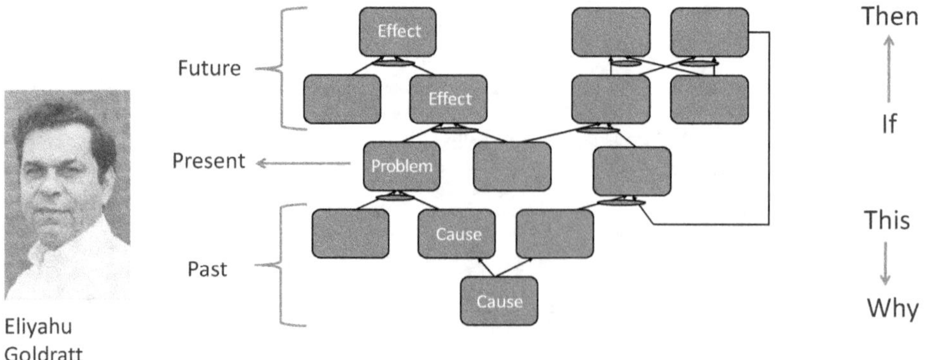

Eliyahu
Goldratt

LSSI
LEAN SIX SIGMA INSTITUTE

Example SOS

Develop a current reality tree

Find the cause (Solve)

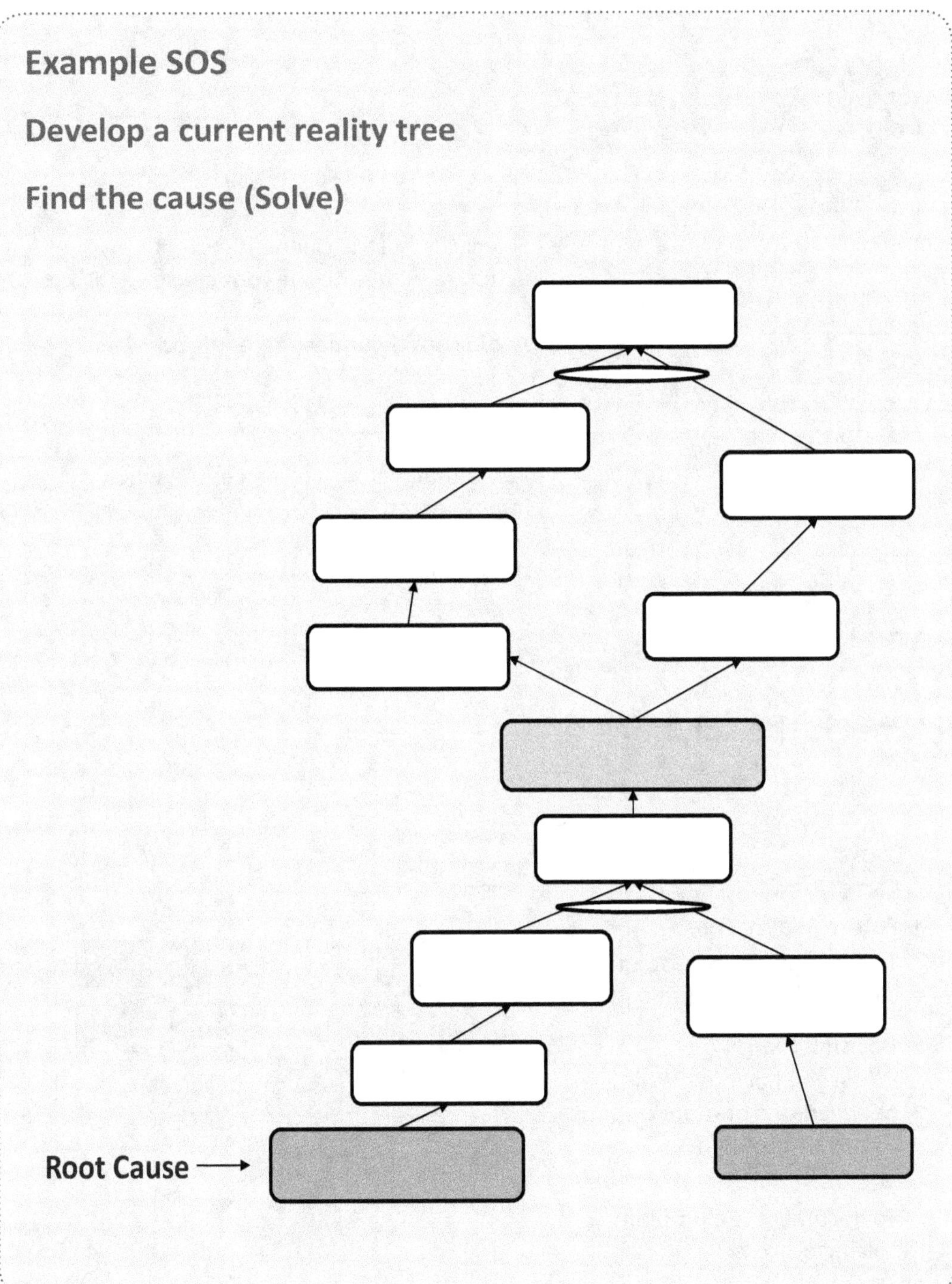

3   Solution

Define the problem

Find the cause

Solution

- Select the best permanent correct action to **eliminate the root cause**.

- **Avoid** causing **undesirable effects.**

- **Plan and implement** corrective actions.

- Verify that actions are **successful** when implemented.

- **Document** the case.

What is the solution?

Tools

- **Future Reality Tree**
  To establish the best solution sustained in actions and effects.

- **Decision Matrix**
  When you have to decide between two or more options to solve a problem.

- **A3**
  To document the problem solving process.

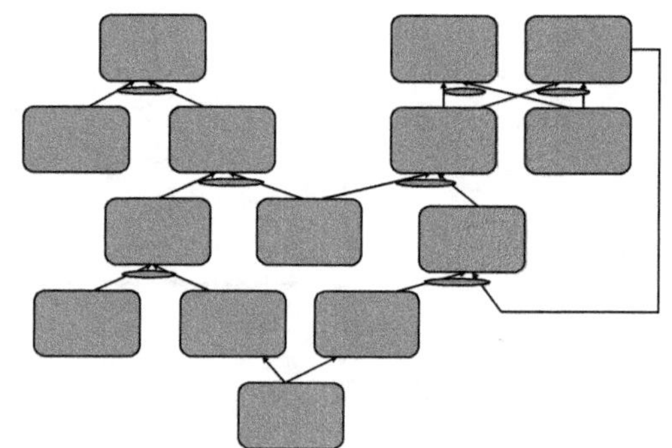

Example SOS

Develop a Future Reality Tree

Solution (Solve)

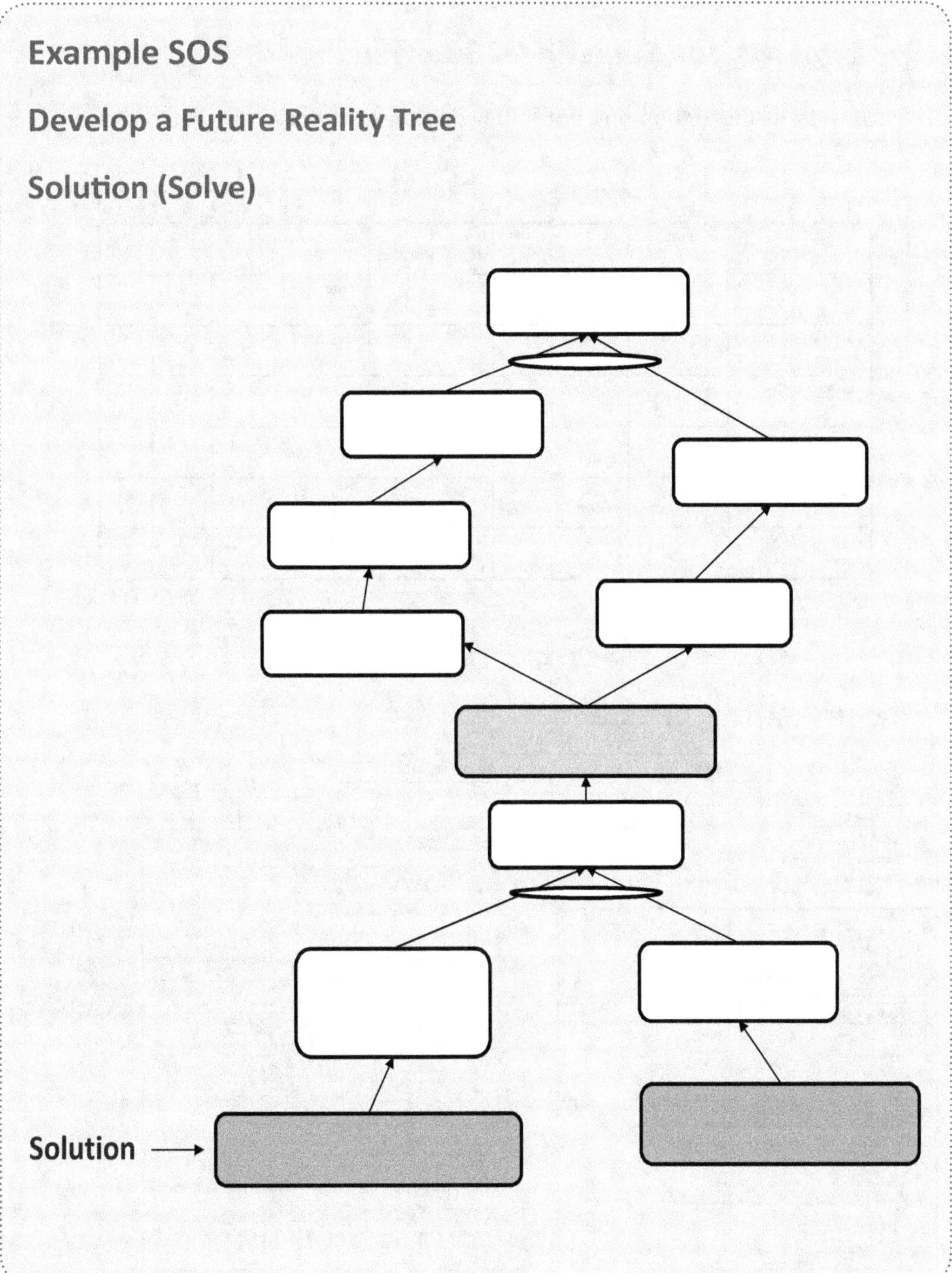

Decision Matrix: Selecting a Solution

If there is more than one potential solution to choose from, then use the following matrix:

Criteria	Importance	Alternative A			Alternative B		
		Evaluation	Value	Pts.	Evaluation	Value	Pts.
Safety	10	Visual fatigue	7	70	None	10	100
Defect Reduction	9	Reduced by 75%	8	72	Eliminated	10	90
Implementation Time	7	3 months	3	21	1 - 2 weeks	10	70
Operating Cost	5	Approximately $150/month	6	30	Approximately $25/month	9	45
Implementation Cost	3	Approximately $4,500	8	24	Approximately $5,000	6	18
Impact on Other Areas	2	None	10	20	None	10	20

Total **237**   Total **343**

Document the problem

Title: On time delivery, improving reliability

initials   *Owner*

1. Background

Why are we talking about it?
- **Customers are complaining**
- **Late deliveries**
- **Low machine reliability**

2. Current Conditions

What's the problem, where do we stand?
- **Orders are not delivered on time**

3. Target/Goal(s)

-*What is the specific change you want to accomplish now?*
- **Zero late deliveries**
- **Zero breakdowns**

4. Analysis

What is the root cause(s) of the problem?
- *Lack of preventive maintenance*
- *Operators don´t have the correct training*

Choose the simplest problem-solving tool for this issue:

Proposed Countermeasure(s)

Your proposal to reach the future state, the target condition.
- **Implement Total Productive Maintenance**
- *Develop a training program*

Plan

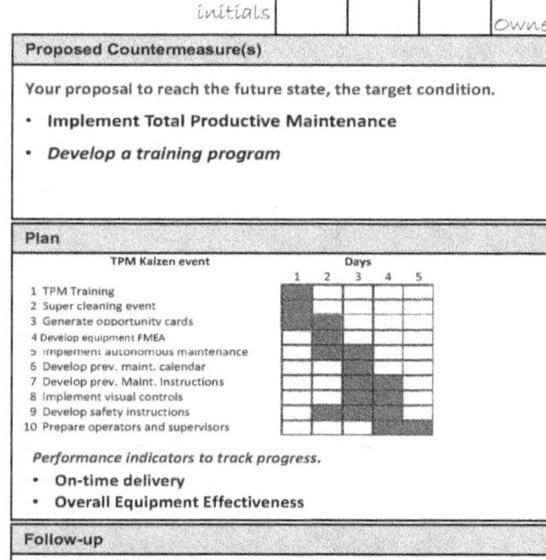

Performance indicators to track progress.
- **On-time delivery**
- **Overall Equipment Effectiveness**

Follow-up

- **Analyze box score in weekly meetings**
- *Gemba walks to analyze day by the hour boards*

We will cover the **A3** during the Yellow Belt Training

What we accomplish?

- Apply the problem-solving process to:

    - Define the problem properly.
    - Identify the root cause and effects.
    - Define actions that eliminate the problem.
    - Efficiently document the problem-solving process.

- Now it is very important to consider:

    - Use the simple problem-solving method.
    - Teach our classmates, students and family how to solve problems in an easy way.
    - Constantly improve our problem-solving process.

Example SOS

Bayside is one of our best customers. Lately, we haven't been able to deliver a single order to them on time. Our facility is a mess. Nothing is ever produced as planned.

The production supervisor blames maintenance personnel for being too slow when fixing maintenance issues. The maintenance staff blames the operators for not taking care of the machines and letting them breakdown constantly. The bottom line is that we are not delivering products on time to our customers, and they are assessing the possibility of going with other more reliable suppliers.

Every day, we try our best to meet our production schedule. However, issues keep coming up, and as the production manager, I spend much of my time resolving them.

In the last few days, we have had to pay for excessive maintenance costs and overtime to ensure that our orders are complete. However, we still can't meet our expected delivery dates and requirements.

I really don't know what is going on with the company. I am beginning to feel desperate and am not sure what the solution is. I have morning meetings every day with my production personnel and we review the production schedule. The meetings are chaotic since everyone is placing blame on each other and no one can agree on the best problem solving method.

In the maintenance report, I have noted high reliability/performance fuses are being changed frequently. Lately, I have had to approve urgent purchase orders for fuses to avoid stopping the production machines.

I think we need to establish a preventive maintenance plan, but with all the problems we are facing, I don't see how we can put one together since there is not enough time to focus on both production and maintenance.

The operators are constantly reporting that the machines are overheating, but I think they are just using the machines as an excuse to evade their responsibility for not meeting production and delivery requirements. I have been wanting to launch a training program to teach the operators how to operate the machines correctly, but we haven't had time since we are almost always behind schedule.

At this point, I don't know what the solutions are to address our problems and I am totally overwhelmed. I need to solve our issues quickly or we might have to completely shut the plant down due to low productivity.

5S Housekeeping

Learning objectives

1. Understand the benefits of working in a clean and orderly environment.
2. Learn how to implement the 5S discipline

Content

> Background
> What is 5S Housekeeping?
> Benefits
> Procedure
> Examples

Background

Why is order important?

I cannot find my keys!

Where did I put that document?

Where are those materials?

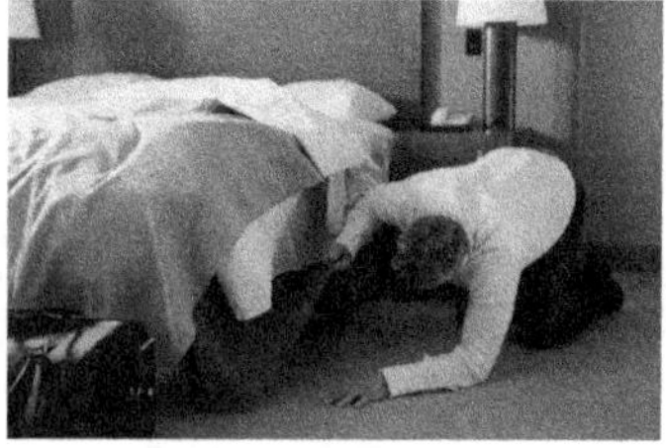  

- Culture and habits are the most important elements of agile thinking (Lean Thinking).

- 5S was developed by Hiroyuki Hirano and is considered a stepping stone to other improvement tools or systems.

- Therefore, it is said that a good improvement event is one that starts with 5S.

Hiroyuki Hirano

LSSI
LEAN SIX SIGMA INSTITUTE

Origin of the 5Ss   1950

- Ford Motor Company developed the CANDO program.
- The Japanese, who visited the Ford Michigan plants, adopted it (Hiroyuki Hirano).

C leaning up   = *Seiri*

A rranging   = *Seiton*

N eatness   = *Seiso*

D iscipline   = *Seiketsu*

O ngoing Improvement = *Shitsuke*

Toyota improved Ford's design

Seiri	**S** ort
Seiton	**S** traighten
Seiso	**S** hine
Seiketsu	**S** tandardize
Shitsuke	**S** ustain

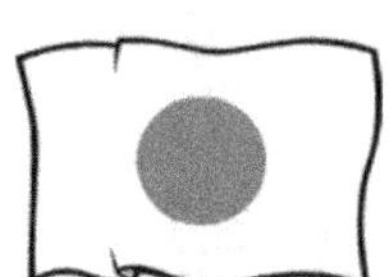

What is 5S Housekeeping?

- 5S is a **discipline** that improves productivity in the workplace by standardizing **housekeeping habits** (orderliness and cleanliness).

What is **NOT** 5S Housekeeping?

- A methodology that is only applicable to manufacturing environments.
- A program to impress visitors and customers.
- A spring cleaning event.
- A system that has little impact on efficiency and customer satisfaction.

Benefits

- Find anything in less than 30 seconds
- Improved employee productivity
- Improved personal satisfaction
- Safer work environment
- Higher Quality

LSSI
LEAN SIX SIGMA INSTITUTE

Procedure

 A **5S program** is well-developed with the successful completion of the following steps:

Sort	Straighten	Shine	Standardize	Sustain
Separate the necessary items from the unnecessary items.	Organize the necessary work items by establishing a specific place for each item.	Clean the workspace and keep it neat.	Define methods to ensure that the procedures and activities are implemented consistently.	Make a habit out of 5S activities to ensure that work areas are more productive.

Sort – Seiri

Sort	Straighten	Shine	Standardize	Sustain

Sort: Remove all the items from the workplace that are not necessary for performing productive operations.

Sorting process:

1. Recognize areas of opportunity
2. Define the selection criteria
3. Identify the selected items
4. Make the selected items available

1. Recognize areas of opportunity

Sort > Straighten > Shine > Standardize > Sustain

- Warehouses
- Common areas
- Offices
- Production floor
- Briefcases
- Binders
- Computers

2. Define the selection criteria

You must decide what to do with the items that are **not needed.**

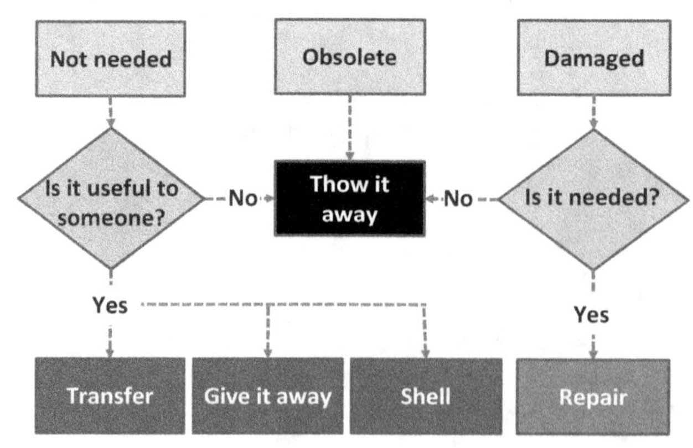

- Select what is not needed.

- Go through all work areas, shelves, drawers, etc. Keep only essential items. Store or discard everything else.

3. Identify the selected items

The items categorized as **not needed** must be clearly labeled and confined in a quarantine area.

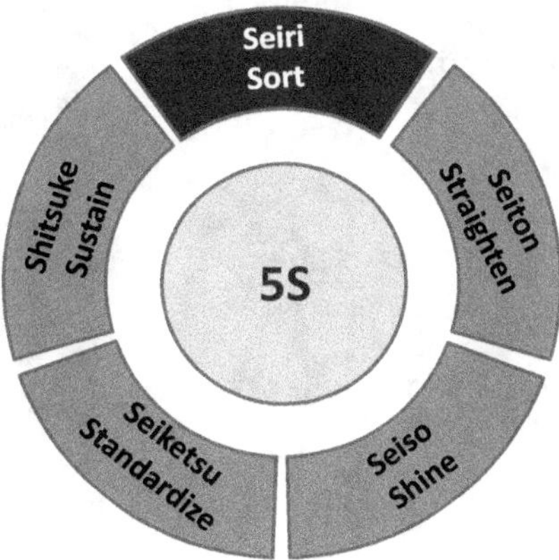

Seiri **Principle**

«Only what is needed, only the amount needed and only when you need it.»

Straighten – Seiton

Sort > **Straighten** > Shine > Standardize > Sustain

Straighten: Organize necessary work items and establish a specific place for each item. This will facilitate item identification, location, availability, and return after use.

Straightening process:
1. Prepare the work area
2. Establish a specific place for each item
3. Establish rules and follow them

Key elements
- All needed items have a designated location.
- The need to search for items is eliminated.

Value
- Everything is organized and accessible.
- There is a place for everything.
- After use, items are returned to where they belong.

LSSI
LEAN SIX SIGMA INSTITUTE

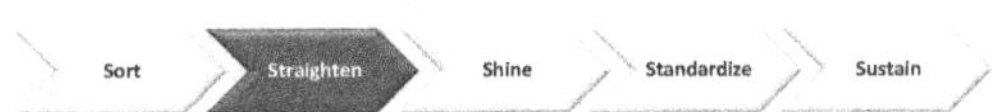

- Determine how long it takes to find the items.
    - **Can you find any item in less than 30 seconds?**
- When organizing, focus on:
    - Defining the location for the parts, tools, supplies, and materials based on their function.
    - Clearly identifying the items' names and locations.
    - The ability to quickly and easily retrieve the items.
- **Deliverable:**
    - A list of necessary items, where they can be found, and locations that are clearly marked.

1. Prepare the work area

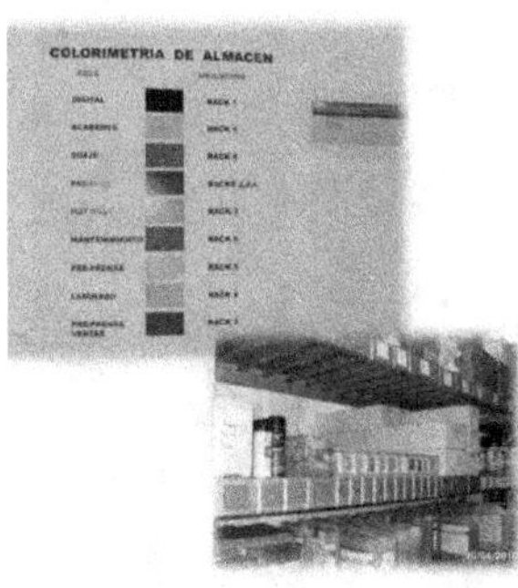

Color Codes for 5S

	Physical Health Hazard Exposure area
	Fire & Emergency Equipment
	Operational Clearance Area
	Permanent Location for Equipment
	Defects, Scraps, Rework, Red Tag area
	Working Areas & Aisleways
	Finished Goods, Completed Documentation/Paperwork
	Temporary Storage Location, Waiting for approval

2. Establish a specific place for each item

"Anyone" can immediately see, retrieve and return any item.

Question	Answers
What?	Define which items are necessary (select)
	Identify the items
Where?	Define their correct location
	Mark their locations to make them identifiable
How many?	Define the quantity of items
	Identify the number of items needed

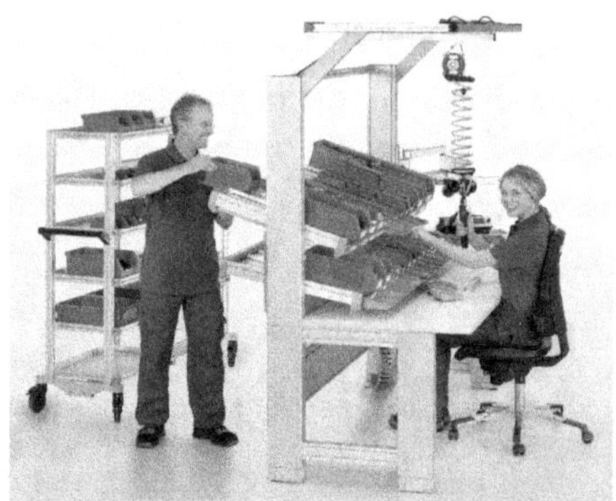

▶ What?

- Define which items are required

- Use removable labels to clearly identify an item and use another label to specify where it should be kept

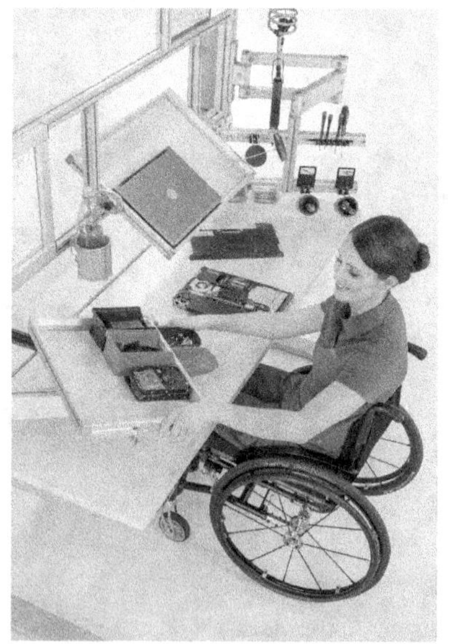

Provide specific and accessible locations for each item

▶ Where?

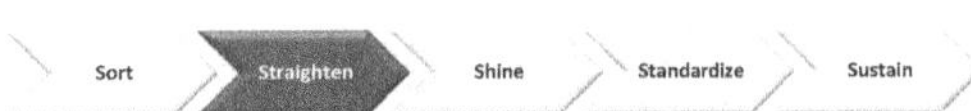

Store all items that are used together in the same location.

Store items with similar functions together.

Avoid storing items in enclosed spaces.

Each item is in its place

Cabinet Identification

- Use letters to identify cabinets

- Arrange the cabinets in rows and column

- Name files and folders

▶ How many?

Seiton Principle

«A place for everything, and
everything in its place.»

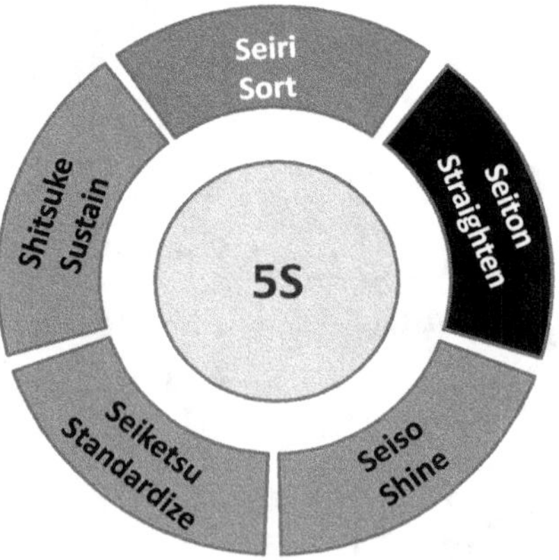

Shine – Seiso

Sort → Straighten → **Shine** → Standardize → Sustain

Shine: Very simple. Clean the workspace! Remove all the dirt.

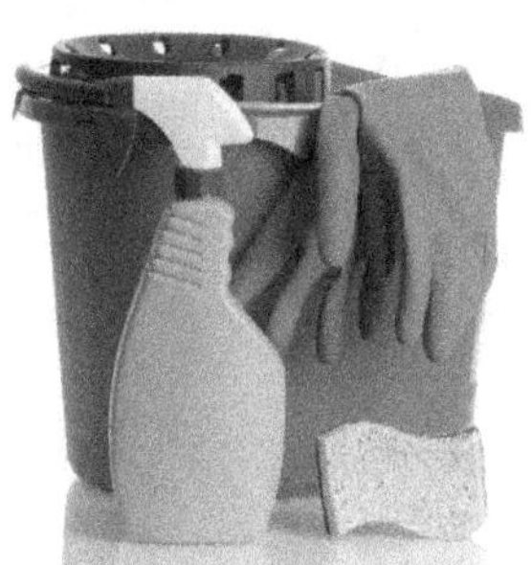

Cleaning process:

1. Create a cleaning schedule

2. Define cleaning methods

3. Develop discipline

Cleaning process

In Japan, children start the day cleaning their schools as a way of respecting and caring for the environment where they will learn the knowledge for life.

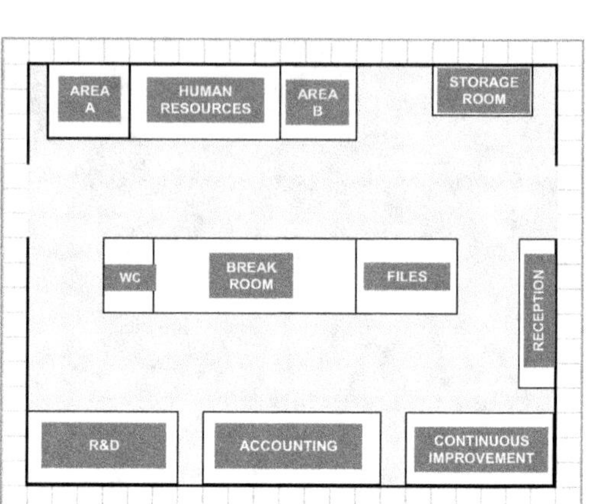

- To create a cleaning schedule, start by determining what must be cleaned.

- A good method for organizing activities is to use a map of the entire work area.

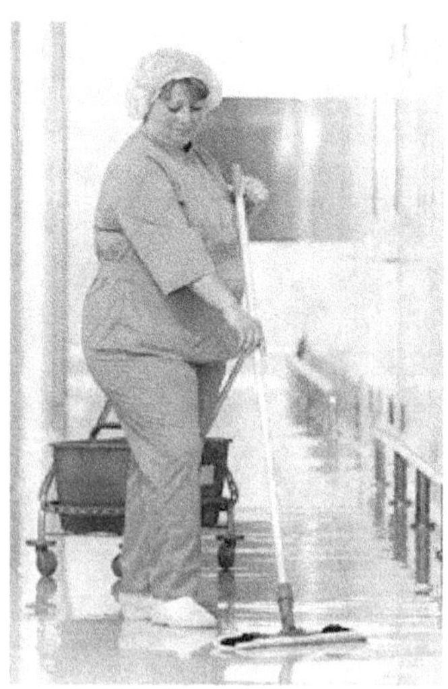

Shine – Useful tips

- Identify sources of dirt
- Always inspect while cleaning
- Repair leaks to prevent soiling
- Paint areas, equipment, floors, walls, and ceilings
- Improve lighting in the work areas

1. Create a cleaning schedule

Determine who is responsible for the cleaning activities, and define when and how often each activity should take place.

Cleaning Schedule				
Area	*Items*	*Responsible*	*Shift*	*Frequency*
Prens #1	Floors	J. Hobbs	1st	Daily
	Prenss	M. Hilton	2nd	Weekly
	Lamps	H. Patrick	3rd	Weekly
	Conveyor	J. Chase	2nd	Daily

2. Define cleaning methods

- Make a list of all cleaning activities
- Make a list of the items, supplies, and equipment needed
- Document the cleaning activities

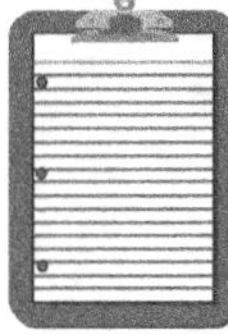

▶ Step approach to cleaning

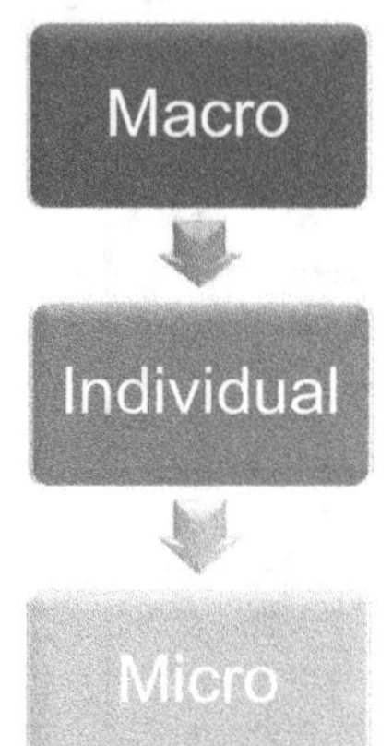

Macro — Common areas: surfaces, walls, ceilings, lights, storage areas, bathrooms, shelves, filing cabinets, etc.

Individual — Individual work stations: chairs, drawers, computers, shelves, etc. Clean things under your table!

Micro — Measuring instruments: micrometers, calibrators, Vernier calipers, microscopes, etc.

Seiso **Principle**

«The cleanest place is not the one cleaned the most, but the one that gets dirty the least.»

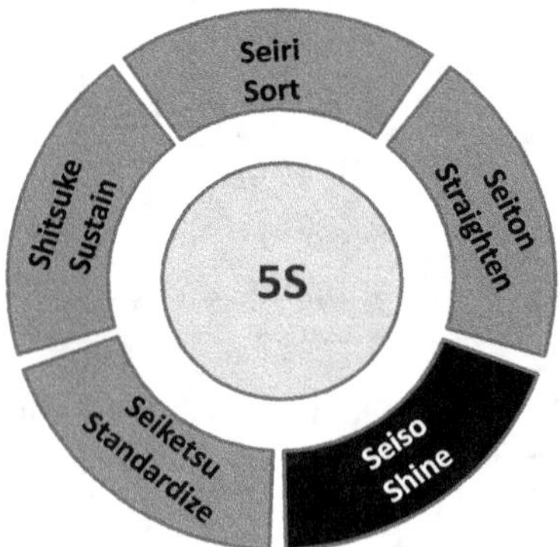

Standardize – Seiketsu

Sort → Straighten → Shine → **Standardize** → Sustain

Standaize: Ensure that procedures, practices, and activities are implemented consistently and on a regular basis. Ensure that the *Sort*, *Straighten* and *Shine* stages are maintained in the work areas

Standardize process:
1. Integrate the 5S activities into your regular work day
2. Evaluate the results

1. Integrate the 5S activities into your regular work day

- Establish procedures
- Develop a standardization manual
- Perform inspections

▶ Evaluate the areas

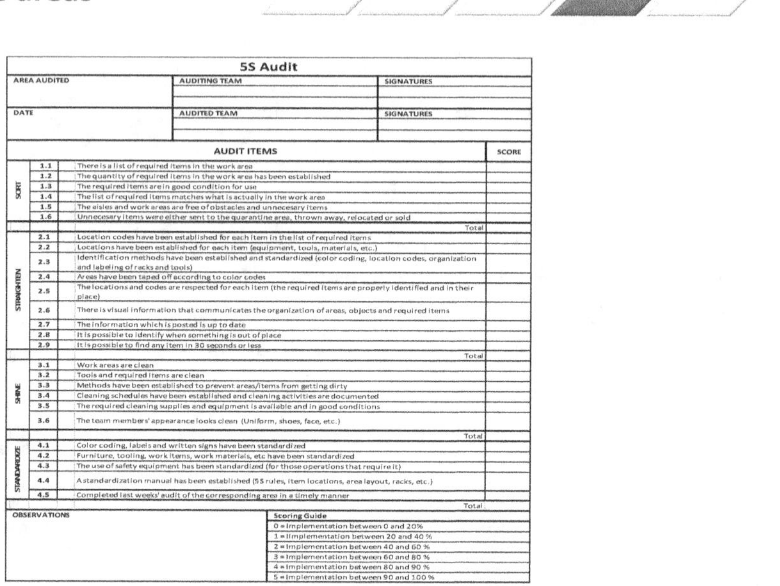

5S Audit			
AREA AUDITED	**AUDITING TEAM**	**SIGNATURES**	
DATE	**AUDITED TEAM**	**SIGNATURES**	
AUDIT ITEMS			**SCORE**
SORT	1.1	There is a list of required items in the work area	
	1.2	The quantity of required items in the work area has been established	
	1.3	The required items are in good condition for use	
	1.4	The list of required items matches what is actually in the work area	
	1.5	The aisles and work areas are free of obstacles and unnecesary items	
	1.6	Unnecesary items were either sent to the quarantine area, thrown away, relocated or sold	
		Total	
STRAIGHTEN	2.1	Location codes have been established for each item in the list of required items	
	2.2	Locations have been established for each item (equipment, tools, materials, etc.)	
	2.3	Identification methods have been established and standardized (color coding, location codes, organization and labeling of racks and tools)	
	2.4	Areas have been taped off according to color codes	
	2.5	The locations and codes are respected for each item (the required items are properly identified and in their place)	
	2.6	There is visual information that communicates the organization of areas, objects and required items	
	2.7	The information which is posted is up to date	
	2.8	It is possible to identify when something is out of place	
	2.9	It is possible to find any item in 30 seconds or less	
		Total	
SHINE	3.1	Work areas are clean	
	3.2	Tools and required items are clean	
	3.3	Methods have been established to prevent areas/items from getting dirty	
	3.4	Cleaning schedules have been established and cleaning activities are documented	
	3.5	The required cleaning supplies and equipment is available and in good conditions	
	3.6	The team members' appearance looks clean (Uniform, shoes, face, etc.)	
		Total	
STANDARDIZE	4.1	Color coding, labels and written signs have been standardized	
	4.2	Furniture, tooling, work items, work materials, etc have been standardized	
	4.3	The use of safety equipment has been standardized (for those operations that require it)	
	4.4	A standardization manual has been established (5S rules, item locations, area layout, racks, etc.)	
	4.5	Completed last weeks' audit of the corresponding area in a timely manner	
		Total	

OBSERVATIONS	Scoring Guide
	0 = Implementation between 0 and 20%
	1 = Implementation between 20 and 40 %
	2 = Implementation between 40 and 60 %
	3 = Implementation between 60 and 80 %
	4 = Implementation between 80 and 90 %
	5 = Implementation between 90 and 100 %

2. Evaluate the results

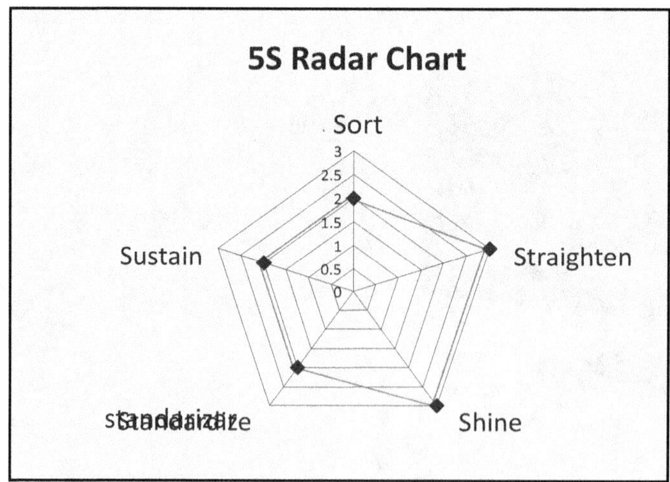

Seiketsu **Principle**

«Say what you do,
do what you say,
and prove it.»

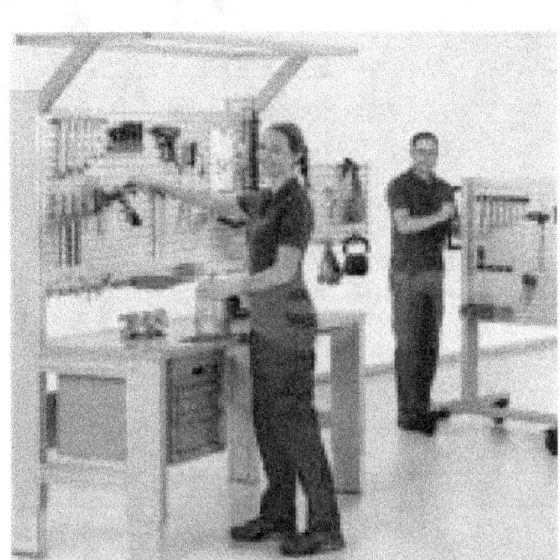

Sustain – Shitsuke

Sustaining never ends:
- Have follow-up / monitoring meetings
- Improve standards
- Conduct Gemba Walks
- Invite people who are outside your area
- Have contests
- Publicly acknowledge the successes

Suggestions for implementation

Preparation
- Management training
- Train all staff
- Define the implementation team
- Define pilot area(s)
- Divide areas
- Create visual control boards
- Design a logo and theme
- Take pictures of the areas
- Kick-off day

Implement 1st S
- Apply first 5S evaluation
- Photos of current state
- Training on 1st S
- Red cards
- Sort and classify
- Verify red cards
- Evaluation (check list)
- Pictures of improvements

Implement 2nd S
- Progress review and training on 2nd S
- Start organizing and labeling
- Verify
- Evaluation (check list with pictures of 2nd S)
- Pictures for future evaluations

Implement 3rd S
- Progress review and training on 3rd S
- Establish cleaning schedules
- Verify
- Evaluation (check list with pictures of 2nd S
- Pictures of improvements

Implement 4th S
- Create standardization manual
- Create evaluation forms/templates
- Create order and cleanliness regulations

Examples

In the industry

Manufacturing plant

Warehouse

Workshops

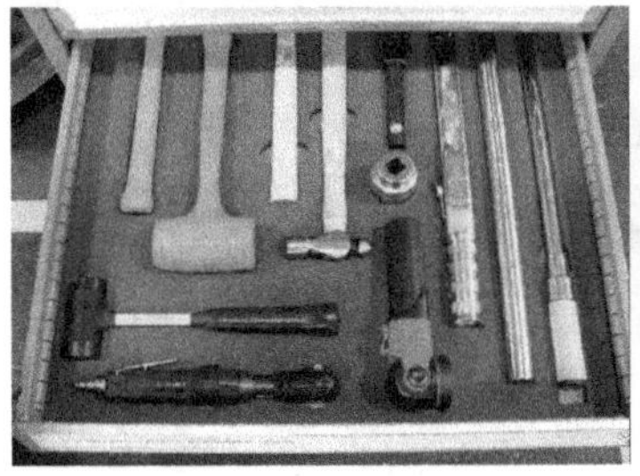

Workstation / Storage

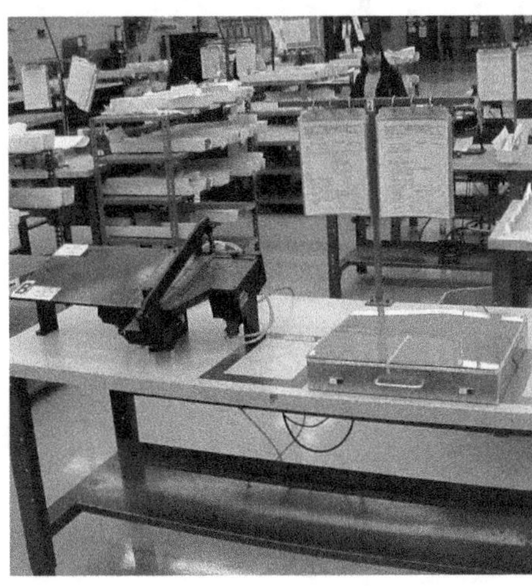

All materials are identified and in their designated places.
Wheels are installed under the storage units for easy movement.

Laboratory

In documents and files

In office

Andon

Learning objectives

1. Understand how visual management works as an essential part of the Lean transformation.
2. Leverage visual tools to improve operational structure and stability, reduce variation, and increase efficiency.
3. Apply visual tools in your daily routines to improve efficiencies in both your work and personal life.

Content

> Background
> What is Andon?
> Benefits
> Procedure
> Examples
> Exercise

Background

Long ago, early humans painted on cave walls as a form of communication and establish a legacy.

Historically, armies recognized one another by their flags and uniforms.

How do humans perceive information?

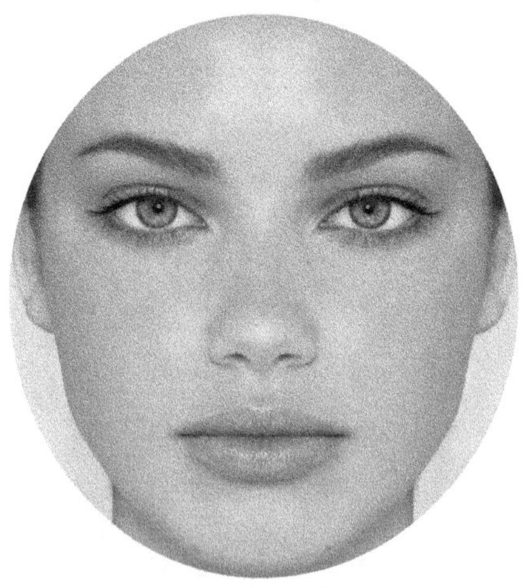

83 % by Sight

11 % by Hearing

4 % by Smell

1 % by Touch

1 % by Taste

Origin of Andon

- In ancient Japan, an Andon was a **lamp**.

- It was made of sheets of paper placed around a base, with a candle inside.

- An Andon was used as a **visual signal** to communicate a message over long distance.

What is Andon?

- Andon is a signal that incorporates **visual, auditory, and textual elements,** and is used to notify people of quality issues or stoppages due to specific reasons.

- Information provided by these signals can be used to identify or indicate a **regular or irregular condition** at the workplace, which might require further action.

- Andon provides real-time information and feedback on the status of a process.

- These signals are efficient, self-regulating, and managed by the operators.

What is NO Andon?

- A presentation of screens and graphics to impress corporate visitors or customers
- An opportunity to fill up space on bare walls for decorative purposes
- A one-time effort, where visual elements or information become obsolete over time
- An isolated application of Leader Standard Work

LSSI
LEAN SIX SIGMA INSTITUTE

Key Points

- Visual management is an essential part of a Lean management system.
- For visual management to be effective and sustainable, it must be integrated with:

  - Strategic management
  - Management follow-up (Gemba walks)
  - Situation analysis (Kata)
  - Standardized work
  - Project management
  - Daily management

  - Results management
  - 5S Housekeeping
  - Continuous flow
  - Quick preparations
  - Total Productive Maintenance
  - Kanban
  - Etc.

Which of the following ANDON elements can you identify in the photo?

- Materials
- Methods
- Machines
- Workforce
- Measurements
- Environment
- Safety

Form of communication

- A distinctive aspect of visual communication is that it helps to guide the activities of group members, so that everyone is working in the same direction.

- **An Andon can be a:**
  - Signal
  - Sound
  - Label
  - Screen
  - Trend chart
  - Color scheme
  - Etc.

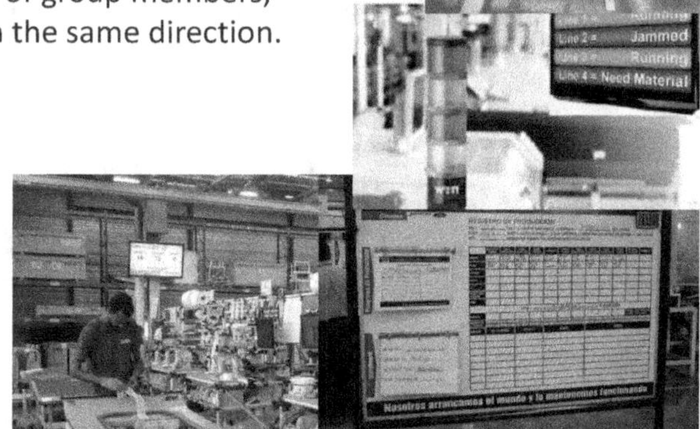

Andon example - Turning off car lights

Visual Control Levels combined with Poka-yoke

1. Share Information	Include instructions to "turn off the lights before turning off the engine" in the car's owner's manual.
2. Share established standards	Write the instructions on the car's dashboard so that it is easy for the driver to see them: "The lights should be turned off before leaving the car."
3. Incorporate standards in the workplace	Install a red light near the instructions so that both are easily seen by the driver.
4. Notification of irregular condition	Install a bell that sounds immediately when you open the car door if the lights are on.
5. Detection of irregular condition	Install a device that prevent the keys from being removed from the ignition if the lights are on.
6. Prevent irregular condition	Install a device that automatically turns off the lights when the engine is turned off.

- Improves **Quality**
- Reduces **Costs**
- Improves **Response Time**
- Improves **Safety**
- Improves **Communication**

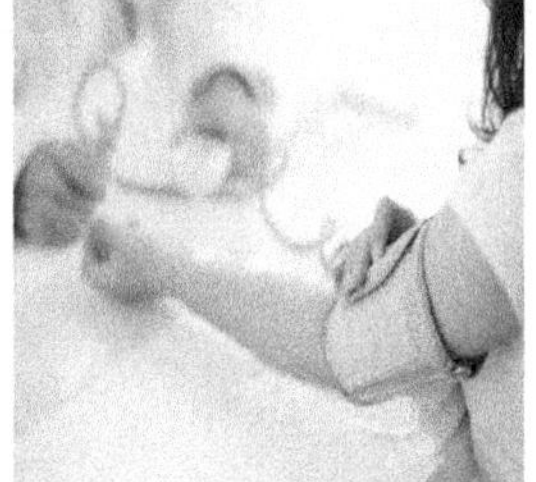

- Provides a way to bring **Immediate attention** to a problem
- Offers a **simple mechanism** to communicate information
- Improves **accountability**
- Increases the **speed and quality** of decision-making

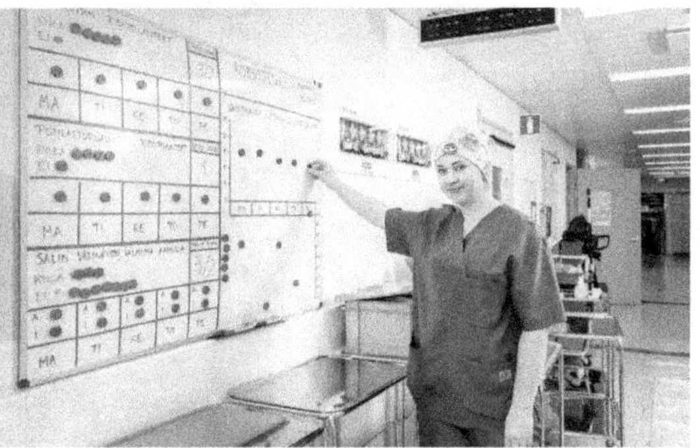

Procedure

1. Identify the information you want to know and the errors you want to avoid.

2. Design a simple visual way to guide and manage the activities of the group members.

3. Test the method – Seek feedback from the involved group members.

4. Train the entire group so that everyone is using the system.

5. Review and improve the system regularly.

Andon is widely applicable in both Services and Manufacturing.

Services and production

- Hospitals and clinics
- Restaurants
- Laboratories
- Manufacturing facilities
- Logistics operations
- etc.

Hospitals

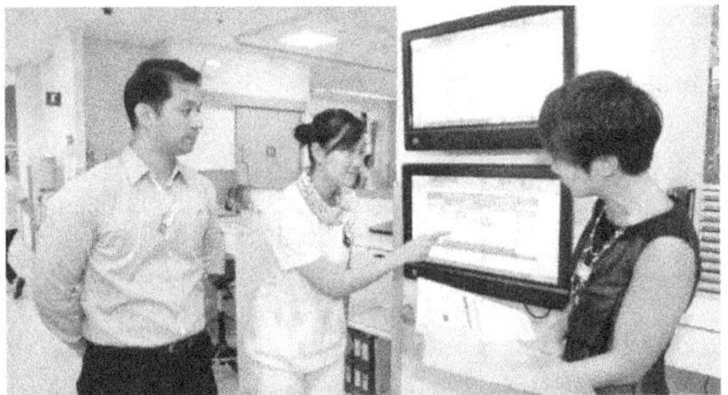

Hospital admissions

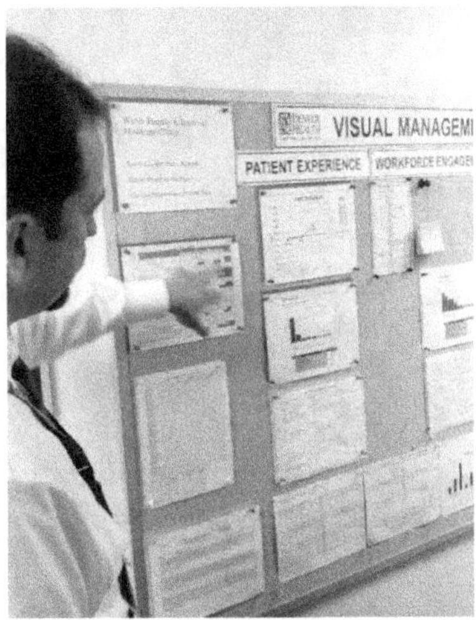

Dashboard

Agile meetings

- Andon Boards.
- Only relevant information is discussed.
- All participants are well-informed.
- All participants contribute ideas.
- A plan is suggested.
- Everyone shares common goals.

Source: Products Verde Valle.

Andon in manufacturing cells

Use Andon to compare the actual results against the goals every hour.

- Leaders and operators meet every day at the beginning of the shift.

- Goals and requirements are established.

- During the shift, the operators update the information every hour. Decisions are made based on the results.

			MACHINE #23			
HOUR	TARGET	ACTUAL	CUMMULATIVE TARGET	CUMMULATIVE ACTUAL	DEFECTS	COMMENTS
7:00 – 8:00	95	90	95	90	1	Morning meeting went over – material not secured during startup
8:00 – 9:00	100	100	195	190	0	
9:00 – 10:00	100	100	295	290	0	
10:00 – 11:00	100	100	395	390	0	
11:00 – 12:00	75	75	470	465	0	
12:00 – 1:00	75	40	545	505	0	Changeover
1:00 – 2:00	100	90	645	595	3	Changeover – Startup issues, incorrect program
2:00 – 3:00	100	100	745	695	0	
3:00 – 4:00	85	85	830	780	0	

Andon in Product Family / Value Stream

- The Value Stream team meets to analyze results.

- Both the current state and future state VSMs for the next 2-4 months are shown.

- The strategies, structure, and talent program are analyzed.

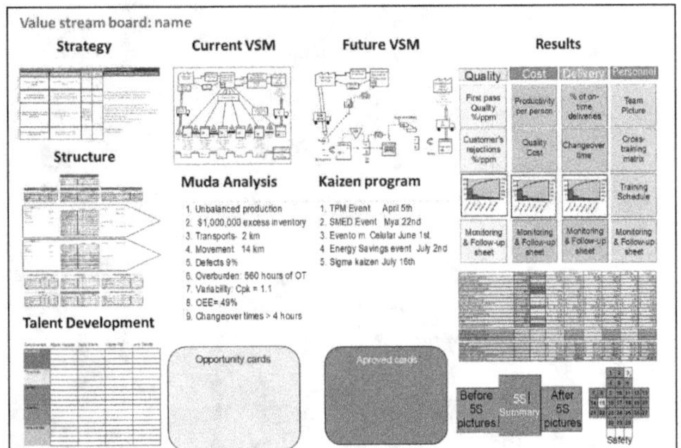

Tips for creating a visual space

- Mark all inventory areas.

- Mark the places where the equipment belongs with labels.

- Indicate visually the amount of paperwork allowed.

- Label all cabinets, shelves, etc., with their designated content.

Safety Andons

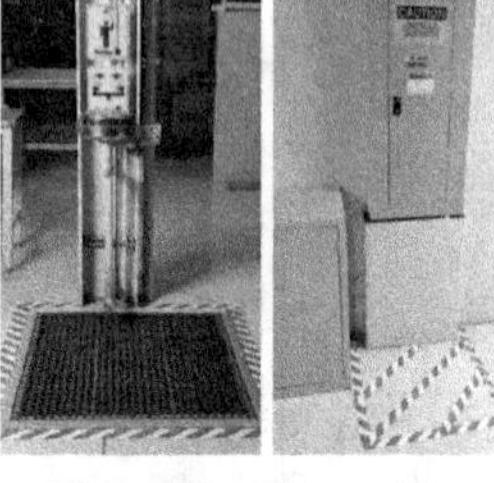

Hazardous materials

Area that required use of personal protective equipment (PPE)

Labels that indicate danger

Walkways

Control Andons

Pressure Control

Oil-Level Control

Tension Control

Office Andons

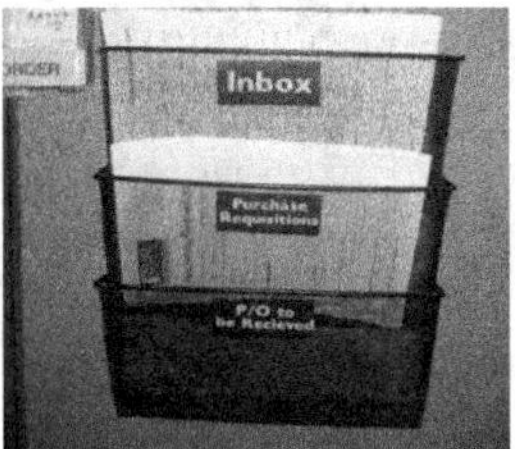

Document Trays

Files

Fire Extinguisher

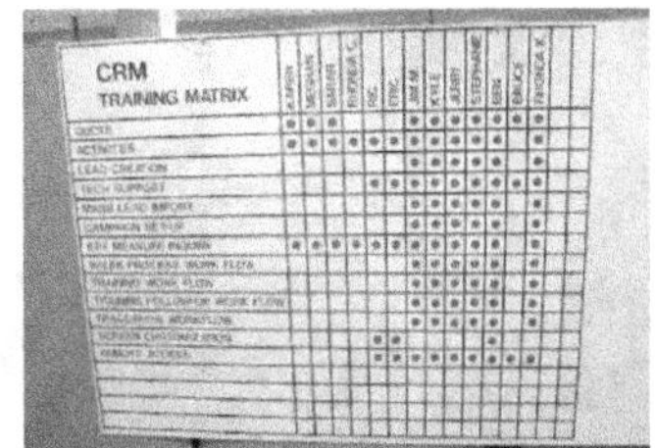

Multi-skill Matrix Status

Personnel Assignments

Operations Andons

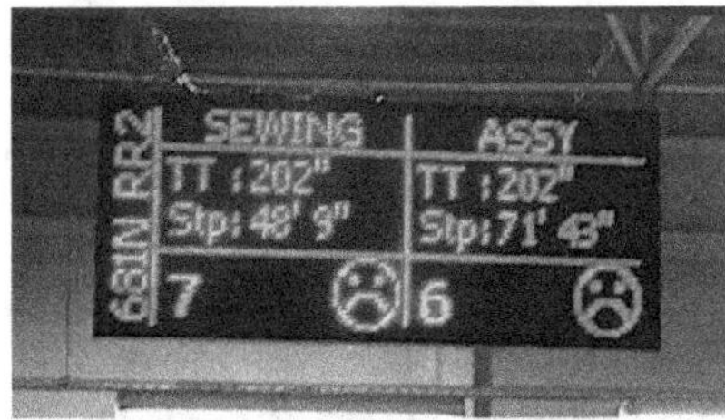

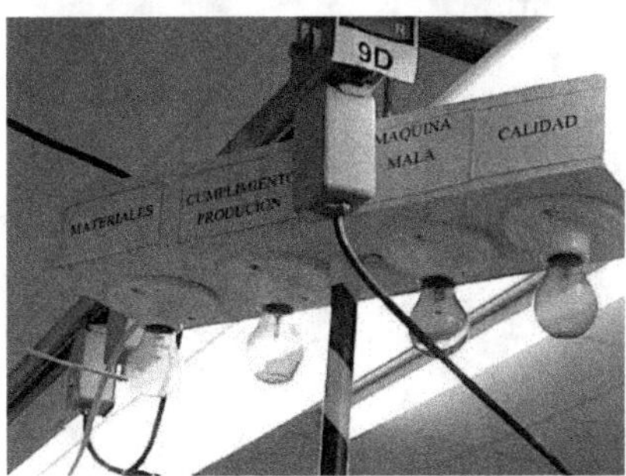

Examples of visual controls

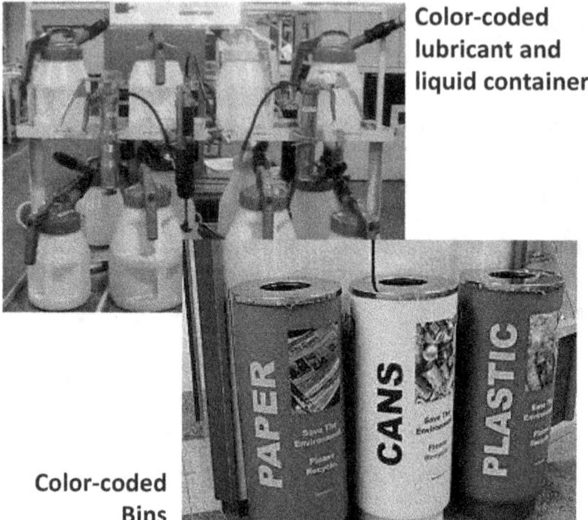

Color-coded lubricant and liquid containers

Color-coded Bins

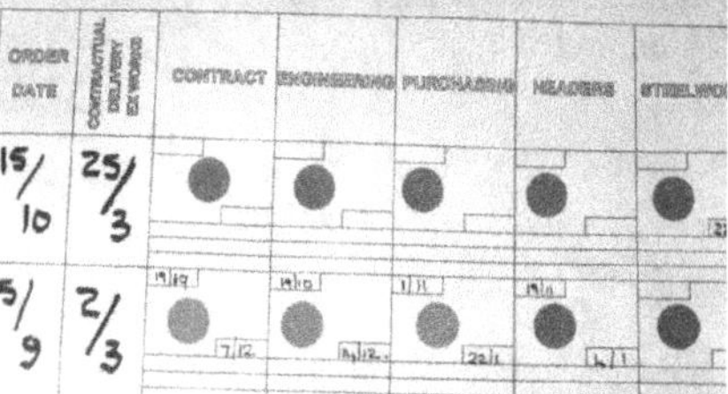

Fuguai Tagging Opportunity Cards

ORDER DATE	CONTRACTUAL DELIVERY EX WORKS	CONTRACT	ENGINEERING	PURCHASING	HEADERS	STEELWORK
15/10	25/3	●	●	●	●	●
5/9	2/3	●	●	●	●	●

Color-coded Project Status sheets

Visual signal Andons

- The visual warning sensors inform the operator that there is a problem.

- These sensors use colors, alarms, and / or lights to get the workers' attention.

- They may be combined with a contact or energy sensor to get the workers' attention.

LSSI
LEAN SIX SIGMA INSTITUTE

Healthcare Andons

- **Color-coded** Andons indicate the status of different patient areas.

- An Andon used in a **team meeting** to help guide actions.

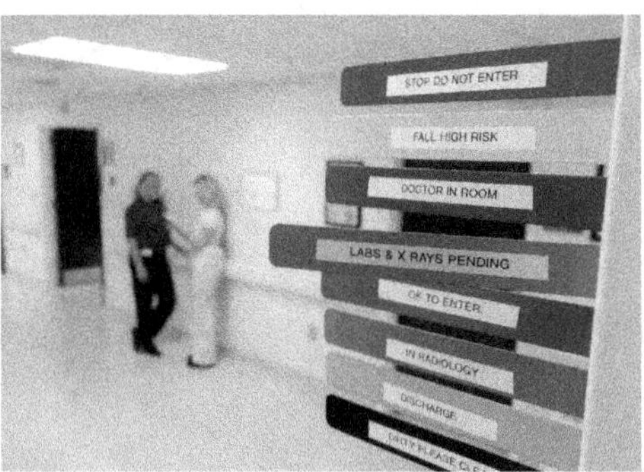

1. In your work area, identify opportunities to apply visual management and the corresponding Andon types.

2. Design a simple visual way to show what you have learned in this session.

3. Test the method you develop. Seek feedback from others who are involved in the system.

Standard Work Instructions

Background

Standard working methods were developed by Taiichi Ohno and Shigeo Shingo at Toyota during the 1950s and 1960s.

Shigeo Shingo

Taiichi Ohno

«Where there is no standard, there can be no Kaizen.»
Taiichi Ohno

What is a Standard?

A **standard** is a rule or example that provides clear explanations.

- Continuous improvement methods depend on identifying, setting, and improving standards.

- Standards form the baseline to analyze new opportunities for improvement.

LSSI
LEAN SIX SIGMA INSTITUTE

The lack of standards creates confusion and frustration

Which is the right plug?

Which dial turns a specific burner?

Evolution of the "Stop" sign

There were no standards for road signs

- Today, the "Stop" sign is recognized all over the world

- However, in the early days, do you know what it was like?

Lack of standards was the problem

*A lack of standards caused collisions,
injuries, and disorganization.*

Types of standards

- Regulations

- Quality Standards

- Specifications

- Technical Standards

- Process Standards

- Manuals

- Notices

- Memos

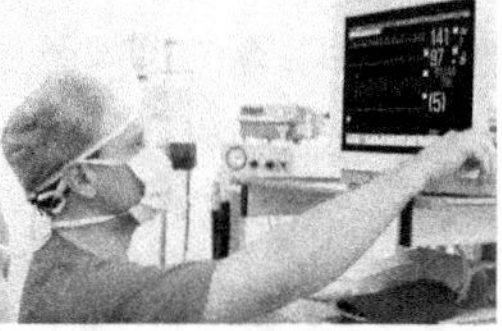

A good standard should be visual and help identify
abnormal situations in the processes.

LSSI
LEAN SIX SIGMA INSTITUTE

What is a Standard Work Instruction?

Standard Work Instructions (SWI) are instructions designed to ensure that processes are consistent, timely, and repeatable.

- They are printed and placed near the work station.

- The objectives and actual results of the use of the SWI are improvements in:

  - Increase in Quality of the finished product or service

  - Consistency of the finished product or service

  - Increase in process performance

  - Employee safety

Work instructions

WORK INSTRUCTION				LSSI LEAN SIX SIGMA INSTITUTE
Area:	**Operation:**	**Type of Product or Service:**	**Prepared by:**	Pg. 1 of 1
NO. — SEQUENCE OF OPERATIONS	**KEY POINTS**	**KEY POINTS REASONS**	**ILLUSTRATIONS**	
1 — Pick up the material.	1.- Use both hands to pick up the material.	1.- Hold material firmly to avoid an incident.	(2)	
2 — Place the material on the work table.	1.- Use clamps to fix the piece in place.	1.- Prevents movement, which prevents defects and/or incidents.		
3 — Place tips facing toward the edges.	1.- Make sure that the piece is properly balanced.	1.- Facilitates cutting.	(3)	
4 — Cut the piece to the desired length.	1.- Sharpen the cutting tool.	1.- Facilitates cutting.		
5 — Place cut pieces on the next table.	1.- Place them with the labeled side up.	1.- Facilitates identification.	(4)	
6				
7				
CHANGES — Date / Rev / ption of Change / Elim. / Approved	**SAFETY CONSIDERATIONS** — -Safety equipment must be used at all times.	**SAFETY CONSIDERATIONS** — -Safety equipment must be used at all times.	**SIGNATURES** — Date / Shift / Supervisor / Operator	

It is recommended that operators, service providers, engineers, quality personnel, and HR staff all participate in the creation of work instructions to ensure all aspects are included.

Components of standard work

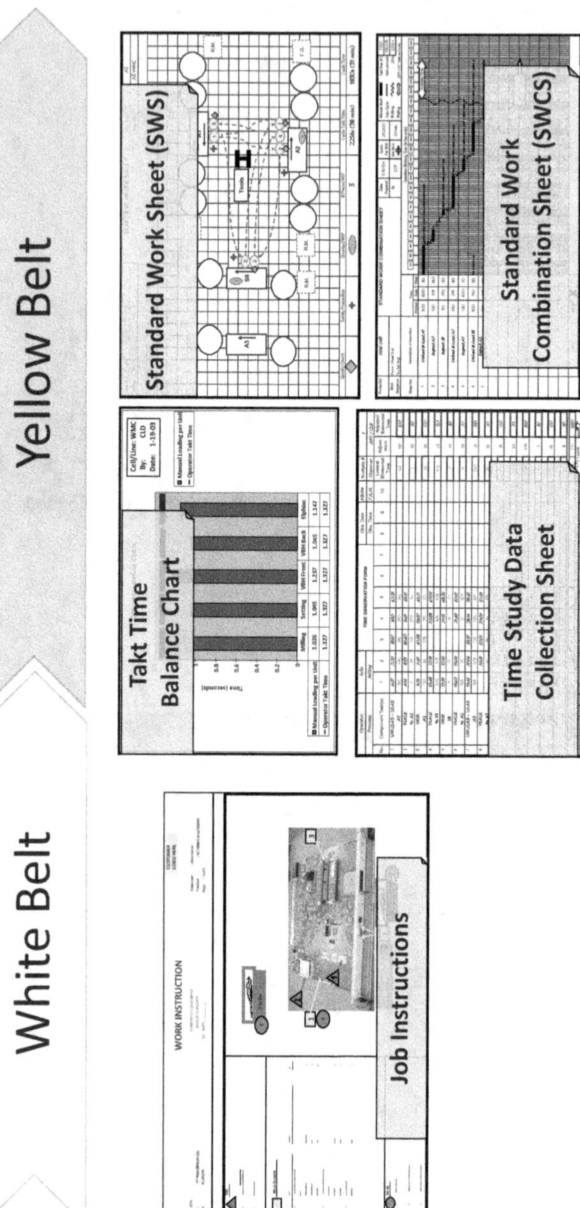

Development of talent through TWI Standards

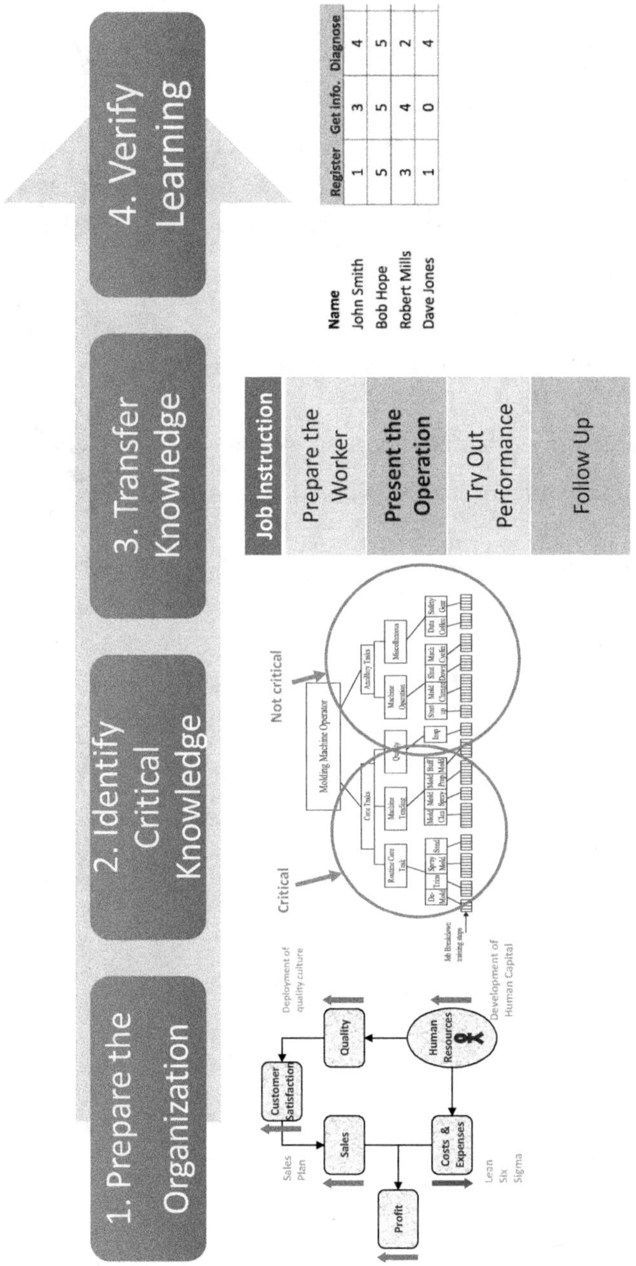

1. Prepare the Organization

2. Identify Critical Knowledge

3. Transfer Knowledge

4. Verify Learning

Job Instruction

- Prepare the Worker
- **Present the Operation**
- Try Out Performance
- Follow Up

Name	Register	Get info.	Diagnose
John Smith	1	3	4
Bob Hope	5	5	5
Robert Mills	3	4	2
Dave Jones	1	0	4

Critical

Not critical

Molding Machine Operator

Deployment of quality culture

Development of Human Capital

Job Breakdown: training steps

Customer Satisfaction — Quality — Human Resources — Sales — Costs & Expenses — Profit

Sales Plan

Lean Six Sigma

TWI (Training Within Industry)

Benefits

- Achieve process stability

  Standardization ensures that procedures are always performed identically to meet **safety**, **quality**, and **speed** standards.

- Provides a clear description of the activities in the workstation.

- Indicates the key points related to the operation.

- Establishes a baseline to evaluate and manage processes and assess their performance.

- Ensures safer and more effective operations.

- Establishes an invaluable information bank.

Note: SWIs are not neccesary for very simple or non-critical processes.

Introduction to *Yellow Belt*

Learning objectives

1. Understand the responsibilities of a Yellow Belt.
2. Understand how tools are used in the adaptation and improvement cycles.
3. Explain what tools are used in projects.

Content

> Lean principles
> Responsibilities
> When are the tools used?
> Methodology of improvement cycles

Lean principles

The 4 P's

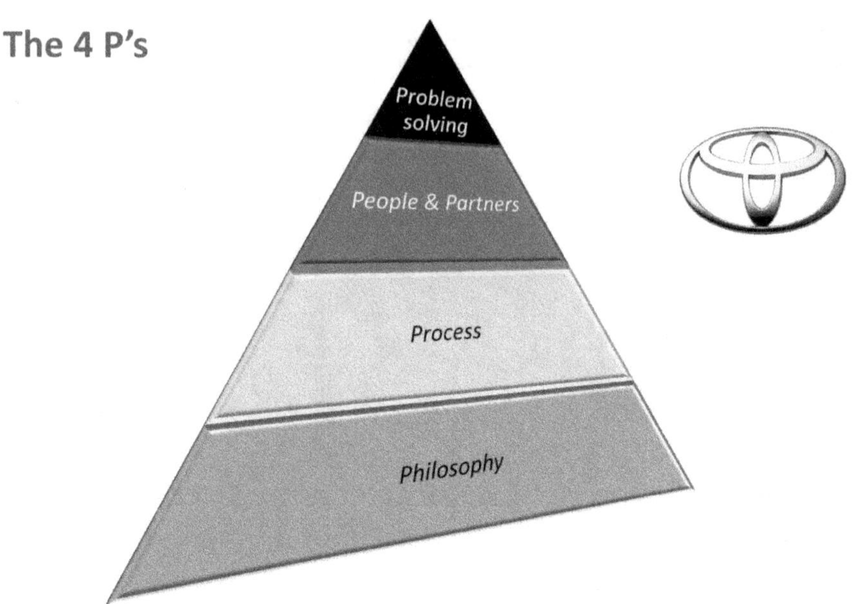

Philosophy

1. Base management decisions on a Long-term philosophy

Process

2. Create process flow
3. Use "Pull" systems
4. Level out workload
5. Stop when needed to avoid defects
6. Standardize processes
7. Visual control
8. Only use reliable technology

Developing our people and suppliers

9. Develop leaders
10. Develop and challenge your people
11. Respect your suppliers by challenging them

Solving problems generates learning

12. See for yourself
13. Make decisions
14. Learn through Kaizen

LSSI
LEAN SIX SIGMA INSTITUTE

Responsibilities

20 to 50 YBs for every 100 employees

Experts in Lean Methodologies and Tools

As an individual contributor

- Keep their work organized, standardized, and ensure the quality of their work
- Use the YB tools to solve problems and improve their work continuously
- Do their work with quality and on time

As a team leader

- Lead kaizen and problem solving teams
- Train and coach White Belts
- Follow up on project activities

Knowledge

- DMAIC methodology and Lean tools for speed and quality

Selection of implementation project leader and team

The speed and success of the implementation largely depends on:

- Selecting **the right project leader**. It must be someone who **is trusted and respected**, and has knowledge of the processes.

- Selecting the **right team.**

- **Having enthusiastic and supportive leadership** by senior management.

When are the tools used?

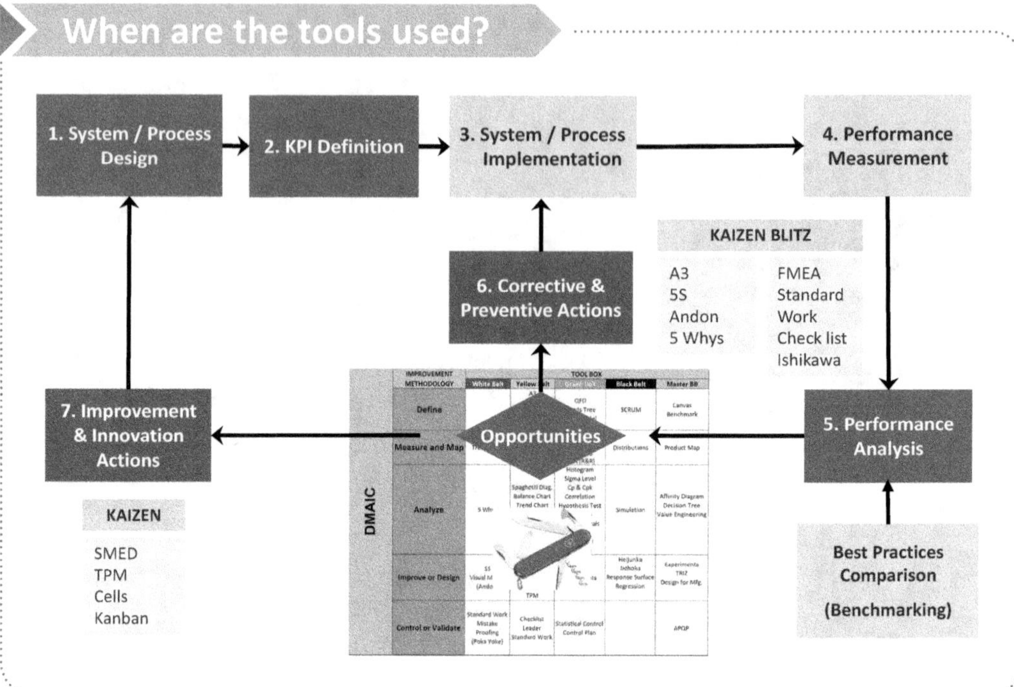

Methodology of improvement cycles

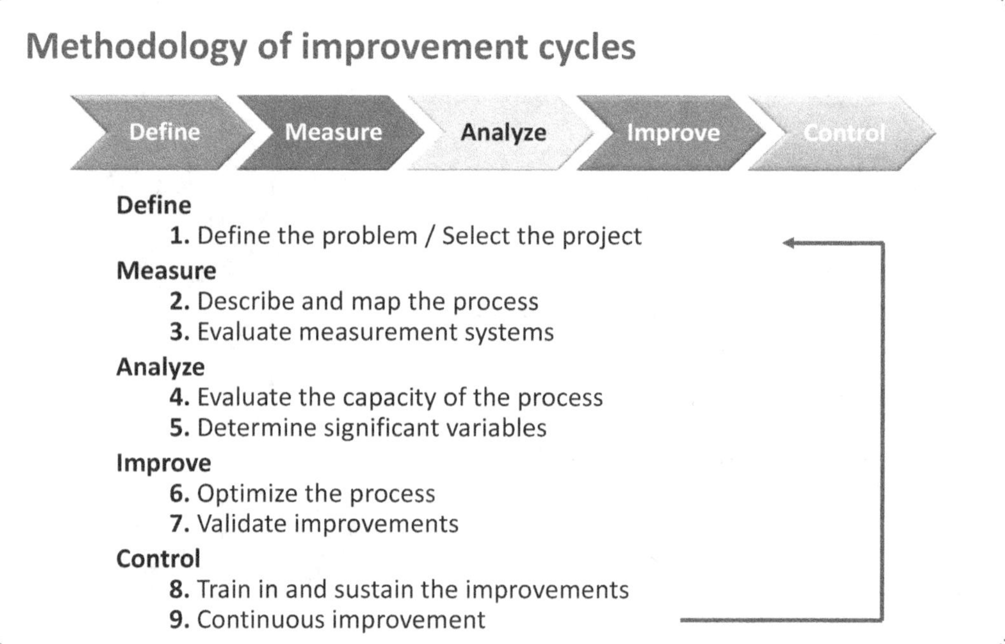

Define
1. Define the problem / Select the project

Measure
2. Describe and map the process
3. Evaluate measurement systems

Analyze
4. Evaluate the capacity of the process
5. Determine significant variables

Improve
6. Optimize the process
7. Validate improvements

Control
8. Train in and sustain the improvements
9. Continuous improvement

Yellow Belt

Lean Management + Lean Basic + Lean Improvement Tools

Lean Management Tools (Lean Management)

- Business Model "Canvas"
- Strategic Planning : Hoshin Kanri
- Value Stream Management
- Talent Development

Lean Basic Tools (White Belt)

- Problem Solving
- 5S Housekeeping
- Visual Management (Andon)
- Standard Work Instruction

Yellow Belt

Lean Management + Lean Basic + Lean Improvement Tools

Define

- 4-Quadrant Analysis
- Project Definition: A3

Measure and Map

- Data Collection
- Overall Equipment Effectiveness (OEE)
- Current State Value Stream Map (VSM)

Analyze

- Spaghetti Diagram
- Balance Chart
- Waste Analysis
- Failure Mode & Effects Analysis (FMEA)

Improve

- *Kaizen*
  - Continous Flow
  - Quick Preparations (SMED)
  - Total Productive Maintenance (TPM)
  - *Kanban.*
- Future Value Stream Map (VSM)

Control

- Standardized Work
- *Poka yoke.*
- *Kata.*

4-Quadrant Analysis

12

Learning objectives

1. Understand how to develop a 4-Quadrant Analysis, measure any type of key performance indicator and analyze it using basic quality tools.
2. Learn how to use three important basic quality tools:

   - Trend chart
   - Pareto chart
   - Cause and effect diagram (Fishbone Diagram & 5 Why's)
   - Action List

Content

> Background
> What is a 4-Quadrant Analysis?
> Benefits
> Key elements
> Procedure

Background

- Many companies fail because they do not have well defined goals or targets.

- These organizations tend to embark on large-scale waste elimination efforts, looking for improvement opportunities in all areas at the same time.

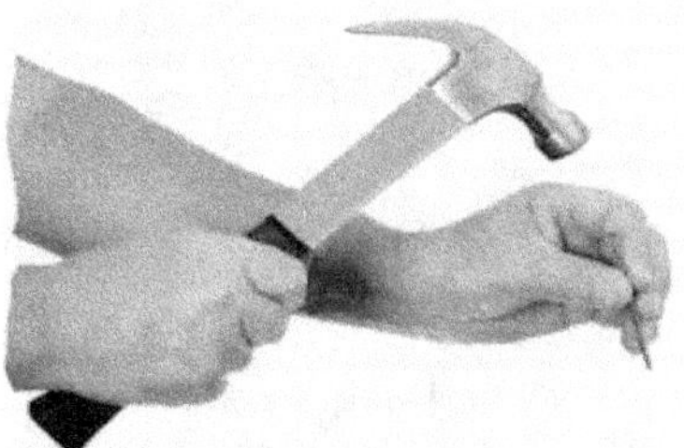

«It is tempting, if the only tool you have is a hammer, to treat everything as if it were a nail.» Abraham Maslow

What is a 4-Quadrant analysis?

- A **4-Quadrant analysis** is a Lean method used to support agile decision making.

- It involves **analyzing root causes** and their impact to objectively understand any situation.

Benefits

- On-the-spot **problem solving**

- **Better understanding** of any metric or indicator

- Focus on **the most important** aspects of an operation

- Improved **decision-making** based on data

Box Score → 4 Quadrants

BOX SCORE	Objective	13-may	20-may	27-may	03-jun	10-jun	17-jun
Units per person	21	14,00	16,00	18,00	20,00	19,00	23,00
On-time deliveries	100%	100%	100%	100%	100%	100%	100%
Lead time (days)	4	3	4	1	3	4	5
Days from door to door	3	6	12	23	14	9	7
First pass quality	95%	80%	80%	80%	85%	85%	85%
Sigma level	5	4,10	4,30	4,11	4,32	4,70	4,34
Quality costs	$ 250	$ 2.345	$ 3.112	$ 645	$ 345	$ 1.245	$ 3.124
Average product cost	$ 300	$ 343	$ 337	$ 362	$ 338	$ 337	$ 325
Inventory value	$ 545.000	$ 3.004.234	$ 2.334.756	$ 2.945.893	$ 2.564.392	$ 1.945.678	$ 1.234.975
Inventory turns	12	4,50	4,00	6,70	7,10	8,30	9,00
Maintenance costs	$ 500	$ 2.820	$ 645	$ 2.323	$ 976	$ 1.733	$ 756
5S Evaluation	100%	100%	100%	100%	100%	100%	100%
OEE	85%	70%	73%	75%	79%	81%	81%
Demand		500	600,00	550,00	495,00	620,00	545,00
Production Capacity		650	650,00	650,00	650,00	650,00	650,00
Available capacity		23%	8%	15%	24%	5%	16%
Revenue		$ 432.050	$ 384.870	$ 422.456	$ 389.754	$ 389.455	$ 456.032
Material Costs		$ 189.000	$ 125.679	$ 167.453	$ 133.456	$ 133.234	$ 197.034
Conversion Costs		$ 131.200	$ 130.242	$ 132.000	$ 132.426	$ 128.034	$ 111.342
Value Stream Profit		$ 111.850	$ 128.949	$ 123.003	$ 123.872	$ 128.187	$ 147.656
Value Stream ROS		25,89%	33,50%	29,12%	31,78%	32,91%	32,38%

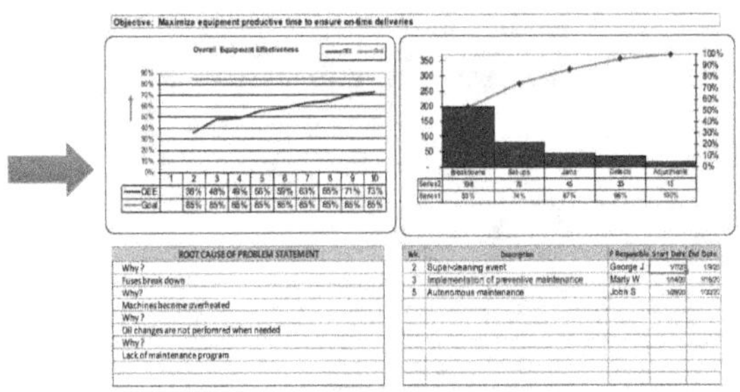

Every KPI from the Box Score should be linked to a 4Q report in order to visually understand any situation in more depth, at any time.

Key elements

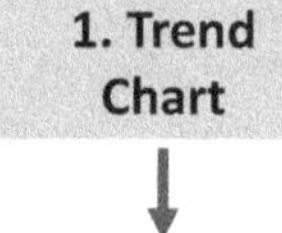

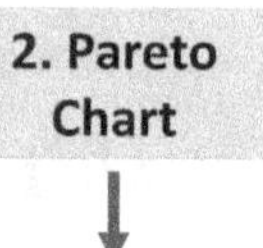

Objective: Maximize equipment productive time to ensure on-time deliveries

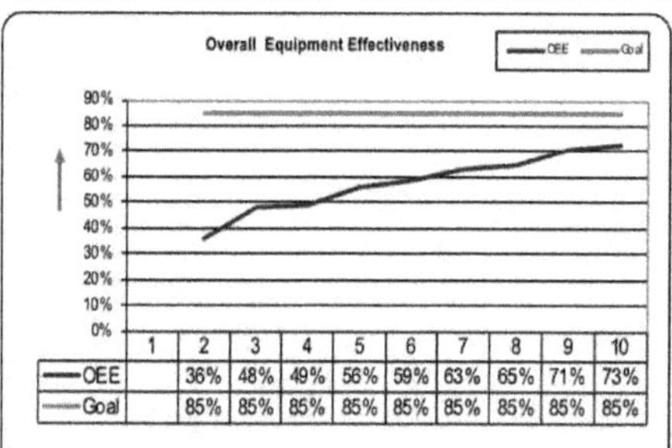

	1	2	3	4	5	6	7	8	9	10
OEE		36%	48%	49%	56%	59%	63%	65%	71%	73%
Goal		85%	85%	85%	85%	85%	85%	85%	85%	85%

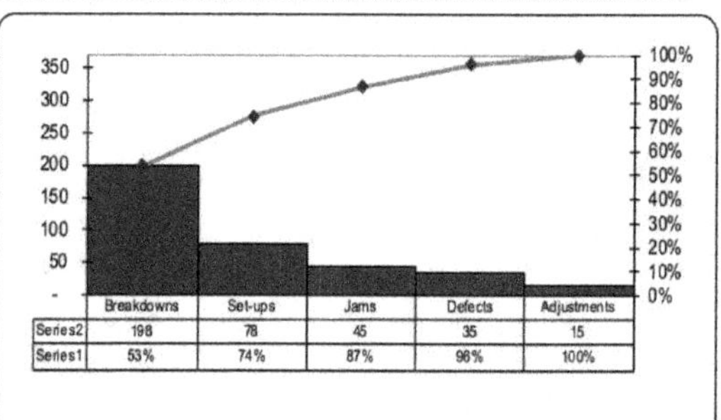

	Breakdowns	Set-ups	Jams	Defects	Adjustments
Series2	198	78	45	35	15
Series1	53%	74%	87%	96%	100%

ROOT CAUSE OF PROBLEM STATEMENT
Why ?
Fuses break down
Why?
Machines become overheated
Why ?
Oil changes are not perfomred when needed
Why ?
Lack of maintenance program

Wk.	Description	P Responsible	Start Date	End Date
2	Super-cleaning event	George J	1/7/20	1/9/20
3	Implementation of preventive maintenance	Marty W	1/14/20	1/16/20
5	Autonomous maintenance	John S	1/28/20	1/30/20

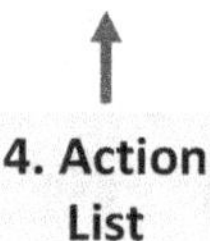

3. Cause & Effect Analysis

4. Action List

Procedure

1. What is the current status of a KPI (**Trend chart**)?
   - What is the problem?
   - What are the historical results?
2. What is the most important aspect of the KPI that needs to be evaluated (**Pareto chart**)?
   - What **20%** of the issues generate **80%** of the results?
   - What are the 2 or 3 categories that we need to focus on?
3. What is the root cause of the problem (**Cause and Effect**)?
4. What needs to be improved, prevented, or controlled (**Action items**)?

1. Trend chart

A **trend chart** is a graphical tool used to understand the behavior of a KPI (data) by showing its trend during any period of time.

	1	2	3	4	5	6	7	8	9	10
OEE		36%	48%	49%	56%	59%	63%	65%	71%	73%
Goal		85%	85%	85%	85%	85%	85%	85%	85%	85%

What does a trend chart tell us?

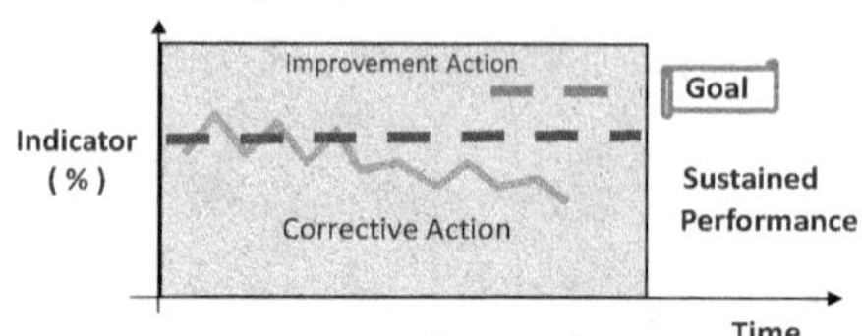

Preventive actions prevent **occurrence**.

Corrective actions prevent **recurrence**.

Improvement actions **surpass** an already sustained performance level.

Control actions **maintain** what has been gained.

How do we draw a trend chart?

1. Collect and record data in an excel spreadsheet
2. Select the columns and titles for the data you want to graph
3. Select the option for a "Line Chart"
4. Create the graph

Analysis of the Indicator: OEE (Overall Equipment Effectiveness)

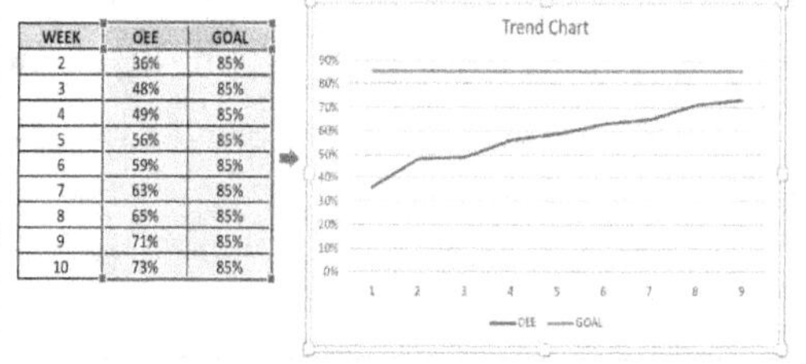

WEEK	OEE	GOAL
2	36%	85%
3	48%	85%
4	49%	85%
5	56%	85%
6	59%	85%
7	63%	85%
8	65%	85%
9	71%	85%
10	73%	85%

2. Pareto chart

- A Pareto Chart is used for counting and categorizing data, in which the categories (represented by bars) are plotted based on occurrences, and in descending order (from left to right) to show the importance of each category.

- Pareto charts are used during the **define and analyze** phases to focus on the most vital resources in the organization (e.g., products, departments, problems, defects, causes, etc.) to help optimize performance.

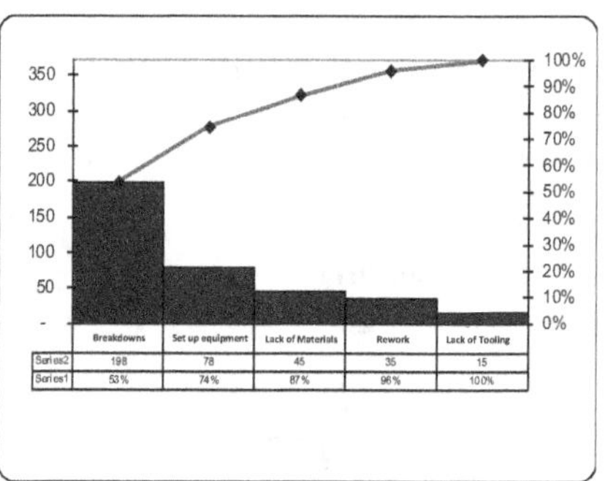

«Vital few and the trivial many.» Dr. Joseph Juran

How do we create a Pareto chart?

1. Determine what problem(s) you will investigate and how you will collect data
2. Design a data collection sheet
3. Collect data and organize it based on occurrences, and in descending order
4. Calculate the cumulative totals
5. Calculate the cumulative occurrences and percentages
6. Construct the graph

**Analysis of the Indicator: OEE
(Overall Equipment Effectiveness)**

Causes	Count or Frequency	Cumulative Frequency	Percentage	Cumulative Percentage
Breakdowns	198	198	0.53	0.53
Setups	78	276	0.21	0.74
Lack of Material	45	321	0.12	0.87
Rework	35	356	0.09	0.96
Lack of Tooling	15	371	0.05	100%
Total	371		100%	

Example

**Analysis of the Indicator: OEE
(Overall Equipment Effectiveness)**

Causes	Count or Frequency	Cumulative Frequency	Percentage	Cumulative Percentage
Breakdowns	198	198	0.53	0.53
Setups	78	276	0.21	0.74
Lack of Material	45	321	0.12	0.87
Rework	35	356	0.09	0.96
Lack of Tooling	15	371	0.05	100%
Total	371		100%	

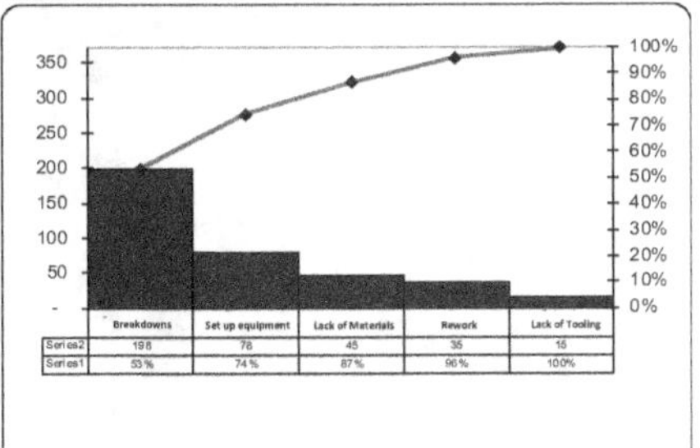

3. Cause and effect analysis

Why's analysis

'Why' should be answered up to 5 times in a consecutive manner in order to find the root cause of the problem statement (the #1 category on the Pareto Chart).

Analysis of the Indicator: OEE.
Problem Statement: Machines break down

ROOT CAUSE OF PROBLEM STATEMENT
Why?
Fuses break down
Why?
Machines become overheated
Why?
Oil changes are not performed when needed
Why?
Lack of a maintenance program
Why?

4. Action items

Results

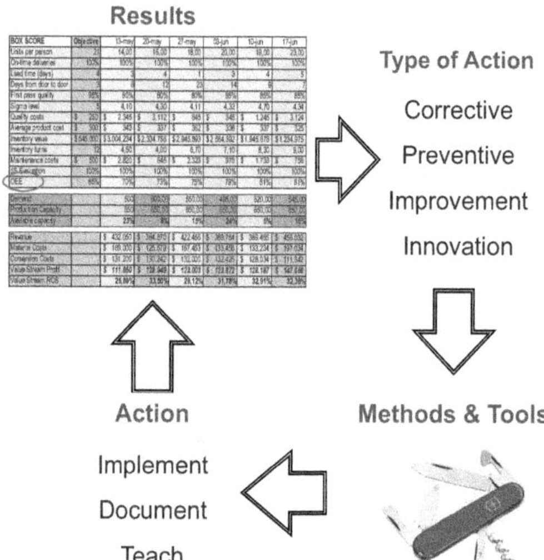

BOX SCORE	Objective	13-may	20-may	27-may	03-jun	10-jun	17-jun
Units per person	21	14,00	16,00	18,00	20,00	19,00	23,00
On-time deliveries	100%	100%	100%	100%	100%	100%	100%
Lead time (days)	4	3	4	1	3	4	5
Days from door to door	3	8	12	23	14	8	7
First pass quality	95%	90%	90%	80%	85%	85%	85%
Sigma level	5	4,10	4,30	4,11	4,32	4,70	4,34
Quality costs	$ 250	$ 2.345	$ 3.112	$ 645	$ 545	$ 1.245	$ 3.124
Average product cost	$ 300	$ 343	$ 337	$ 362	$ 336	$ 337	$ 325
Inventory value	$ 545.000	$ 3.004.234	$ 2.304.756	$ 2.045.893	$ 2.564.392	$ 1.945.876	$ 1.234.975
Inventory turns	12	4,50	4,00	6,70	7,10	8,30	9,00
Maintenance costs	$ 500	$ 2.820	$ 646	$ 2.320	$ 975	$ 1.733	$ 796
5S Evaluation	100%	100%	100%	100%	100%	100%	100%
OEE	65%	70%	73%	75%	78%	81%	81%
Demand		500	600,00	550,00	485,00	620,00	645,00
Production Capacity		650	650,00	650,00	650,00	650,00	650,00
Available capacity		23%	8%	15%	24%	6%	16%
Revenue		$ 432.060	$ 384.870	$ 422.466	$ 388.784	$ 385.465	$ 456.002
Material Costs		$ 189.000	$ 125.579	$ 167.463	$ 133.458	$ 133.234	$ 197.034
Conversion Costs		$ 131.200	$ 130.342	$ 132.000	$ 132.426	$ 128.034	$ 111.542
Value Stream Profit		$ 111.860	$ 128.949	$ 123.003	$ 123.872	$ 128.187	$ 147.646
Value Stream ROS		25,88%	33,50%	29,12%	31,78%	32,91%	32,38%

Type of Action

Corrective

Preventive

Improvement

Innovation

Action

Implement

Document

Teach

Methods & Tools

Improvement Methodology	Tool Box		
	White Belt	Yellow Belt	Green Belt
Define		A3	QFD Needs Tree Kano Model
Measure and Map	Trend chart	Data Collection OEE VSM	SIPOC Basic Statistics Sampling MSA (R&R)
Analyze	5 Whys	Spaghetti Diag. Balance Chart Trend Chart Pareto Chart	Histogram Sigma Level Cp & Cpk Correlation Hypothesis Test Box Plots Conf. Intervals Variance Multi-Vari
Improve or Design	5 S Visual Management (Andon)	Continuous Flow Kanban Quick Changes (SMED) TPM	Experiments
Control or Validate	Standard Work Mistake Proofing (Poka Yoke)	Checklist	Statistical Control Control Plan

LSSI
LEAN SIX SIGMA INSTITUTE

Kata boards

- The most important use of any type of analysis is to make the best improvement decisions, solve a problem, or control a situation.

- During **Kata Cycles**, the **4-Quadrant Analysis** process will contribute to the **formulation of a hypothesis** and the **generation of experiment ideas**.

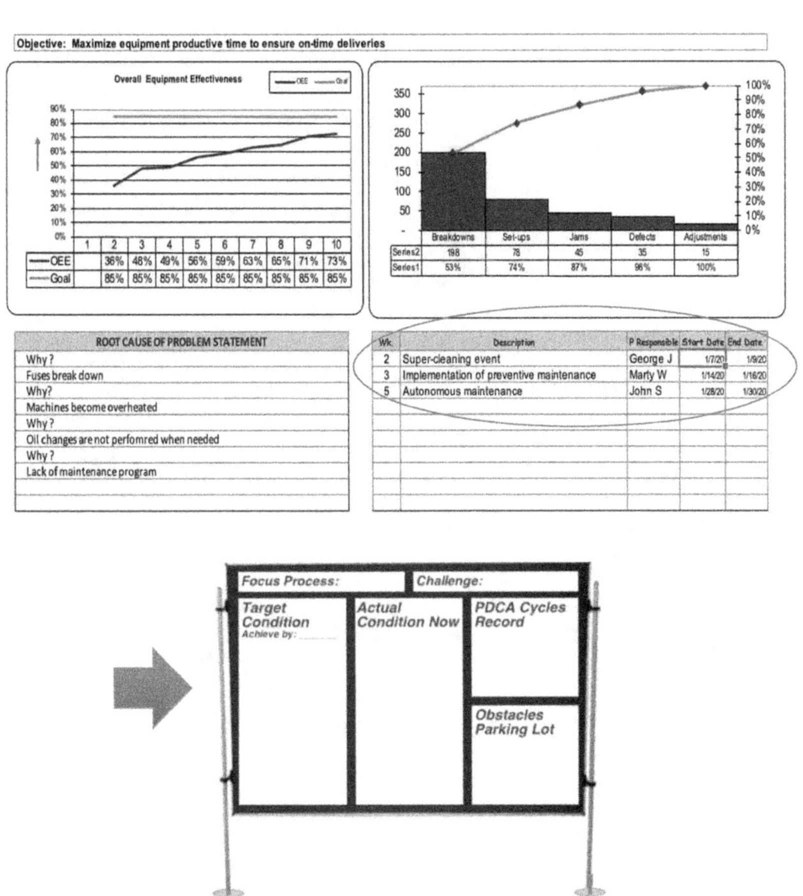

Objective: Maximize equipment productive time to ensure on-time deliveries

Overall Equipment Effectiveness

	1	2	3	4	5	6	7	8	9	10
OEE		36%	48%	49%	56%	59%	63%	65%	71%	73%
Goal		85%	85%	85%	85%	85%	85%	85%	85%	85%

	Breakdowns	Set-ups	Jams	Defects	Adjustments
Series2	198	78	45	35	15
Series1	53%	74%	87%	96%	100%

ROOT CAUSE OF PROBLEM STATEMENT
Why ?
Fuses break down
Why?
Machines become overheated
Why ?
Oil changes are not perfomred when needed
Why ?
Lack of maintenance program

Wk.	Description	P Responsible	Start Date	End Date
2	Super-cleaning event	George J	1/7/20	1/9/20
3	Implementation of preventive maintenance	Marty W	1/14/20	1/16/20
5	Autonomous maintenance	John S	1/28/20	1/30/20

Project Definition: A3

13

Learning objectives

1. Understand the importance of project planning and documentation.
2. Understand A3 key elements.
3. Learn how to create an A3 in a simple way, to quickly document projects for an executive summary.

Content

> Background
> What is an A3?
> Benefits
> A3 elements
> Procedure
> Example

Background

- Projects are the way we tactically execute strategy

- Almost every company implements projects

- Project pitfalls:

    - Not linked to their business strategies and have team members who do not fully understand the projects' benefits

    - Not define them correctly from the start

- Proper project definition is the foundation for successful project execution

What is an A3?

- An **A3** is used to document and provide an **executive summary** of each improvement project.

- It is a **simple and well-structured** way to present a report.

Origins of A3

- **A3** is an international standard name for the paper size: 11" x 17". It is called Tabloid or Ledger.

- The concept was developed by Toyota to describe the process of reducing **report-writing** to just **one page**.

- An **A3** is the integration of developing a one-page report and the thinking process applied to **problem-solving**.

LSSI
LEAN SIX SIGMA INSTITUTE

Applications of A3

Initially, **A3s** were only used for simple and common problems. Now we use **A3s** for:

- Strategic projects
- Simple projects
- Problem-solving
- Kaizen implementation
- Lean Six Sigma implementation

- Improvement projects are aligned with and prioritized according to the company's strategies.

- Provides a standardized data-driven method to identify improvement projects.

- Project definition ensures that the number of projects assigned to an area or department does not exceed the resources available for their implementation.

- An **A3** provides team members, at all levels, a structure and methodology for effective **problem-solving**.

A3 elements

1. **Title**: Identifies the name of the problem, theme, or issue
2. **Control reference**: Number or code for document tracking
3. **Owner**: Identifies who owns the problem or situation
4. **Date**: Date of issue and latest revision
5. **Background**: Establishes the business case or context
6. **Current conditions**: Describes the current situation and known information about the problem
7. **Objectives**: Identifies the desired outcome
8. **Analysis**: Analyzes the current state and root cause of the problem
9. **Proposed countermeasures**: Proposes corrective or improvement actions to reach the objectives
10. **Plan**: Presents the action plan and schedule required to reach each goal
11. **Follow-up**: Establishes follow-up meetings to ensure results, identify problems, develop new countermeasures, and communicate improvements

Procedure

	Control Reference	
	Owner	
	Date	

Title:

1. Background

Why is the problem important?

2. Current Conditions / Baseline

What is the problem?

3. Scope / Objectives

What specific outcomes are required?

4. Analysis

What is/are the root cause(s) of the problem?

Left side: Current State

5. Recommendations

What is/are our proposed countermeasure(s)?

6. Plan

What activities will be required for implementation, and who will be responsible for what and when?

7. Results and Follow-up

How will we know if the implemented actions have reached the goals? What remaining issues can we expect?

Right side: Future State

1. Background: define the business case or problem statement

1. Background
Business Case

- Developing a "**Business Case**" helps us **identify** our company's problems or areas of opportunity.

- It provides a **summarized description** of the characteristics of a situation or problem.

- It is used to estimate the **potential value** of implementing a project.

Define the business case or problem statement

A **Business Case** is a general definition of the area of opportunity assigned to the project team.

As a company, the performance of ______________ in the area of___________ is not meeting ___________. This is causing problems resulting in ______________ (problems), which cost us approximately______________ per year.

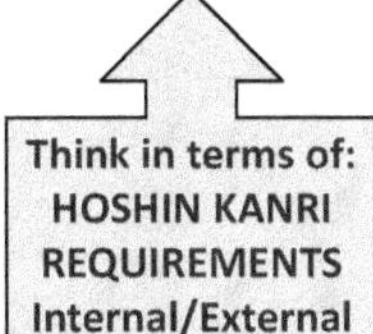

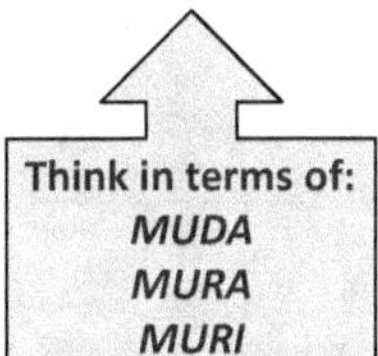

Business case examples

As a company, the performance of **accounts receivable** in the area of **invoicing** is not meeting **our goal of 47 payment days**. This is causing problems resulting in **lack of liquidity and exceeding the established budget**, which cost us approximately **$4 million** per year.

As a company, the performance of **quality** in the **assembly** area is not meeting **our goal of 97% quality**. This is causing problems resulting **in insufficient floor space, late deliveries, and high quality-related costs**, which cost us approximately **$1 million** per year.

As a company, the performance of **on-time deliveries** in the area of **medical products** is not meeting **our production schedule or budgeted operating costs**. This is causing problems resulting in **loss of customers and contracts, and decreased sales**, which cost us approximately **$850,000** per year.

2. Current conditions / baseline

Control Reference
Owner
Date

Title:

1. Background

2. Current Conditions / Baseline

What is the problem?

3. Scope / Objectives

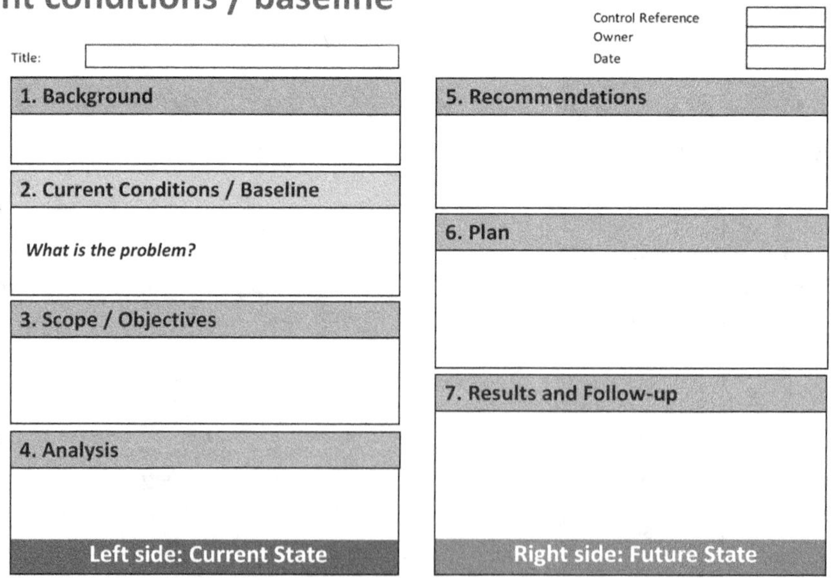

This topic was taught in the White Belt training (problem solving methodology)

4. Analysis

Left side: Current State

5. Recommendations

6. Plan

7. Results and Follow-up

Right side: Future State

Define the current conditions and establish the baseline

Baseline

- At this step, we should have an idea of the magnitude of the problem or opportunity.

- The magnitude should be expressed in units (hours, orders, percent late, etc.)

- Next, we determine the current performance levels (baselines) and desired performance levels (objectives/goals).

- It is important that we verify that we are using long-term information when estimating the baseline.

3. Establish the scope and objectives

3. Scope / Objectives
What specific outcomes are required?

For projects with poorly defined scopes like "Eliminating world hunger".

- The scope is so big and ambiguous that it **is impossible to manage** and the team may become discouraged.

- It is **difficult to relate** the project results to the activities.

Characteristics of projects with appropriate scopes:

- The project is **large enough** that it is challenging for all the participants.

- The team believes that the **solution is achievable** and within their area of responsibility.

What is a CTQ?

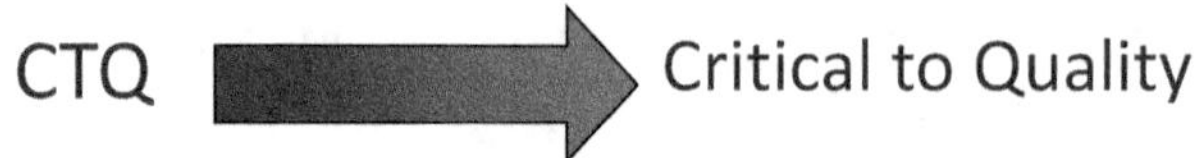

**A CTQ is a characteristic of a product or service
that must meet a critical customer requirement.**

CTQs are identified by conducting a Voice of the Customer (VOC)
analysis and documenting it as a function of the business case.

Establish the objectives

The **objective** is a more specific statement of the results expected from
the project. Here are some examples:

- Improve lead time from 20 days to 5 days by December 2020.

- Improve on-time delivery from 67% to 75% by December 2020.

- Increase quality from 90% to 95% by January 2021.

- Reduce price from $5 to $ 4.85 by July 2020.

Establish the scope, baseline and objectives

| Scope / Baseline / Objectives | *What specific outcomes are required?* |

BUSINESS CASE	SCOPE	CTQ's	BASELINE	OBJECTIVE	SAVINGS
As a company, the performance of on-time deliveries in the area of medical products is not meeting our production schedule or budgeted operating costs. This is causing problems resulting in loss of customers and contracts, and decreased sales, which costs us approximately $850,000 per year.	Family of blood pressure monitors	On-Time Deliveries	85 %	95 %	$ 800,000
		Reasonable Prices	$ 120.00	$ 100.00	

Voice of the Customer

4. Analysis

Title: [   ]

Control Reference [ ]
Owner [ ]
Date [ ]

| 1. Background | | 5. Recommendations |

| 2. Current Conditions / Baseline |

| 3. Scope / Objectives |

| 6. Plan |

4. Analysis

What is the root cause(s) of the problem? Choose the simplest problem-analysis tool that clearly shows the cause-and-effect relationship.

e.g., Current VSM, FMEA, Balance Chart, Spaghetti Diagram, 5 Why's Fishbone Diagram, CRT, etc.

| 7. Results and Follow-up |

Left side: Current State

Right side: Future State

Recommendations, action plan and follow up

Control Reference
Owner
Date

Title:

1. Background

2. Current Conditions / Baseline

3. Scope / Objectives

4. Analysis

Left side: Current State

5. Recommendations
What is/are our proposed countermeasure(s)? e.g., Future VSM, TPM, Kanban, Continuous Flow, SMED, etc.

6. Plan
What activities will be required for implementation, and who will be responsible for what and when? Gantt Chart

7. Results and Follow-up
How will we know if the implemented actions have reached the goals? What remaining issues can we expect? Gemba Walks/Box Score

Right side: Future State

What is a Gantt Chart?

- A Gantt Chart is a project planning tool that **graphically depicts the tasks** that need to be completed in a project.

- It was invented by Henry L. Gantt in 1917.

- The Gantt Chart also provides a graphical way of assessing **project progress**.

A Gantt Chart allows you to:

- Schedule project activities and tasks

- Quickly evaluate project progress at any time

- Monitor a project's completion with respect to time and activities

- Assign team member project responsibilities (i.e., tasks and activities)

Elements

Vertical axis: Project activities to be completed

Horizontal axis: Calendar or timeline with units of measure that are most appropriate for the project: e.g., hours, days, weeks, months, etc.

The position of each box in the chart indicates the start and end date for each activity.

Each activity is represented by a box. The length of the box indicates the activity's duration.

Add the number of days expected to complete each activity.

LEAN SIX SIGMA PROJECT GANTT CHART
PROJECT #

	Duration	Start	End	1	2	3	4	5	6	7	8	9	10	11	12	13	14	15	16	17	18	19	20
DEFINE	**13**	**1/1/2018**	**1/14/2018**																				
Define the project, create a project charter	7	1/1/2018	1/8/2018																				
Define the process and problem metrics	3	1/4/2018	1/7/2018																				
Form the team	2	1/6/2018	1/8/2018																				
Project approval	1	1/7/2018	1/8/2018																				
MEASURE	**16**	**1/7/2018**	**1/23/2018**																				
Describe the process	2	1/7/2018	1/9/2018																				
Measure process performance	2	1/9/2018	1/11/2018																				
Measurement systems analysis	2	1/11/2018	1/13/2018																				
Define the baseline	10	1/21/2018	1/31/2018																				
Revise and update project status	0	1/21/2018	1/21/2018																				
ANALYZE	**28**	**1/21/2018**	**2/18/2018**																				
Analyze the process	8	1/21/2018	1/29/2018																				
Analyze the sources of variation	10	1/31/2018	2/10/2018																				
Determine significant variables	10	2/10/2018	2/20/2018																				
Revise and update project status	0	2/10/2018	2/10/2018																				
IMPROVE	**25**	**2/10/2018**	**3/7/2018**																				
Determine new operating conditions	10	2/10/2018	2/20/2018																				
Estimate the benefits of the improved process	5	2/15/2018	2/20/2018																				
Determine and adjust the failure modes	5	2/15/2018	2/20/2018																				
Implement and verify process changes	5	2/20/2018	2/25/2018																				
Revise and update project status	0	2/20/2018	2/20/2018																				
CONTROL	**17**	**2/20/2018**	**3/9/2018**																				
Implement control actions	9	2/20/2018	3/1/2018																				
Implement a control plan with the process owner	2	2/22/2018	2/24/2018																				
Implement a monthly achievements plan analysis	5	2/22/2018	2/27/2018																				
Document lessons learned	1	2/23/2018	2/24/2018																				
Formal project completion	0	2/23/2018	2/23/2018																				

Title: Improve on-time delivery and equipment reliability

Background:
description of the characteristics of a situation →

1. Background

As a company, the performance of on-time deliveries in the area of medical products is not meeting our production schedule or budgeted operating costs. This is causing problems like loss of customers and contracts and decreased sales, which cost us approximately $850,000 per year.

Problem and actual impact →

2. Current Conditions / Baseline

What is the problem? What is the current situation?

- Orders are not delivered on time

3. Scope / Objectives

SCOPE	CTQ's	BASELINE	OBJECTIVE	SAVINGS
Family of blood pressure monitors	On-Time Deliveries	85 %	95 %	$ 800,000
	Reasonable Prices	$ 120.00	$ 100.00	

Root cause(s):
Definition of causes of the problem. →

4. Analysis

What is/are the root cause(s) of the problem?

- Lack of preventive maintenance
- Operators don't have the correct training

Choose the simplest problem-solving tool for this issue:
E.g., - 5 Whys, fishbone diagram, CRT, etc.

Actions:
Activities, person responsible and commitment dates →

5. Recommendations

What is/are our proposed countermeasure(s)?
- **Implement Total Productive Maintenance**
- **Develop a training program**

6. Plan

What activities will be required for implementation and who will be responsible for what and when?

TPM Kaizen event

1 TPM Training
2 Super cleaning event
3 Generate opportunity cards
4 Develop equipement FMEA
5 Implement autonomous maintenance
6 Develop prev. maint. calendar
7 Develop prev. Maint. Instructions
8 Implement visual controls
9 Develop safety instructions
10 Prepare operators and supervisors

Days: 1 2 3 4 5 — equipment

Performance indicators to track progress
- **On-time delivery**
- **Overall Equipment Effectiveness**

Follow up:
Verify results →

7. Results & Follow-up

- **On-time deliveries improved by 15%**
- **Breakdowns reduced by 10%**
- **Analyze the Box Score used in weekly meetings**
- **Implement Gemba walks to analyze day-by-the-hour boards**

How to fold an A3

- Since an **A3** paper is larger than the most commonly used office paper, it is difficult to file and add to report binders.

- Toyota adopted a specific way of folding an **A3** report that resulted in an 8.5" by 11" paper so that it could be placed in regular binders.

1. Fold in half from right to left

2. Fold in half from left to right

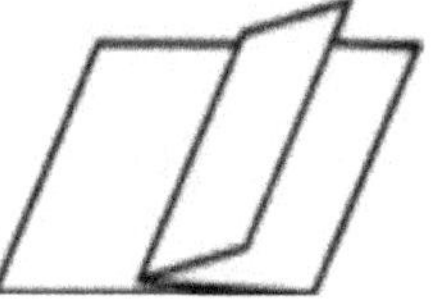

3. It is ready to file in a binder

Data Collection

Background

Data gathering

- In Lean Six Sigma, data is the basis for quality decision-making.

- Data gathering must be as clear and simple as possible to prevent errors.

Common data collection errors

- **Measurement**: errors following procedure of instruments' calibration.

- **Operational**: failure to follow instruction manuals, lack of training, missing data, and errors collecting data.

- **Influence from interaction**: the process of measuring could have a negative effect over the performance of a given operation.

- **Perception/Bias**: those who collect the data tend to see what they want to see.

- **Sampling**: the data collected does not represent the entire process.

Benefits

- Effective knowledge of those data elements that are relevant to establish current state conditions.

- The acquisition of wider knowledge about the process and the personnel in charge through the data collection allows for a more efficient project execution.

- Recognize potential opportunities to improve the quality of the data generated in processes and verify that the data collected is accurate.

Procedure

1. Identify the data sources

2. Collect the data

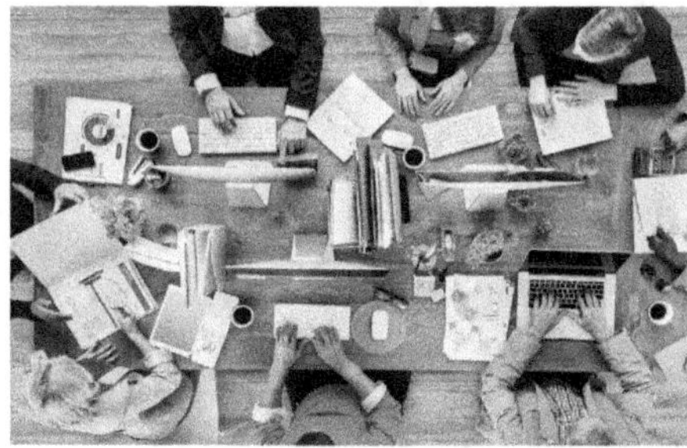

1. Identify the data sources

Information flow	Material flow

Examples

- Monthly or weekly demand
- Forecasts
- Order confirmations
- Order processing
- Etc.

- Cycle times for each operation (C/T, cycle time)
- Setup times (C/O, changeover time)
- Overall Equipment Effectiveness (OEE)
- Number of workers
- Work in process (WIP) Inventory levels (i.e., the most common quantities)
- Transportation methods between suppliers, operations and clients
- Scrap rate and/or rework

2. Collect the data

- In its different forms, data collection allows for the obtainment of data in a more reliable fashion and furthers the use of more sophisticated tools.

Types
- A. Post-its
- B. Time study sheet
- C. Photos and videos

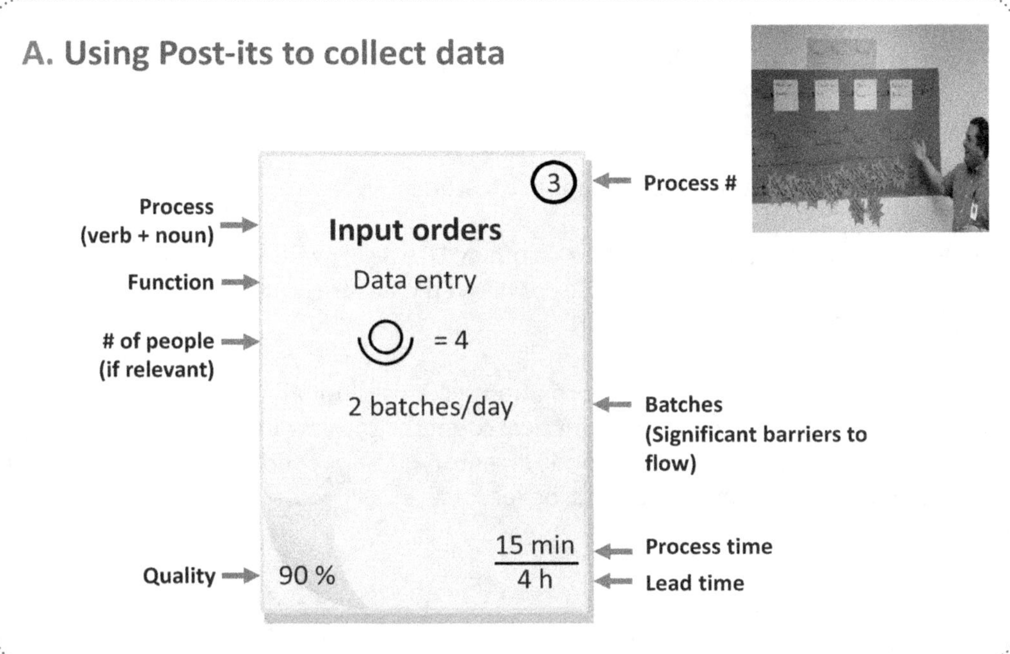

B. Time study - data collection sheet

Process	LSSI LEAN SIX SIGMA INSTITUTE	TIME STUDY DATA COLLECTION SHEET Dashboards Manufacturing	Date			Process #	
			Time			Observer	

No.	Work elements	Measure point	1	2	3	4	5	6	7	8	9	10	11	12	13	14	15	Lowest repeated time
1	Cutting	Cutting Station	21	20	22	22	25	22	23	21	22	22	20	27	22	22	21	22
			22	22	23	22	22	21	22	22	20	25	22	23	22	22	22	
2	Painting	Painting Station	47	45	45	43	47	45	45	45	43	49	45	45	43	45	45	45
			45	47	45	43	45	45	45	40	45	45	43	45	45	43	41	
3	Driling	Driling station	19	17	21	19	19	21	19	19	20	21	19	19	25	19	21	19
			23	19	19	19	21	20	19	19	21	19	19	21	20	19	19	
4	Electronic Assembly	Assembly Station 1	65	65	63	63	67	63	63	63	61	63	65	63	67	63	67	63
			63	63	65	63	63	67	65	63	63	63	61	62	63	65	63	
5	Upload Software	Upload softawere tab	22	23	23	22	22	22	21	22	25	23	22	22	23	25	22	22
			21	22	23	22	21	23	22	23	22	22	25	22	22	22	22	
6	Control Modul Assembly	Assembly Sation 2	33	32	35	32	32	35	33	32	32	32	35	32	32	35	32	32
			35	32	32	35	32	32	35	32	33	32	32	32	35	32	33	
7	Final Assembly & Testing	Assembly Sation 2	134	137	135	139	130	131	134	134	133	135	134	137	131	134	129	134
			134	137	134	131	130	130	134	134	133	134	134	137	134	133	134	
8	Packaging & Shipping	Packaging Station	51	49	49	47	51	49	49	50	51	49	49	50	53	49	49	49
			45	50	49	49	47	49	49	51	49	53	49	49	51	49	49	
Cycle Time																		386

Data collection tips

- Collect recent, factual data. Do not use historical records.

- Walk around the production floor or office. Use a stopwatch to time each step of the process. Trust what you measure, not what you are told.

- The inventory data stored in information systems is not always reliable. Make sure to perform physical counts of the raw materials, work-in-process, and finished goods inventory. Do not count units. Instead, count containers, pallets, boxes, etc.

LSSI
LEAN SIX SIGMA INSTITUTE

Overall Equipment Effectiveness (OEE)

What is OEE (Overall Equipment Effectiveness)?

Overall Equipment Effectiveness is one of the most important indicators for any process.

- It represents the **percentage of time spent** adding value for customers.

- Processes able to work according to their production cycle without producing defects are considered efficient.

OEE = Availability X Efficiency X Quality

- **Availability** is the percentage of time that a process system is fully operational (no defective products or services are generated).

- **Efficiency /Performance** is the percentage of time that the process runs at standard speed.

- **Quality** is the percentage of good products or services generated as compared to the total products or services generated.

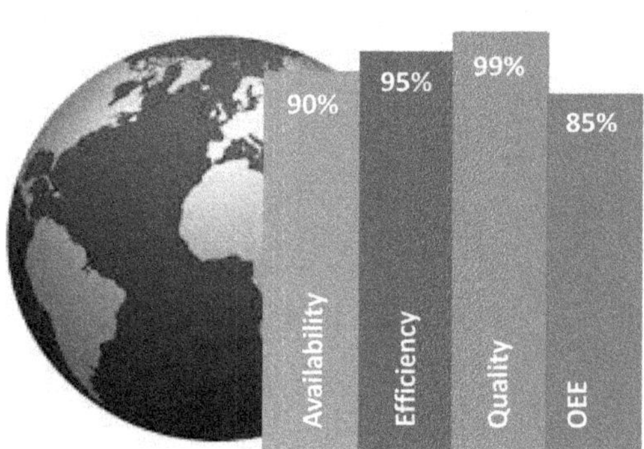

6 Big losses of OEE

1. **Stops**: The process or equipment is scheduled for production but is not running due to a failure. It needs to be repaired or adjusted.

2. **Setup and adjustments**: The process or equipment is stopped for changeovers or setups.

3. **Small stops**: Micro stops due to seizing or failures. They tend to be so brief that they are hard to monitor and record (i.e. less than 5 minutes.)

4. **Reduced speed**: Time loss that occurs when the process or equipment runs slower than its theoretical maximum speed.

5. **Setup rejects**: Time spent generating rejects as the process stabilizes after a changeovers or adjustment.

6. **Production rejects**: Time spent generating rejects during steady-state production.

Procedure

1. Record the downtime during a workday

2. Count the number of rejects and rework generated during the workday

3. Calculate **Availability**: Operating Time / Available time

4. Calculate **Efficiency**: Units Produced / (Operating time X Capacity)

5. Calculate **Quality**: Good Units on the First Pass / Total Units Produced

6. Calculate **Overall Equipment Effectiveness**

7. Share the results with the team and make decisions for improvement

Example

The following results were obtained during one regular workday for the diagnosis process:

Day-by-the-Hour Board

Goal 73 units **Date:** 01/01/20
Capacity 10 units per hour

Hours	Goal	Actual	Accumulated	Downtime (minutes)	Type	Defects
8 to 9	10	10	10			
9 to 10	8	7	17	10	Break	
10 to 11	10	10	27			
11 to 12	10	5	32	20	Setups	
12 to 1	5	4	36	30	Lunch	
1 to 2	10	11	47			
2 to 3	10	2	49	30	Breakdown	3
3 to 4	10	11	60			
Total	73	60		90		3

Overall Equipment Effectiveness

Goal 73 units **Date:** 01/01/20
Capacity 10 units per hour

Hours	Goal	Actual	Accumulated	Downtime (minutes)	Type	Defects
8 to 9	10	10	10			
9 to 10	8	7	17	10	Break	
10 to 11	10	10	27			
11 to 12	10	5	32	20	Setups	
12 to 1	5	4	36	30	Lunch	
1 to 2	10	11	47			
2 to 3	10	2	49	30	Breakdown	3
3 to 4	10	11	60			
Total	73	60		90		3

Total time = 480 min.

Available Time = 440 min. | Planned Downtime 40 min.

Operating Time = 390 min. | Downtime 50 min.

Net Operating Time = (390 x .97) = 378 min. | Speed loss 12 min.

Fully Productive Time = (378 x .95) = 359 min. | Quality loss 19 min.

$$\text{Availability} = \frac{\text{Operating Time}}{\text{Available Time}} = 390 / 440 = \textbf{89 \%}$$

$$\text{Efficiency} = \frac{\text{Units Produced}}{\text{Operating time x Capacity}} = \frac{63 \text{ units}}{(390 \text{ min}/60 \text{ min}) \times 10 \text{ units}} = \textbf{97 \%}$$

$$\text{Quality} = \frac{\text{Good units on the first pass}}{\text{Total units produced}} = \frac{60 \text{ units}}{63 \text{ units}} = \textbf{95 \%}$$

OEE = 359 / 440 = **82 %**

OEE = **Availability X Efficiency X Quality**
OEE = $0.89 \times 0.97 \times 0.95 = $ **82 %**

Calculate OEE for a laundry service business

- Total Time = 480 min.
- Planned Downtime = 30 min. for lunch
- Breakdowns = 10 min.
- Preparation Time = 20 min.
- Capacity = 80 lb / hour
- Total pounds processed = 510 lb
- Rework = 25 lb

Calculate :

1. Availability
2. Efficiency
3. Quality
4. OEE

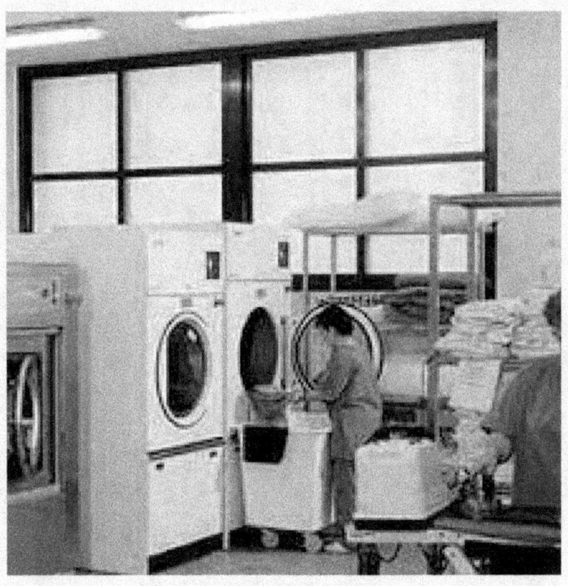

Current State Value Stream Map (VSM)

Learning objectives

1. Understand the importance of developing a Value Stream Map (VSM) for each end-to-end process to be improved.
2. Learn the general procedure to map any kind of process.
3. Learn to identify process bottlenecks and critical areas of opportunity.

Content

> Background
> What is a current state VSM?
> Benefits
> Key elements
> Procedure and exercise

Background

One of the main reasons why Lean Six Sigma fails is:

- Implement tools **everywhere** and at the same time, without establishing a precise **focus** that considers the business needs.

We call it *"Popcorn kaizen"*.

Very few people in any organization are able to respond all the following questions correctly:

- What is the current demand for our products or services?

- What is our current capacity?

- What are the bottlenecks in our system? Where are these restrictions located?

- What is the production cost for each of our products or services?

- Are we making or losing money?

Lean principles

- Specify **value** from the customer's perspective

- Identify the **Value Stream** for each product or service family

- Ensure **Continuous Flow** for each product or service by eliminating waste

- Deliver only when the customer wants it (Pull system), ensuring Just-In-Time

- Seek **perfection**

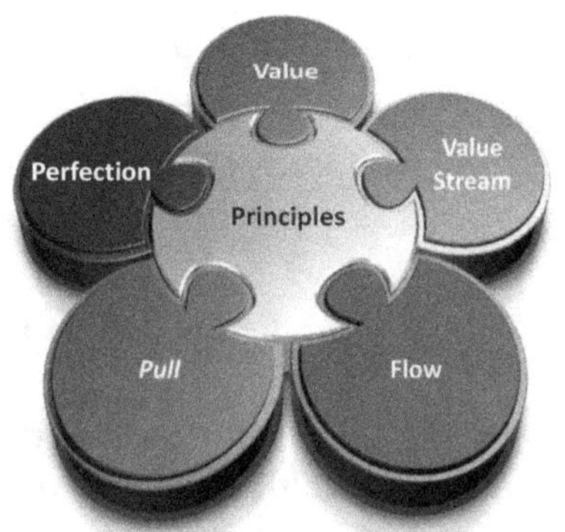

Source: *Lean Thinking,* por James P. Womack y Daniel T. Jones.

What is a current state VSM?

It is a **graphical representation** of the steps of the process and the information flow. This tool allows to understand the process flow and identify waste, with the purpose to develop improvement plans.

A **Value Stream** includes all activities required to satisfy customer requests, from the customer order to delivery.

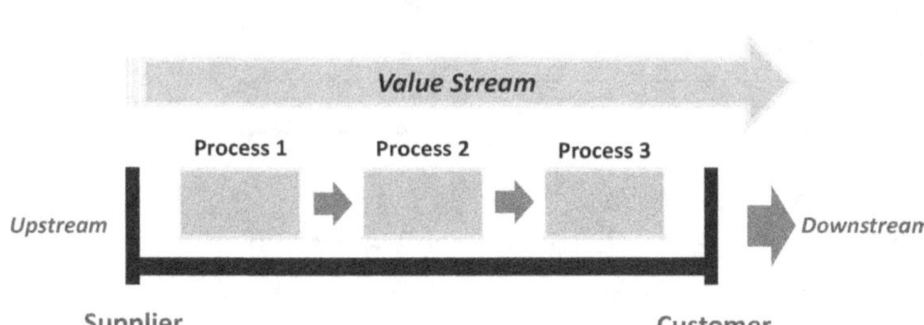

Types of maps

Current State VSM

- A current state VSM is a reference document used to identify the most critical forms of **waste** as well as the **improvement opportunity areas**.

Future State VSM

- A future state VSM defines **the best short- to mid-term solution** for the operation, proposing the **improvements** to be incorporated into the productive system.

VSM provides a general overview of the end-to-end business process.

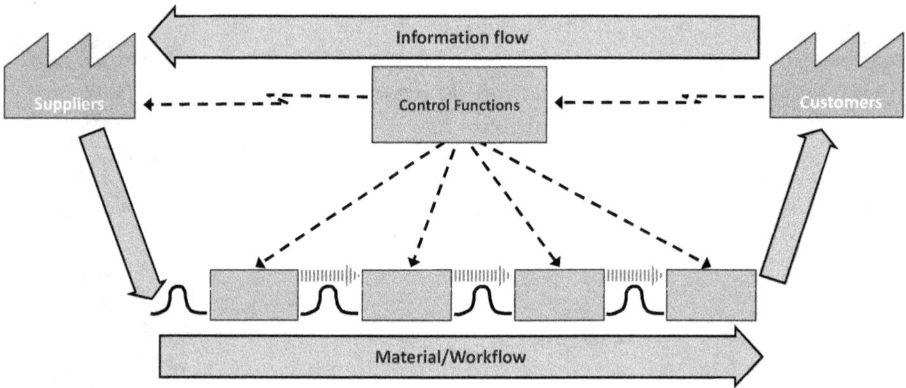

- Establishes the interaction between the material/workflow and the information flow.
- Provides a common visual language to understand a complex system.
- Helps identify those operations that add value to products and services .

LSSI
LEAN SIX SIGMA INSTITUTE

Benefits

- Provides a **graphical method** to understand the entire supply chain in one document

- Helps in the development of an **improvement strategy** for the value stream before implementing changes

- Reveals the process **flow** and the **sources of waste**

- Establishes **a common language** for process analysis

- Promotes a model **to create flow** and **implement Lean Six Sigma** methods and tools

- Support in the detection of **bottlenecks** and **improvement areas**

Key elements: Value Stream Mapping symbols

Symbol	Name	Description
	Process Box	Represents a process or operation through which work or material flows. We typically do not include detailed process steps unless there is significant accumulation of inventory or batching between process steps.
	External Sources	Represents both suppliers and customers. The supplier is the starting point and is typically located on the upper left-hand corner of the map. The customer is the end point and is typically located on the upper right-hand corner of the map.
	Shipments	Represents the transportation of either receiving materials from an external supplier or delivering finished products or services to the customer.
	Data Box	This symbol is located under other symbols to present critical data/information. Normally, it will show data such as shipment frequency, lot size, material information, etc. When it is located under a process box, it typically shows information such as cycle time, changeover time, activity time, lead time, available capacity, batch size, yield, etc.
	Inventory	Represents the inventory level before and after each process. The inventory level is shown under the symbol.
	Employees	Represents one or multiple employees. The number of employees is shown under the symbol.
	Push Arrow	Represents the movement of material from one process to another. It is used when the previous process "pushes" materials to the next process, independently of what is truly needed by the next process.

Symbol	Name	Description
	Material Receipts and Shipments	Represents the movement of finished goods or services to the customer. It can also be used to represent movement of raw materials from suppliers to the facility.
	Electronic Information Flow	Represents the flow of electronic information or data.
	Manual Information Flow	Represents the flow of manual information.
	Go see	Refers to confirming something visually during the process. "Go See" scheduling is a manual count of the inventory to make schedule adjustments.
	Timeline (Value-Added Activities)	Represents a timeline when an activity adds value.
	Timeline (Non-Value Added Activities	Represents a timeline when an activity does not add value.
	Withdrawal arrow	Represents the withdrawal of material from the preceding process.
-FIFO→	FIFO	Represents a "First-in First-out" inventory system.
	Withdrawal Kanban	Used to signal the withdrawal of parts from a supermarket.
	Production Kanban	Used to signal a previous process to produce parts for a downstream process. It is usually in a predefined quantity.
	Kanban Post	Represents the location where Kanban cards are kept.

Symbol	Name	Description
	Signal Kanban	Used to signal a process to change and start the production of a specific part or service. This is normally used when the inventory level in the supermarket goes below the minimum required level.
	Supermarket	Represents a predetermined inventory level which the next process or customer can use or pull from whenever necessary. The supplier process will replenish the supermarket inventory once it is consumed by the next process.
	Buffer/ Safety Stock	Represents the safety stock required to continue production whenever the process encounters issues related to fluctuations in demand or production inactivity. It is a buffer for internal issues and a safety stock for external issues.
	Load Leveling	Used to level the production volume and mix.
	Kaizen	Depicts areas of opportunity and the execution of kaizen events to achieve the future state.

Common mistakes when mapping

- Not preparing Current and Future Value Stream Maps before Kaizen events.

- Creating maps without collecting enough data.

- Developing Value Stream Maps with the incorrect team members or no team at all.

Value Stream Mapping stages

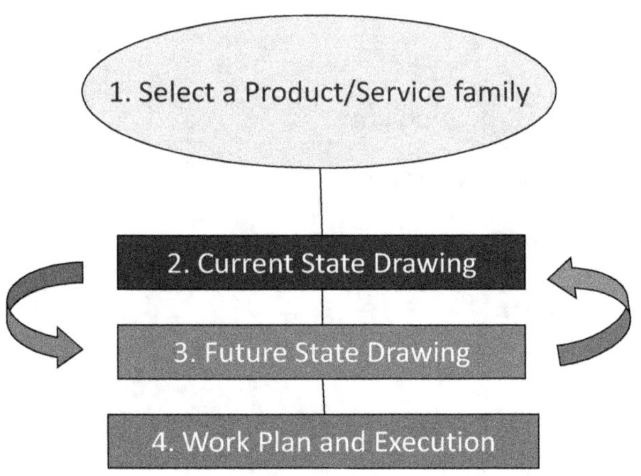

The cycle to develop Value Stream Maps for each of your product/service families is to be performed twice or thrice per year, depending on the specific needs of the organization.

1. Define families

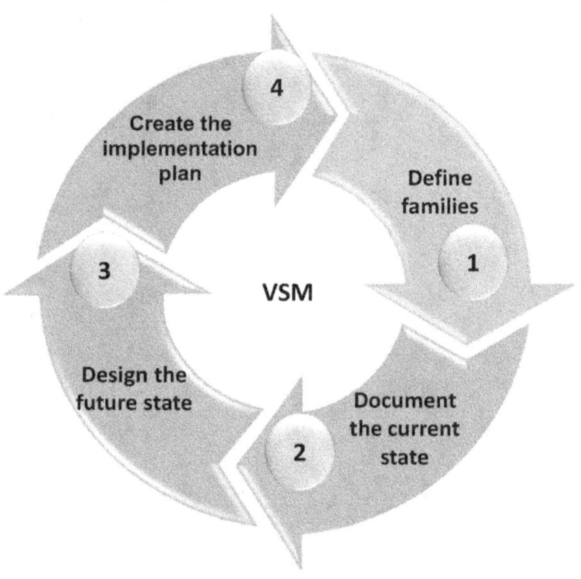

1.1. Define the **scope** of the problem

1.2. Define the **product/service family**

1.3. Complete the **process mapping charter**

1.1. Define the scope of the problem: manufacturing

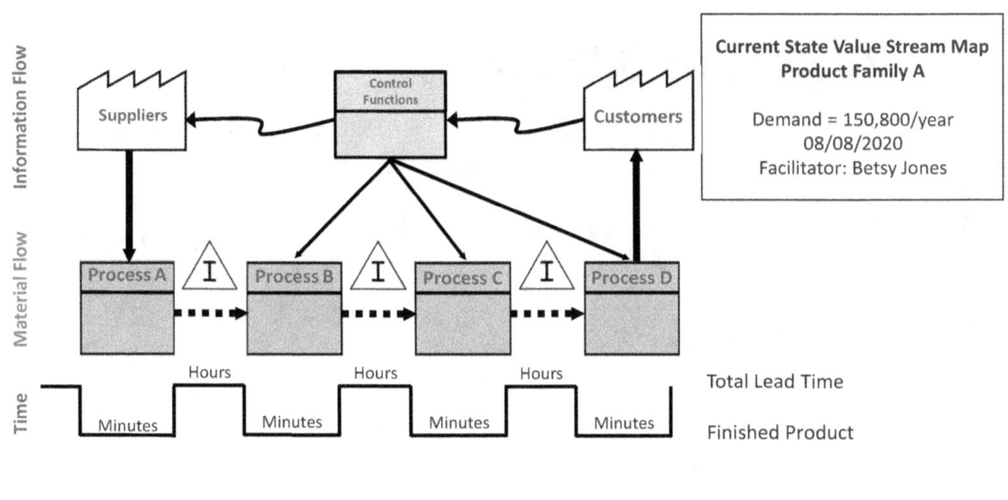

1.1. Define the scope of the problem: office/service

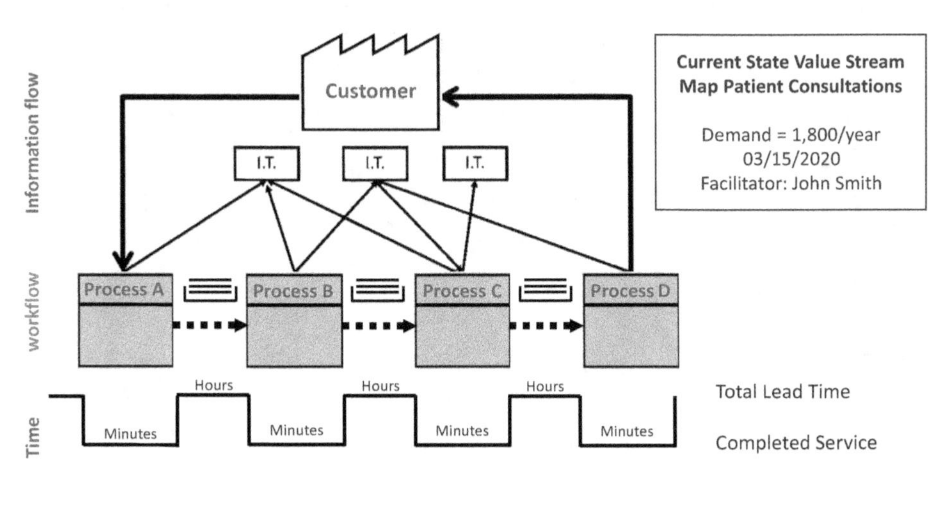

1.2. Define the product family: manufacturing

Group product families by processes, steps/sequence, and similar equipment.

Products	Machining		Punching			Weld.	Assembly		Packaging	
	1	2	3	4	5	6	7	8	9	10
A	X			X		X	X		X	
B	X				X	X	X		X	
C		X				X	X		X	
D		X	X				X		X	
E	X					X	X		X	
F						X	X		X	

Product Family

Products in a family go through the same or very similar processes (same flow) and have similar cycle times.

In this example, the two workstations follow similar assembly and packaging processes, thus they can be considered as a single workstation for their analysis.

1.2. Define the service family

Group service families based on processes, steps/sequence, and similar equipment.

Services	Step 1	Step 2	Step 3	Step 4	Step 5	Step 6	Qty.
Servicie A	X	X	X		X	X	500
Service B	X	X	X		X	X	730
Service C		X		X	X		20
Service D	X		X		X	X	50
Service E		X		X	X		150
Service F	X	X				X	120
Service G	X	X	X	X	X	X	10

1.3. Complete the Process Mapping charter

Value Stream Mapping Charter

Scope		Accountable Parties		Schedule & Logistics	
Value Stream	Value Stream being improved	Executive Sponsor	Director, VP or C-level	Event Date(s)	3 days typically
Specific Conditions	What circumstances are included and excluded? (e.g type of customer, geographic location, etc.)	Value Stream Champion	If needed - often director or manager level	Start/End Times	Start and end times
Customer Demand	How many times is this done per wk, mth, yr?	Facilitator / VSM Manager	Skilled person leading the activity	Location	Need ample wall space
Trigger	What need does the value stream address?				
First Step	Task on first process block	Team Lead	Not always needed	Meals Provided?	Always a nice touch; keeps the team from wandering.
Last Step	Task on last process block				
Boundaries & Limitations	What is the team NOT authorized to change?	Coordinator	The person arranging logistics (reserving the room, ordering food, sending meeting notices, etc.)	Interim Briefing(s)	Aid in consensus building and organizational learning.
FS Implementation	Typically 90-120 days			Briefing Attendees	List required attendees; others are optional.

Current State Problems & Business Needs | Mapping Team

Current State Problems & Business Needs		Function / Role	Name	Contact Information
1	What's driving the need for improvement?			
2		1 Leadership-heavy		
3		2		
4		3		
5		4		

Measurable Target Condition

Measurable Target Condition		Mapping Team		
1	Reduce <defined metric> from X to Y (Z% improvement)	5		
2		6		
3		7		
4		8		
5		9		
		10		

Benefits to Customers | On-Call Support

Benefits to Customers		Function / Role	Name	Contact Information
1	How will internal/external customers benefit as a result			
2	of improvements to the value stream?	1 SMEs that may not be needed full time		
3		2		
4		3		
5		4		

Benefits to Business | Approvals

Benefits to Business		Executive Sponsor	Value Stream Champion	Facilitator / VSM Manager
1	What other benefits will the business or internal customers			
2	realize as a result of improvements to the VSM?			
3				
4		Signature:	Signature:	Signature:
5		Date:	Date:	Date:

2. Document the current state

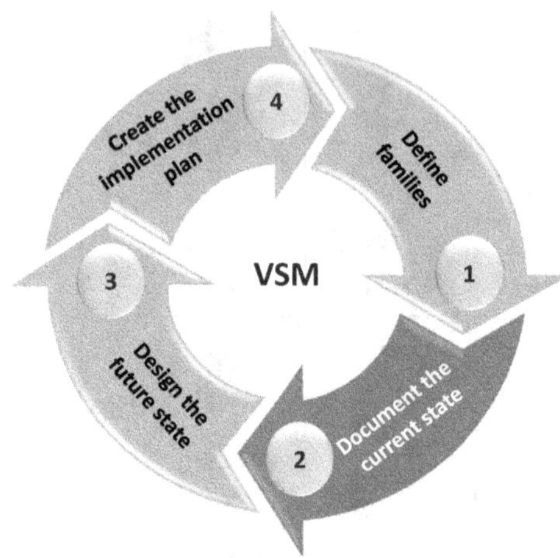

2.1. Create a **Spaghetti Diagram**.

2.2. Draw the **Current State VSM**.

2.3. Calculate **Takt Time**.

2.4. Create a **Balance Chart** to identify the bottleneck.

2.5. Document all forms of **waste**.

2.6. Quantify the **current state**.

Note: This procedure will be explained later using an example.

Manufacturing example

Lean Shop is a mid-sized firm that manufactures the following production control dashboards:

AX - 1	Basic dashboard
AZ - 2	Remote control dashboard
WB -3	WEB dashboard
XR - 4	Colors dashboard
MN - 5	Standard dashboard
MN - 6	Financial dashboard
MN - 7	Overview dashboard

Production process information

We know from internal data that raw materials inventory turnover is 3 days.

OPERATION 1: Cutting
Semi-automatic cutters that require manual feeding of material.
Cycle time: 22 sec
Changeover time: 25 min
OEE: 80%
Operators: 1
WIP Inventory: 712 units

OPERATION 2: Painting
Individual painting booth with heating system.
Cycle time: 45 sec
Changeover time: 5 min
OEE: 95%
Operators: 1
WIP Inventory: 450 units

OPERATION 3: Drilling
Pedestal drills
Cycle time: 19 sec
Changeover time: 0 min (perforations are the same for all dashboards)
OEE: 95%
Operators: 1
WIP Inventory: 632 units

OPERATION 4: Electrical Assembly
Assembly table capable of storing components.
Cycle time: 63 sec
Changeover time: 0 min (hands-on activities only)
OEE: 100%
Operators: 1
WIP Inventory: 310 units

OPERATION 5: Uploading the Software
Computer with device connection that uploads software onto the dashboard chip.
Cycle time: 22 sec
Changeover time: 0 min (only implies selecting the right file on the computer)
OEE: 98%
Operators: 1
WIP Inventory: 110 units

OPERATION 6: Control Module Assembly
Assembly table capable of storing components.
Cycle time: 32 sec
Changeover time: 0 min (hands-on activities only).
OEE: 100%
Operators: 1
WIP Inventory: 217 units

OPERATION 7: Final Assembly & Testing
Assembly table capable of storing components.
Cycle time: 134 sec
Changeover time: 0 min
OEE: 100%
Operators: 1
WIP Inventory: 1,456

OPERATION 8: Packaging & Shipping
Packing table.
Cycle time: 49 sec
Changeover time: 0 min (hands-on activities only)
OEE: 100%
Operators: 1

Phase 1: Define the product or service family

Group product or service families based on processes, steps or sequence, and similar equipment.

In order to define product family for the dashboards, we must first list all part numbers and indicate the operations for which the specific products (dashboards) go through – and record the cycle time for each operation.

Cycle time = the total time from the beginning to the end of an operation or process.

Model	Description	Cutting	Painting	Drilling	Electrical Assembly	Upload Software	Control Module Assembly	Final Assembly & Testing	Packaging & Shipping	Total
AX - 1	Basic dashboard	18	45	12	45	22	30	114	35	**321**
AZ - 2	Remote control dashboard	20	45	14	63	22	24	134	42	**364**
WB -3	WEB dashboard	18	45	19	56	22	31	121	33	**345**
XR - 4	Colors dashboard	22	45	11	50	22	32	119	44	**345**
MN - 5	Standard dashboard	15	45	15	x	x	x	123	47	**243**
MN - 6	Financial dashboard	10	45	15	x	x	x	123	49	**242**
MN - 7	Overview dashboard	6	45	15	x	x	x	123	43	**232**

- This table shows how the first four products go through the same number of operations (same flow). Notice how the last three dashboards do not go through the exact same operations.

- At this point, we have identified two families.

- A family is a group of part numbers that go through the same number of operations or processes and whose total time does not exceed by 30% over the range.

Model	Description	Cutting	Fainting	Drilling	Electrical Assembly	Upload Software	Control Module Assembly	Final Assembly & Testing	Packaging & Shipping	Total
AX - 1	Basic dashboard	18	45	12	45	22	30	114	35	321
AZ - 2	Remote control dashboard	20	45	14	63	22	24	134	42	364
WB -3	WEB dashboard	18	45	19	56	22	31	121	33	345
XR - 4	Colors dashboard	22	45	11	50	22	32	119	44	345
MN - 5	Standard dashboard	15	45	15	x	x	x	123	47	243
MN - 6	Financial dashboard	10	45	15	x	x	x	123	49	242
MN - 7	Overview dashboard	6	45	15	x	x	x	123	43	232

Phase 2: Document the Current State
2.1. Create a Spaghetti Diagram

A **Spaghetti Diagram** is a graphical tool used to represent the movement of people, materials, and information in any type of process (e.g., manufacturing, service, administrative, etc.).

It is an effective tool used to identify:

- Identify the unnecessary movements and transports

- Quantify the travel distances of items and people that are part of any process.

- Prompt relevant layout modifications aimed at reducing or even eliminating unnecessary movement and transport.

LSSI
LEAN SIX SIGMA INSTITUTE

Create a Spaghetti Diagram

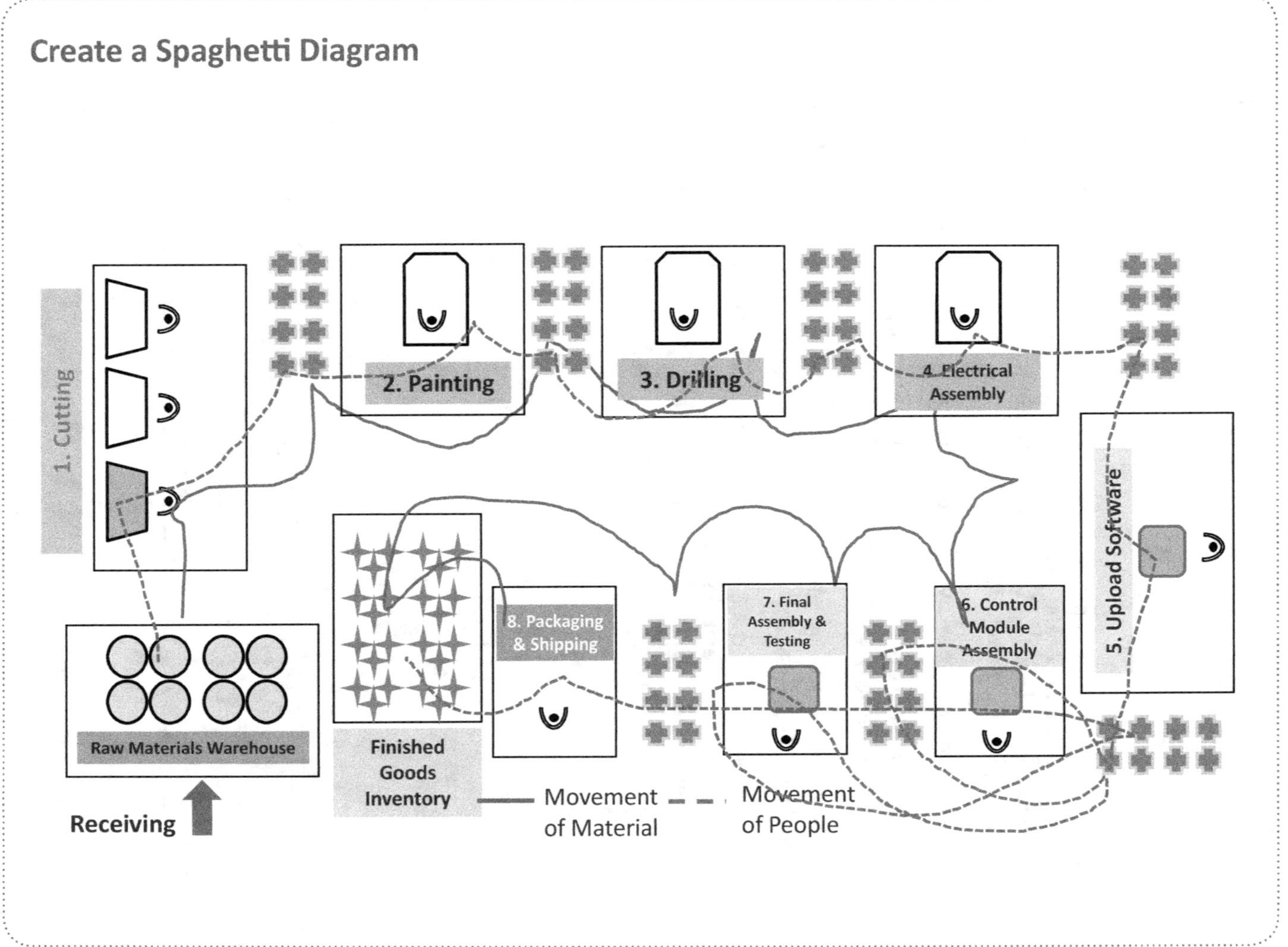

2.2. Draw the Current State Value Stream Map

Procedure

1. Start by drawing the customer symbol in the upper right-hand corner of a two-sheet canvas paper and connecting the flow of information with production control – which in turn communicates the requirements to the supplier by sharing material forecasts.

2. Draw the transportation flows between suppliers and demanders.

3. Draw the sequence of operations and specify cycle times, changeover times, equipment availability, available time, and WIP Inventory – as needed.

4. Draw arrows connecting the production program to each operation to indicate flow of information.

5. Integrate the entire map and evaluate the time spent adding real value. Draw a ladder below the operations: indicate value-added time on the lower steps and non-value-added time on the upper steps. In this case, we convert inventory to days by dividing each inventory by daily demand (341 units).

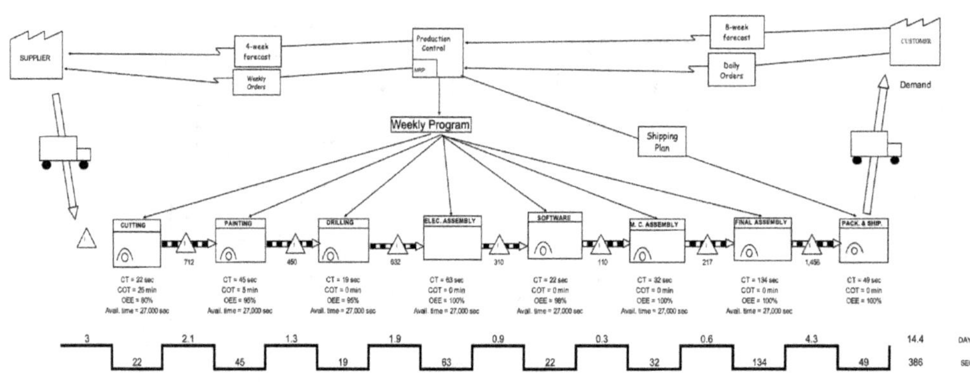

* CT = Cycle time
* COT = Changeover time
* M.C. Assembly = Module Control Assembly [Operation]

2.3. Calculate takt time (speed of demand)

$$\text{Takt Time} = \frac{\text{Available time}}{\text{Demand}}$$

Initial data:

Total time = 8 hr = 480 min

Break time = 30 min

Available time = 450 min * 60 sec / min = 27,000 sec

Monthly demand = 7,510 units

Workdays = 22 days

Daily demand = 7510 units / 22 = 341 units

- Calculate *takt time*.
  Available time = 27,000 sec

- Daily demand = 341 units

- *Takt time* = 27,000 sec / 341 units = 79 sec / unit

- This means that the customer is willing to buy a dashboard every **79 seconds**. This rhythm – or speed – of demand becomes our production goal.

2.4. Create a balance chart

- A **Balance Chart** is an effective graphical tool to **identify:**

  - Waste
  - Overburden
  - Variability

- Used to compare each worker's cycle time against the Takt Time.

- Allows to visualize, contrast, and balance the workloads of every employee in a cell/pod.

The Balance Chart summarizes the real cycle times for each process. This will be explained in further detail during the **Analyze** phase.

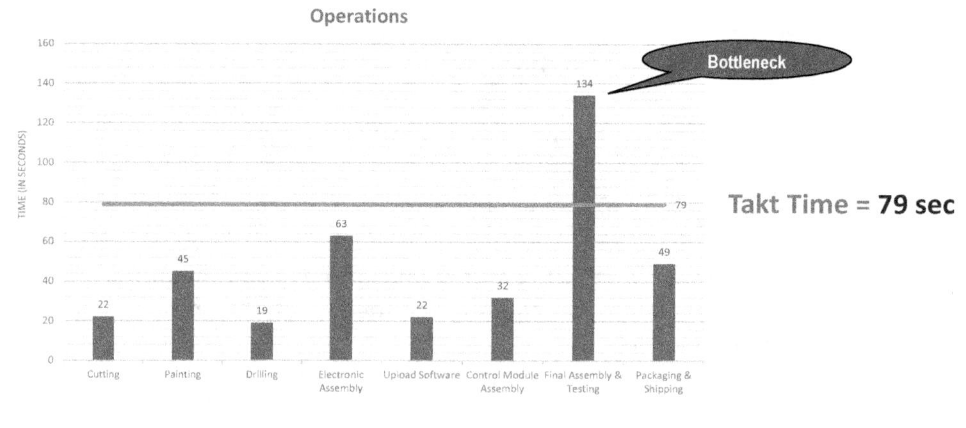

Takt Time = **79 sec**

2.5. Document waste

Form of Waste	Notes	Opportunity	Proposed Actions
Overproduction			
Excess inventory			
Defects or rework			
Unnecessary movement			
Overprocessing			
Waiting and Searching			
Transport			
Talent without action			
Waste of energy			
Pollution / Contamination			

Which activities add value to the process?

Identify value-added and non-value-added activities

Value-added activities

- These are activities that transform a product or service by increasing the benefit the customer is receiving.
- The customer is willing to pay for these activities.

Non-value-added activities

- These are activities that consume time and resources, but do not add value to the product or service, and hence do not add benefit for the customer.
- The customer is not willing to pay for these activities.

Value-added window

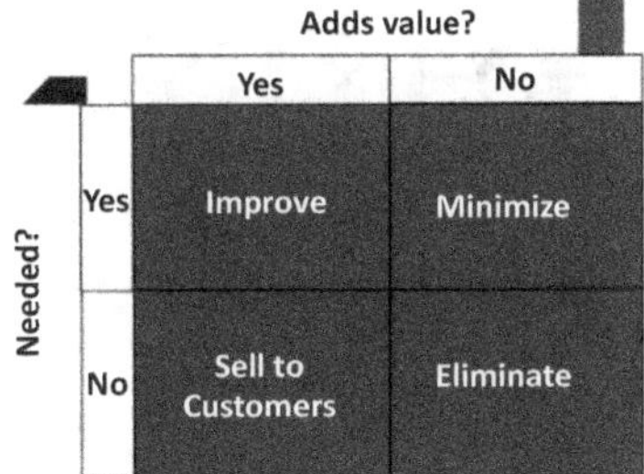

2.6. Quantify the current state

Metric	Current State	Future State (Goal)	Improvement (%)
Space required (sq. ft.)	13,500		
Number of employees	10		
Distance traveled (ft.)	607		
Lead time (days)	14.4		
Raw materials inventory (days)	3		
WIP Inventory (days)	7.1		
Finished Goods Inventory (days)	4.3		
Inventory Turnover	18.3		

Failure Mode and Effects Analysis (FMEA)

Learning objectives

1. Know how to use FMEA to prevent any kind of problem.
2. Know how to identify potential problems (errors) in a system and determine their possible effects.
3. Understand how to use this information to quickly prioritize and focus improvement efforts on prevention, supervision and response plans.

Content

> Introduction
> Background
> What is FMEA?
> Benefits
> When is FMEA used?
> Types of FMEA
> Procedure
> Examples

Introduction

How many problems have we faced, knowing that they could have been avoided by taking preventive action?

- We are all exposed to risks in every day life.

- Throughout every process of service and production there are several types of risk. However, the process that can lead to these risks is often times not analyzed in detail using a structured method.

- Thanks to **FMEA**, risks of various types have been prevented from becoming actual problems.

Background

- FMEA was first used in the 1940s by the U.S. military and later in the 1960s by the aerospace industry during the Apollo mission.

- At the end of the 1970s, the automotive industry began to use FMEA when high costs and liability claims affected some companies.

- Ford was the first American company that implemented the use of FMEA in its quality management systems.

- In 1993 Chrysler, Ford, and GM created the document "Potential Failure Mode and Effects Analysis", which covered the two most current types of FMEA. This document was part of the QS 9000 guidelines (today ISO/TS 16949).

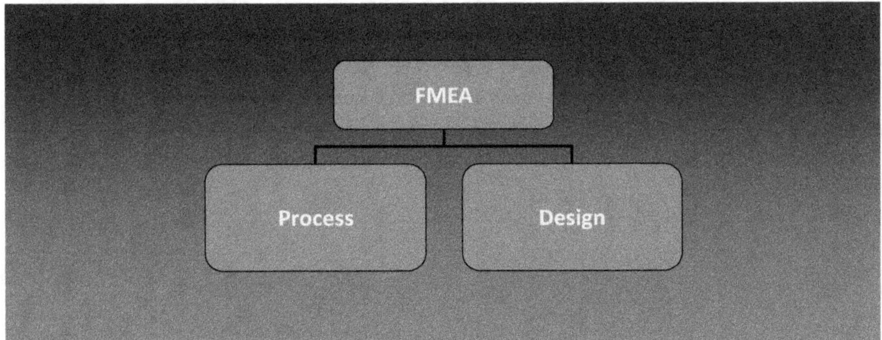

What is FMEA?

It is a formal, analytic, and preventive method to:

1. Recognize and evaluate potential failures of products and processes, as well as the effects of such failures.

2. Identify actions to reduce the probability of potential failures.

3. Document the entire process and maintain the *"know-how"*.

4. Serve as a knowledge bank for the entire company.

Benefits

- Used to identify product and process functions and requirements
- Used to identify all potential failure modes caused by operational deficiencies
- Helps in understanding the effects of possible failure modes on customers
- Used to identify process variables that need to be controlled in order to improve problem detection and reduce occurrences
- Helps us develop a priority list of potential failure modes to establish preventive or corrective actions
- A source for contributing to the development of control plans
- Helps reduce waste and rework
- Helps provide more reliable products and services

When is FMEA used?

- After we solve a problem, and we want to prevent reoccurrence

- When we want to prevent a problem from happening

- When we want to understand a process or product in detail

- When we want to understand what steps in a process or what components in a product need improvement

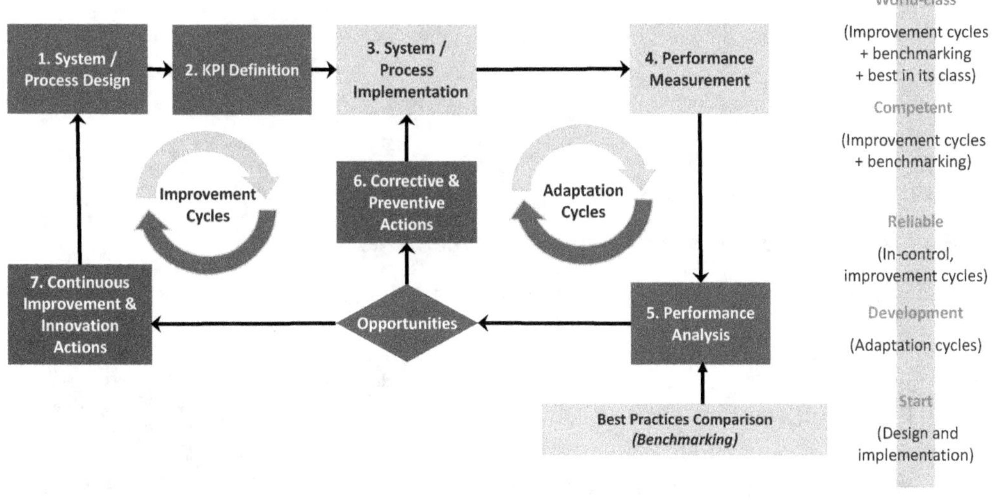

Types of FMEA

Design FMEA is used to:

- Analyze products, high volume tooling or standard machinery.

- Evaluate product sub-systems and components.

- Avoid the need to use process controls to overcome design weaknesses.

Inputs:
- Specifications
- Government requirements
- Physical or technical manufacturing limitations
- Product maintenance limitations

Process FMEA

- Assumes that the product or service will accomplish its final purpose.

- Evaluates each process and its respective elements.

- Is used in the analysis of processes and transactions.

Inputs:
- Process flowcharts
- Results of pilot runs
- Historical data on similar processes (causes of rework and customer rejections)
- Design FMEA (if available)

FMEA Development sequence

Document Development

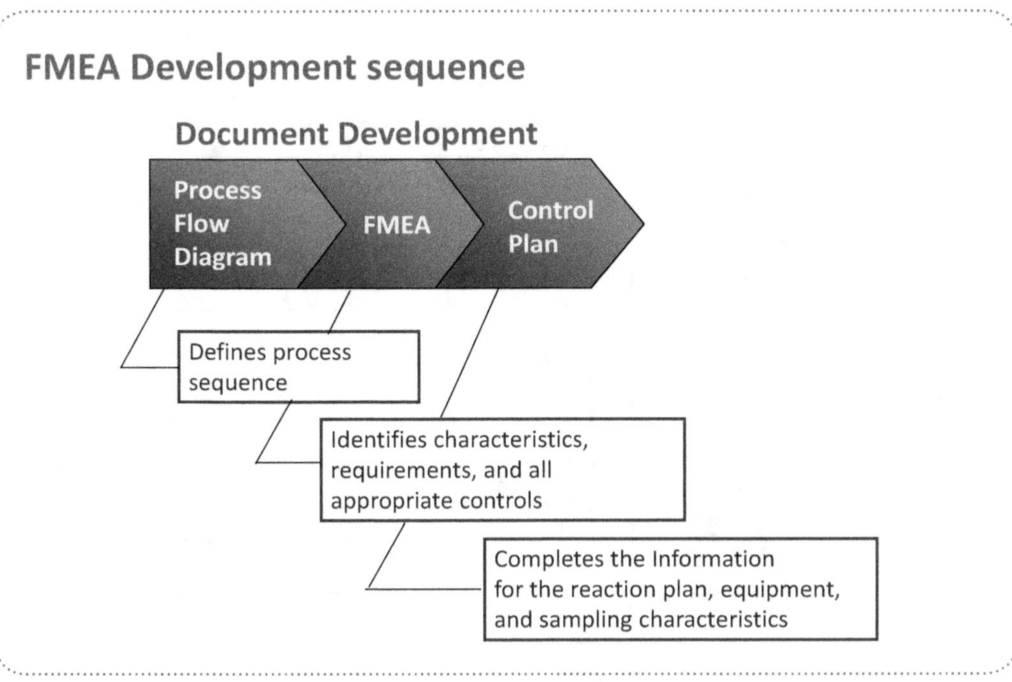

FMEA Content

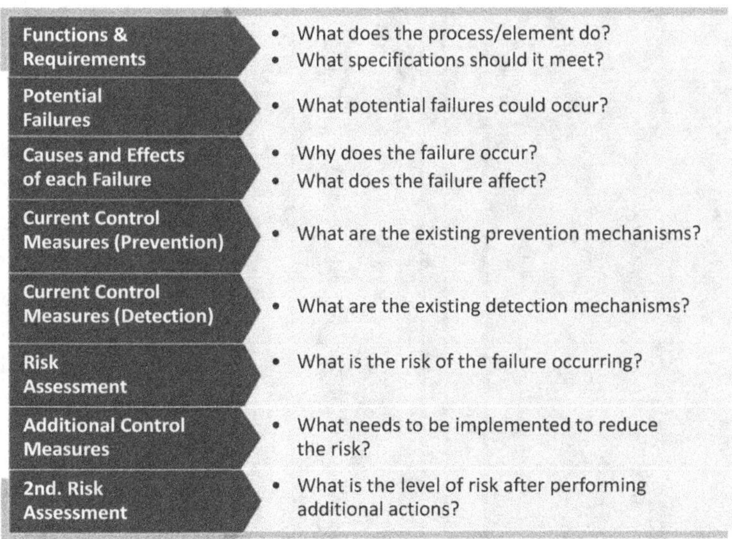

Standard format

System		Subsystem		Component			Number	
Item			Person responsible:				Page #	
Model				Date:		Prepared by:		
Team						Date Created:		Date Modified:

FMEA — **RESULTS**

#	Function/Process Step	Potential Failure	Effect	1 SEVERITY	Potential Causes	2 OCCURRENCE	Existing Controls	3 DETECTION	4 RPN	Recommended Actions	Person Responsible	Implemented Actions	5 SEV	6 OCC	7 DET	8 RPN

Procedure

1. Develop the structure and elements of the system	• For a process FMEA, this is obtained from the service or product assembly process flowchart.
2. Define the function of each process step	• This is key because in the following step you will ask: "What could go wrong for the process not to perform as specified?"
3. Define the failure modes in each process step	• For each element of the FMEA structure we must ask: "What could go wrong?" • What failures are acceptable for the product or process to still be able to fulfill its function? • What cause will trigger a failure?
4. Risk Assessment	• Evaluate the magnitude of risk for each failure and determine if it is necessary to take action to reduce the risk.

1. Develop the structure and elements

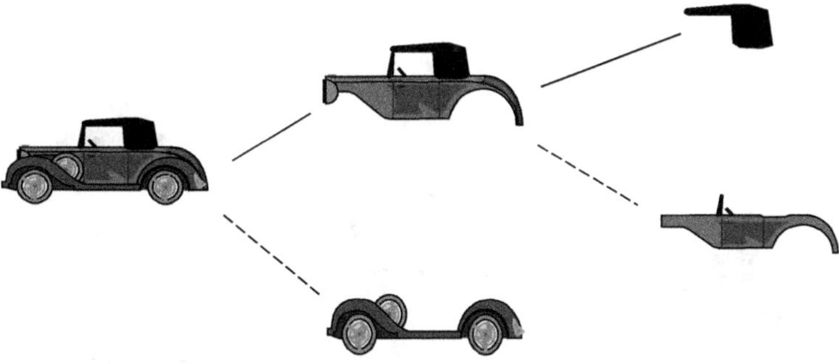

- Create a hierarchical structure (tree diagram)

- Develop the general elements and then move to the specific elements, using as many levels as necessary

2. Define the function of each process step

2.1. Add functions to each element of the system

- Including specifications and requirements is essential
- Use general terms for higher level functions
- Gradually increase detail at lower levels

The description of the function should be stated in terms of a:

$$VERB + NOUN$$

2.2. Generate a function network

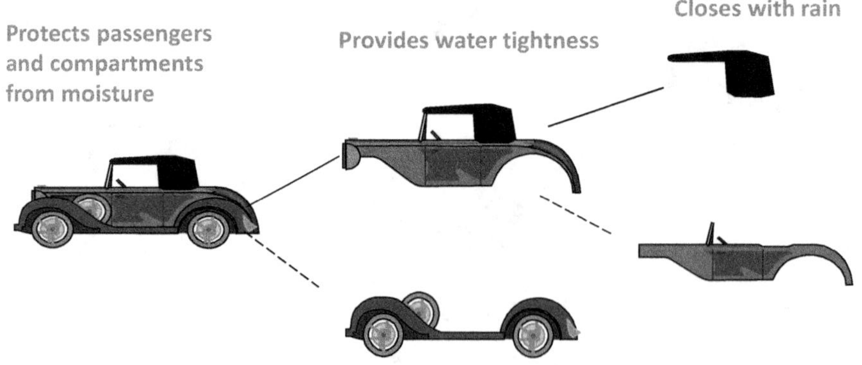

3. Define the failure modes at each process step

A **malfunction** is the failure mode of an element of the system.

3.1. Assign all potential malfunctions for each function, starting from the core element and moving to the lowest level elements in the system.

At this point, do not limit your evaluation of failures based on the probability of them happening!

- In the simplest case, determine the **negation** of the element's **function**.

- Be as precise as possible when describing the characteristics of the failure.

  - Described them in physical or technical terms.

- If there are different failure characteristics with different cause & effect, then categorize them as different failures.

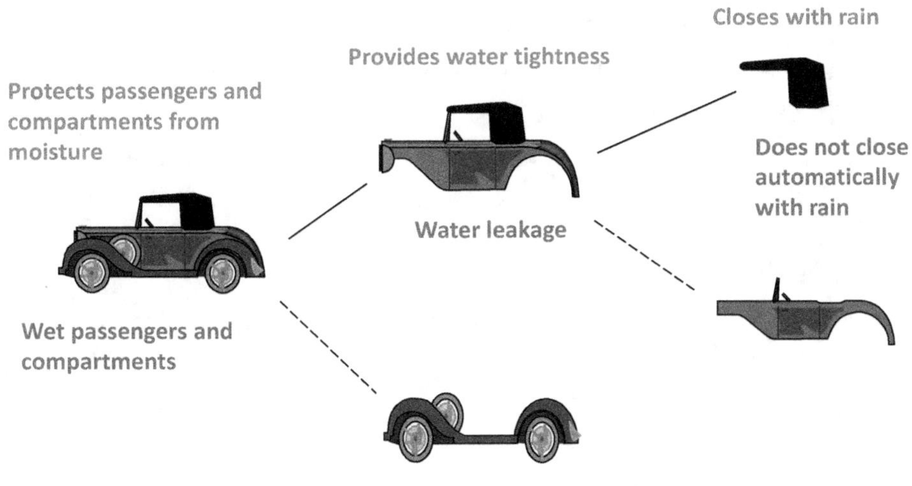

3.2. Generate a failure network

Assign causes (lower level) and effects (higher level) to every failure.

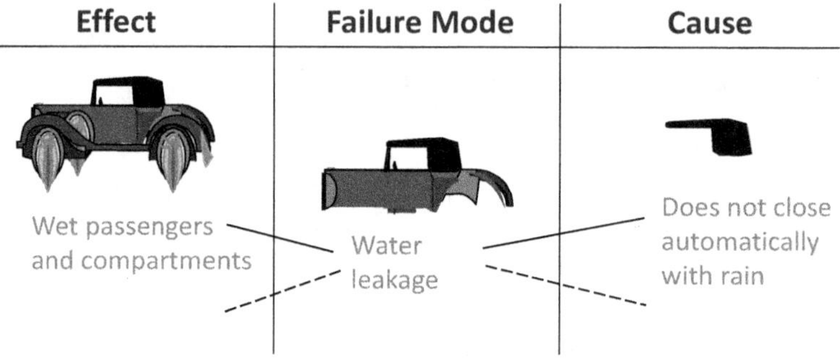

4. Risk assessment

4.1. Control methods

- **Preventive measures** - These are planned activities to avoid an occurrence of a failure.

- **Detection measures** - These are activities for detecting the cause or resulting failure mode.

4.2. Assessment

- **Severity** - With respect to the effect, always use the same evaluation for identical effects.

- **Occurrence** – Probability of failure's cause occurring with respect to preventive control methods.

- **Detection** – Probability of not detecting the cause or failure mode with respect to detection control methods.

- **FMEA RPN** = S x O x D (Severity x Occurrence x Detection)

Rating	Severity	Ocurrence (ppm)	Detection
1	**Minor** (customer doesn´t notice)	x < 1 ppm	**Very high** probability of detecting the defect (always)
2	**Low** (light customer discomfort. Probably will notice small deterioration)	1 < x < 250	
3			**High** probability of detecting the defect (almost always)
4	**Medium** (Some customer dissatisfaction. Notices deterioration of product performance)	250 < x < 12 500	
5			**Moderate** (the defect may be detected)
6			
7	**High** (High customer dissatisfaction. Makes the product useless)	12 500 < x < 50 000	**Low** (the defect probably won´t be detected)
8			
9	**Very High** (Upsets the customer. Makes the product unsafe)	50 000 < x	The defect cannot be detected
10			

RPN: Risk Priority Number

RPN = Severity × Occurrence × Detection

- The implementation of actions reduces the **occurrence**, and/or **detection**.

- **Severity** can only decrease with a change in the design.

- The preferred method for reducing **occurrence** and/or **detection** is to implement **Poka Yoke**, **Six Sigma**, and or **Standardized Work**.

Examples

Design FMEA

#	Function/ Process Step	Potential Failure	Effect	SEV	Potential Causes	OCURR	Existing Controls	DETEC	RPN
Package box	Contains computer	Box opens from the bottom	Computer falls and is damaged	8	Box is not glued properly	4	Gluing instructions Random inspection to verify glueing quality	4	128

Recommended Actions	Person Responsible	Implemented Actions	SEV	OCURR	DETEC	RPN
Automatic glue application by dispenser	John Peters 07/29/2020	Dispenser installation 07/29/2020	8	1	1	8
100% resistance test by automatic pressure device	Lois Smith 07/31/2020	Test device installation 07/31/2020				

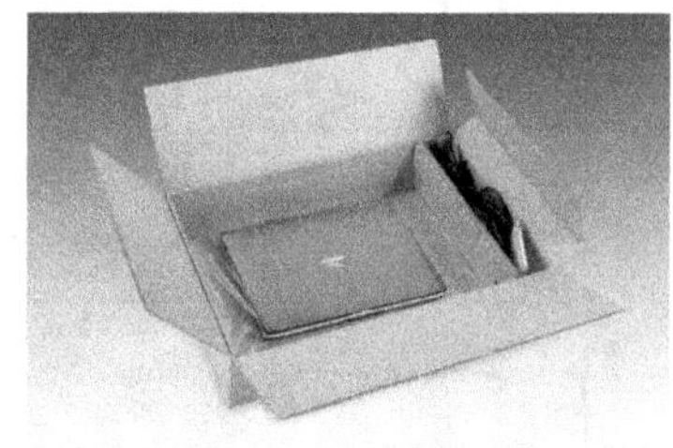

Process FMEA

No.	Process function What is the function of the process?	Failure Mode What could go wrong/ what defect can be generated?		Failure Effect What is the consequence?	Sev.	Failure Mechanism What can cause it?	Occur.	Failure mode Controls What controls do we have to detect the defect?	Det.	RPN
3	Assemble connector and fan to chassis	Inverted connector		Explodes when connected to electric power	9	1. Careless operation 2. Lack of knowledge	4	1. Supervisión 2. Training 3. Finished product inspection	4	144

Recommended Corrective Actions	Responsible Date	Implemented Actions Effective Date	Sev.	Occur.	Det.	RPN
1. Poka-yoke mechanism to ensure the right assembly for the connector	P.J. Fox (10/10/2019)	1. Fixture	9	1	1	9
2. 100% functional testing of the source of the product	M.F. Ruiz (10/10/2019)	2. 100% functional testing				

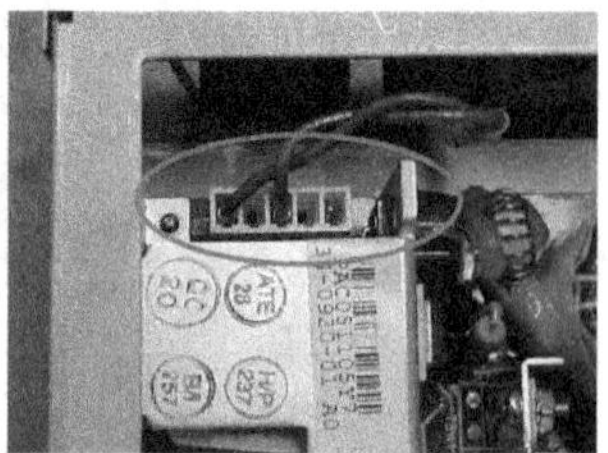

Kaizen

Learning objectives

1. Understand how to apply Kaizen in your personal life and in organizations.
2. Understand the role and importance of Kaizen events in a company's Lean Six Sigma transformation.
3. Learn the procedure for implementing Kaizen events.

Content

> Background
> What is Kaizen?
> Types of Kaizen events
> What is it used for?
> Key elements
> Procedure

Kaizen

Background

Kai = Change   *Zen* = Good or improve

- It has its origin in the Buddhist school of India. It is practiced in China, Japan and South Korea by individuals seeking **personal improvement**.

- The Toyota Motor Company was the first organization to use it as a Lean philosophy and tool.

- Today, many Kaizen concepts and tools come from:

  - The field of Industrial Engineering

  - The teachings of Dr. Edward Deming

  - The book *Gemba Kaizen* by Masaaki Imai

Personal Kaizen philosophy

- **Self-control** is the key to mastering life.

- **Success** starts with individuals and then expands to teams.

- **Enlightenment** is achieved through the cultivation of the mind, body and soul.

- The **goal of life** is to find your purpose and carry it out.

What is Kaizen?

- The Japanese word "**Kaizen**" (改 善) means change *(kai)* to become good *(zen)*.

Kaizen = Change for the Better

«This is not theory ... It's a way of life.»

- For use in organizations, Kaizen means **gradual continuous improvement**

- Everyone is actively **involved**

- *Kaizen* is a **powerful tool** that many leading international organizations use to **improve their people and processes**

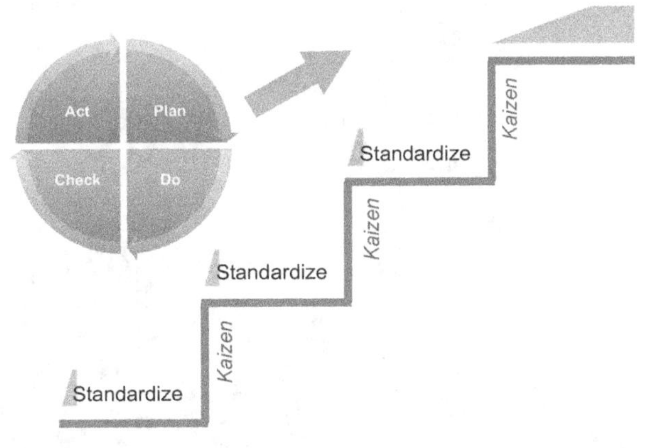

Types of Kaizen events

- ***Kaizen Blitz:*** to make quick improvements or solve simple problems **(3-5 hours)**

- ***Kaizen Events:*** to solve problems and implement Lean tools: TPM, SMED, etc. **(3-5 days)**

- **Six Sigma *Kaizen:*** for complex problems and process / product re-design **(3-5 weeks)**

- Improvements with clients
- Sales improvements
- 5S implementation
- TPM implementation
- Automation
- Layout design
- New product design

- Visual management
- Kanban implementation
- Poka-Yoke
- Continuous flow implementation
- Quick Setup implementation
- Talent Development
- Value engineering implementation (Kaikaku)

Kaizen benefits

- Provides a way to **train employees**, enrich their work experience, and bring out the best in each person.

- Promotes the **personal growth** of employees and the company.

- Improves safety, performance, customer service, therefore **employee satisfaction**.

- Improves **leadership**.

Key elements

- A focus on quality
- Human effort
- Total participation
- A will to change
- Communication

Procedure

Significant improvements in only 5 days!

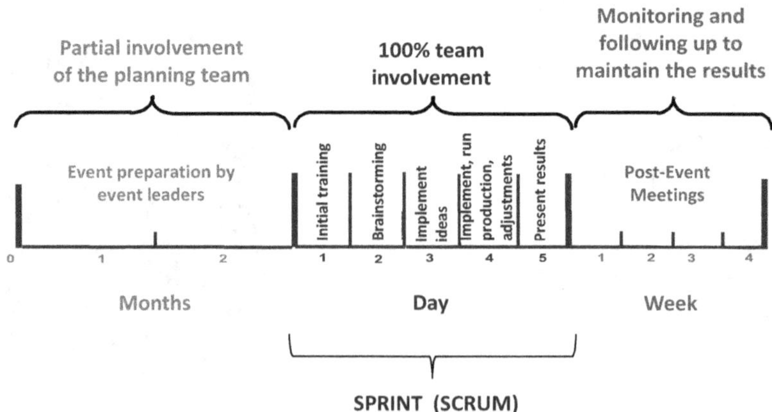

Before the event

Preparation Phase

1. Form the [multidisciplinary] team.

2. Define the objective and scope, and develop the project documentation (Kaizen charter).

3. Define the event agenda and communicate it with team members.

4. Draw the current Value Stream Map (VSM).

5. Provide a brief description of the event (optional; can be the first day of the event).

Relationship between Kaizen and Sprint used in SCRUM

When an agile project is developed based on a future value stream map, each **Kaizen event** represents a **Sprint** in which the team is completely focused and dedicated.

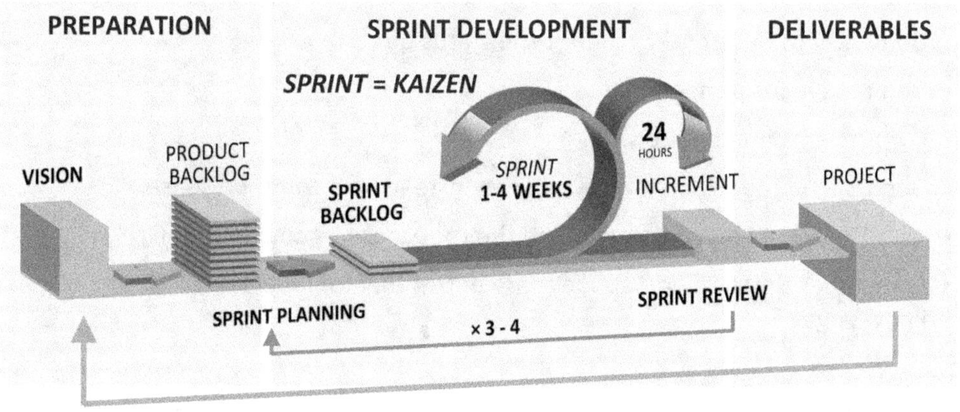

Opportunity cards

- It is important to encourage the team to submit their ideas and, when possible, implement them during the event.

- Improvement ideas should be classified as **opportunity categories A, B, or C**.

  - **A:** These are ideas that can be implemented immediately **(1 to 5 days)**.

  - **B:** These are ideas that can be implemented during or shortly after the event **(1 to 2 weeks)**.

  - **C:** These are ideas that require a greater amount of time to implement and may require special authorization, investment, etc. **(up to 2 months)**.

OPPORTUNITY CARD	
Date:	Number:
Area:	
Opportunity detected: (Muda, Muri, Mura)	
Activity to be performed:	Classification
Equipment:	
Observations:	
Date:	Folio:
Area:	
Opportunity detected: (Muda, Muri, Mura)	
Activity to be performed:	Calssification:
Equipment:	

Improvement principles

- Ignore the traditional or current work methods and consider that there might be a way to do things better.

- Think about how the new method can work and not why it won't work.

- Don't accept excuses – challenge the status quo.

- Don't strive for perfection.

- Fix problems immediately.

- Don't spend money on improvements. Instead, use common sense.

- Ask "Why?" at least 5 times to find the root cause of any problem.

- Remember that 10 people's ideas are better than one person's knowledge.

Continuous Flow

Learning objectives

1. Learn how to design uninterrupted processes.
2. Understand the concept of Work Cells or Office pods.
3. Learn the procedure to develop Continuous Flow.

Content

> Background
> What is Continuous Flow?
> Benefits
> Forms of waste
> Who participates?
> When is it used?
> Procedure
> Examples

Background

- In 1776, Adam Smith, a Scottish economist and philosopher, demonstrated that **dividing labor** into specific tasks would result in increased productivity.

- Frederick Taylor, the father of scientific management, agreed with this concept. In the late 1800s, he introduced the idea of **dedicating specialized labor** to repetitive tasks in order to achieve a more productive flow.

- Henry Ford developed the concept of production lines during the early 20th century, which support the idea of **specialized labor** by using large assembly lines.

- Today, **demand and volume** conditions have changed from large lot sizes of the same product to small lot sizes with a high mix of products. These changes make it difficult for companies to succeed using these early methods.

- As a result, beginning with Shigeo Shingo's first implementations at Toyota, **Lean promotes continuous workflow** as a core principle.

- It is a common practice to **transfer workers** from one value stream to another according with the demand.

What is Continuous Flow?

- Continuous Flow is a process concept designed to significantly improve a facility's layout and create **uninterrupted work flow** between operations.

- As a result, employees' skills and **performance** are optimized, and **response times** are significantly reduced.

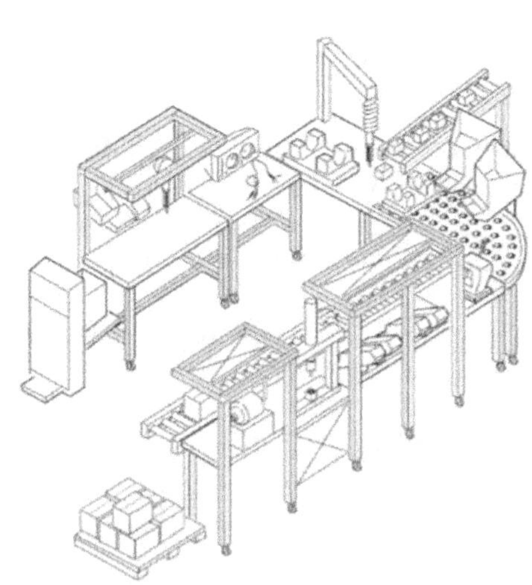

Companies organized by departments

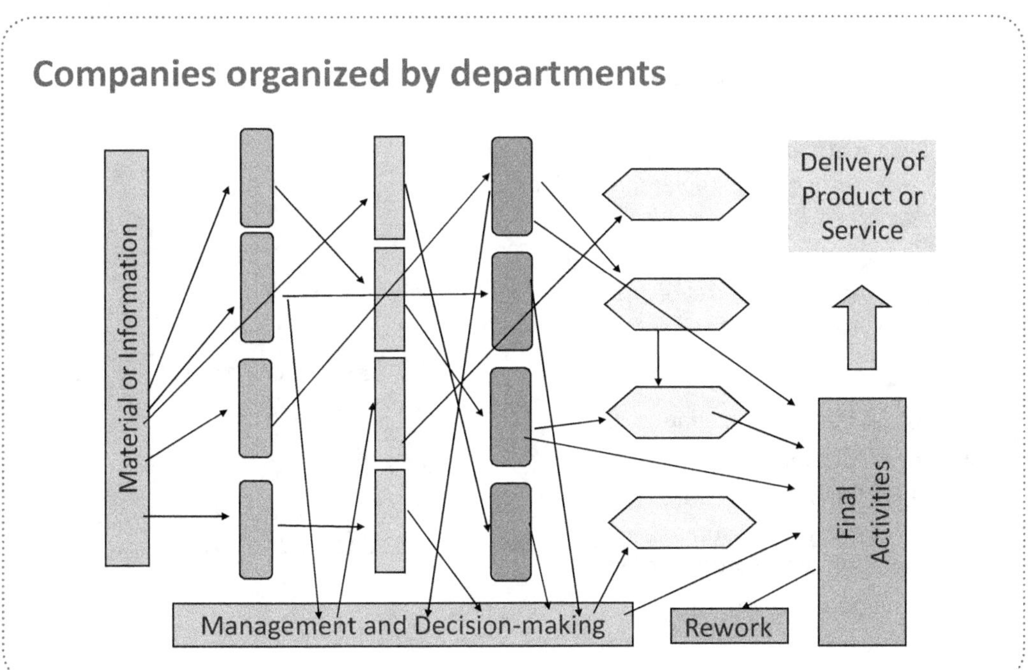

Problems related to organization by departments:

- Defects may not be detected until the service is performed or the product is finished.

- **Material handling** results in an increased number of **defects**.

- People and parts spend **extensive waiting times** between each phase of the process.

- Materials and product inventory **consume too much space**.

What are Workcells or Pods?

- For Lean methodology, **Continuous Flow** is applied through the implementation of **Workcells and Pods**.

- **Workcells and Pods** are work structures that connect the activities of a process according to specific considerations:

  - Workload balancing effectiveness
  - Customer's demand adaptability
  - Process capability baseline enhancement
  - Continuous Flow assurance in the generation of the product or service
  - Layout optimization

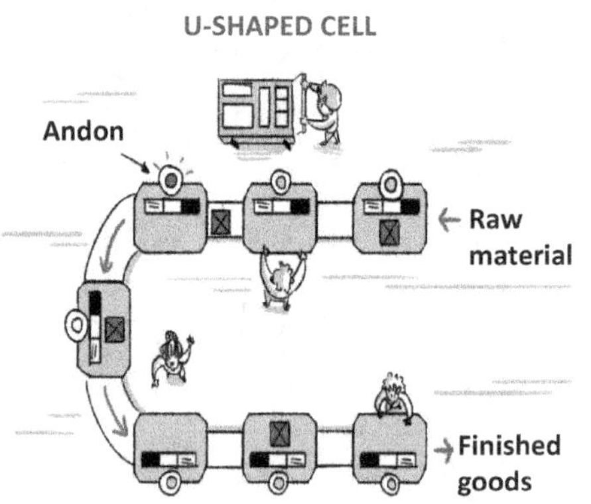

Example of a Work Cell

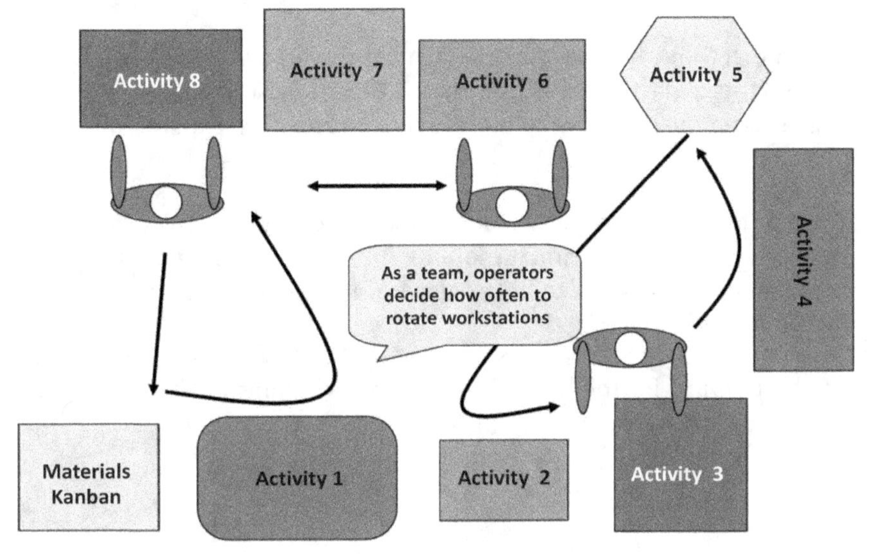

- Significant **reduction** in **response time**.

- Improves **teamwork and communication** – employees are closer to each other and have better opportunities to help one another.

- Ensures a **complete understanding** of the entire work process.

- Promotes a work environment where workers feel a greater **sense of control, ownership, and responsibility** for their activities.

- Leads to greater **employee satisfaction**.

Forms of waste

- **Transport:** Materials or information must travel to other areas where the next step in the process is located. The longer the distance that things are moved, the more effort and resources are expended for no additional value.

- **Space:** There is also a cost associated with storing, managing, and maintaining inventory; and it requires staff, time, funding, and physical space that could be put to better use for other value-added activities.

- **Delays:** Batch processing causes delays while the first unit of service of the batch waits for the last unit of service to be finished before moving to the next process.

Where does an increase in productivity come from?

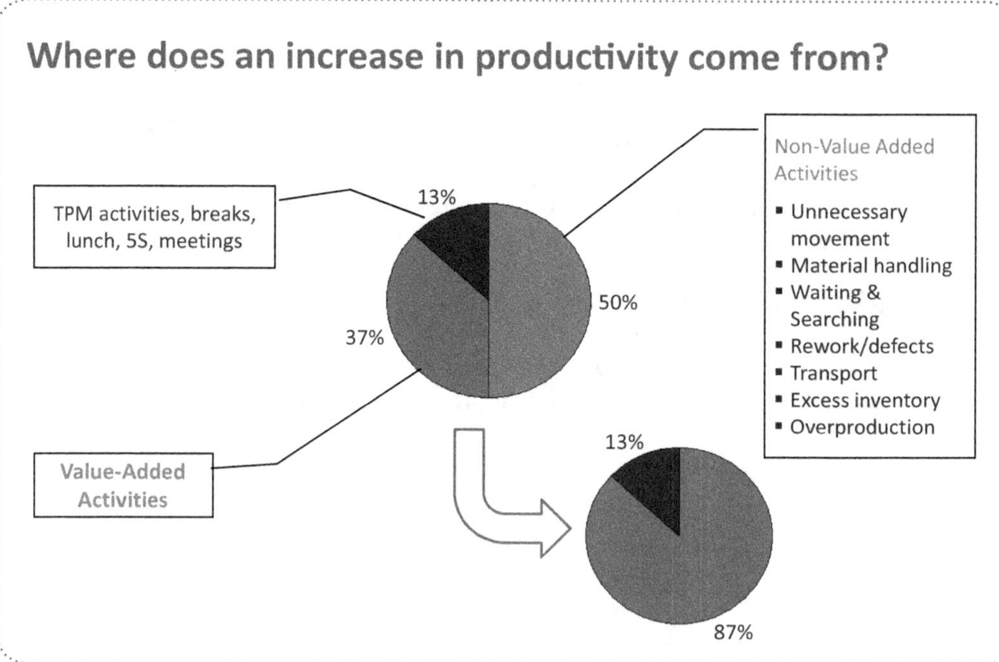

Continuous Flow requirements

- Cells or pods are designed **for every product or service family** (they share the same or similar steps of the process and work teams)

- **Flexible and multi-skilled** workers

Who participates?

- 5 to 12 team members (at least 2 people working in the selected process)
- Maintenance personnel, if applicable
- Quality personnel
- Process engineers, if available
- Supervisors
- Cost accounting staff
- Trainers

When is it used?

- When **lead time** needs to be substantially reduced
- When we need to produce a **higher-mix and lower volume** of products or services
- When the demand for products or services is **difficult to forecast**

Procedure

Before the event

Kaizen events are planned with time in advance. During this planning phase, the following is accomplished:

1. Select a product or service family and draw [current and future] Value Stream Maps.
2. Event opportunities are identified and proposed.
3. Team leader is selected.
4. Event sponsor is selected (this is a person who has authority and can make decisions to support the teams' proposals).
5. Team is selected. Sometimes, customers and suppliers are invited to participate.
6. Event plan and logistics are prepared (e.g., meeting room, event area, tools, etc.).
7. Project documentation is prepared.

During the event

1. Draw a Spaghetti Diagram and analyze waste (Muda) and identify opportunities.
2. Calculate takt time and capacity and determine the number of process workers/operators.
3. **Design and balance** the work cells or Pods.
4. **Simulate** the different options with the team members **in the workplace** (use cardboard boxes, tape on the floor, etc.).
5. **Implement the work** cells or Pods.
6. **Practice** the operation with the team and make changes if necessary.
7. Apply **ergonomics** to the workstations' designs.
8. **Document** the new process and **train** personnel (share knowledge).

❯ Examples

A factory has a manufacturing line for a family of products. The management team decides to transform the process into a manufacturing cell. There are eight operations performed on the line (identified as codes A - H). The cycle times are shown below. The **takt time** for the family is **79** seconds.

Operation No.	Operation Code	Description	Time	Takt Time
1	A	Cutting	22	79
2	B	Painting	45	79
3	C	Drilling	19	79
4	D	Electronic Assembly	63	79
5	E	Upload Software	22	79
6	F	Control Module Assembly	32	79
7	G	Final Assembly & Testing	134	79
8	H	Packaging & Shipping	49	79
		Total cycle time	386	

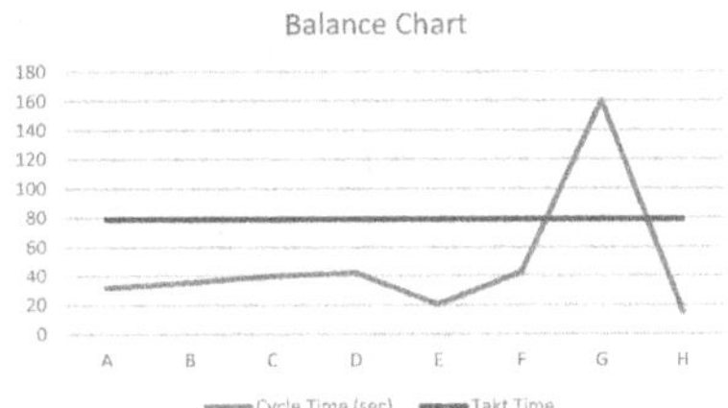

$$\text{Balance Efficiency} = \frac{\text{Sum of "n" cycle times}}{\text{Slowest cycle time * "n"}} = 0.36$$

"n" is the total number of operations

The **Balance Chart** is used to compare each worker's cycle time against the **Takt Time.**

Determine the number of workers

- To determine the number of workers required, divide total cycle time (386 s) by takt time (79 s), which equals **4.88** workers.

- Ideally, 5 workers combined will produce one unit every 79 seconds. This is considering a scenario where that there are no delays or interruptions, workers are utilized 100% of the time, and they are all contributing to multiple operations.

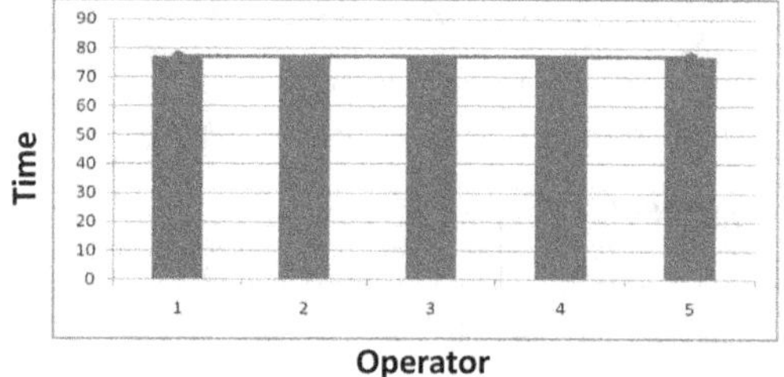

Operator	Cycle time	Takt time
1	77.2	79
2	77.2	79
3	77.2	79
4	77.2	79
5	77.2	79

Balancing of operations

When implementing Continuous Flow, some operations are reassigned in order to obtain the desired takt time.

Operator	Time (s)	Operation Code
1	67	A + B
2	82	C + D
3	77	E + F + part of G
4	77	Part of G
5	83	Part of G + H
Total Cycle Time	386	

Conclusions

- One or more operations are assigned to each worker to most efficiently use their time. However, process improvements should be implemented to reduce the time of operators 2 and 5 so that they can produce faster than the **takt time**.

- It is important to note that this first design is ideal, but that the operations should be further studied to determine the relative ease of combining operations.

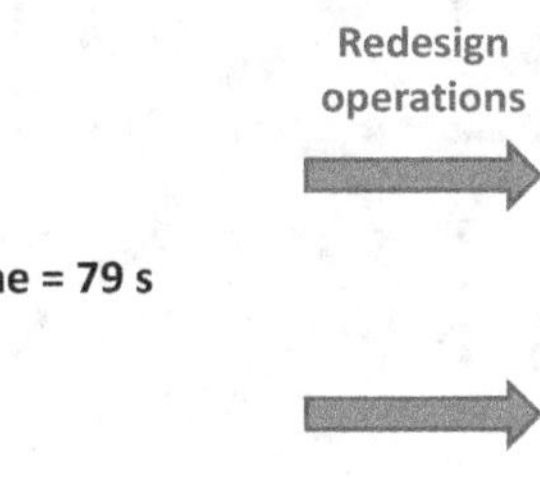

Takt time = 79 s

Operator	Time (s)	Operation Code
1	67	A + B
2	82	C + D
3	77	E + F + part of G
4	77	Part of G
5	83	Part of G + H

Drawing a new Cell

- First draw the inner workstation area and then locate the first and last operation at each end of the U.

- Next, insert the second and second to last operations in succession, until the U is closed.

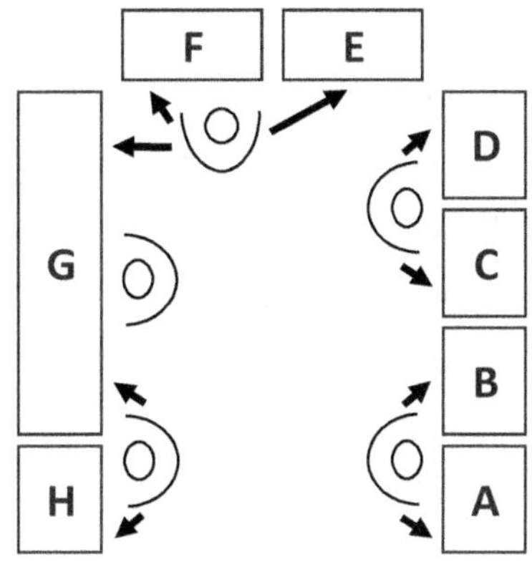

Simulate

Source: Movie "Founder". Mc Donald's system

Ergonomic design considerations

1. Height
2. Space available (reach)
3. Positioning of materials
4. Working below the heart
5. Visual fields
6. Illumination
7. Adjustable positions

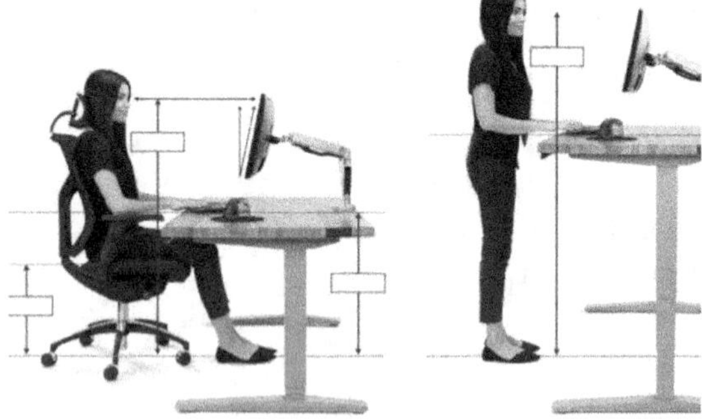

Examples of cells

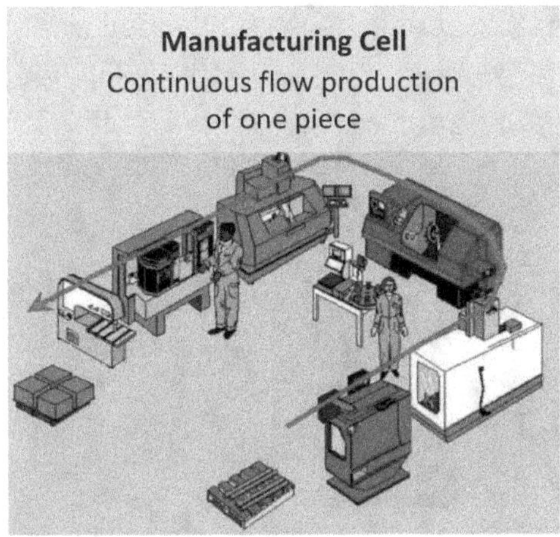

Manufacturing Cell
Continuous flow production
of one piece

Office Cell ("Pod")
Provides a complete service or
process in a continuous flow

Work cell / Vehicle rims

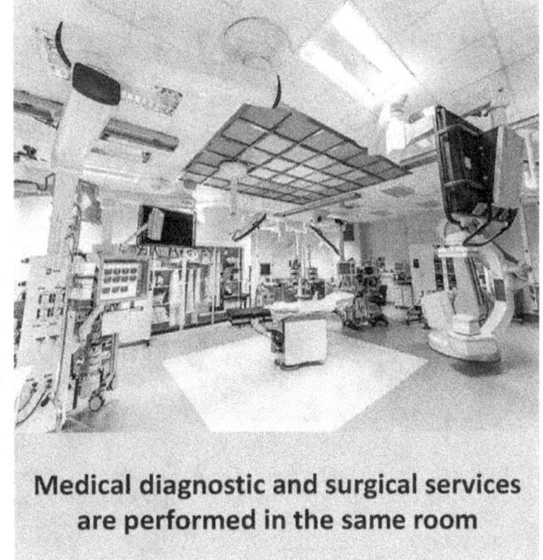

**Medical diagnostic and surgical services
are performed in the same room**

Continuous flow at a Gymnasium

Continuous flow at a restaurant

Every kitchen pod prepares all dishes according to the current demand.

Continuous Flow at a Car Rental Agency

Register and pay

Obtain insurance

Pick up, review and exit

LSSI
LEAN SIX SIGMA INSTITUTE

Quick Setups (SMED)

20

Learning objectives

1. Learn a method that maximizes value-added activities and minimizes non-value added activities by reducing setup times.
2. Understand the benefits of implementing SMED (Quick Setups).
3. Learn a procedure to develop a quick setup event.

Content

> Background
> What is SMED/Quick Setups?
> Benefits
> Important definitions
> Procedure
> Example

Background

- **Taiichi Ohno** joined Toyota in 1943 and later became Production Manager. He analyzed the North American Automotive industry and noticed that companies were using a large number of stamping presses to manufacture multiple vehicle models in order to avoid changing molds. **At that time, mold setup took more than 24 hours.**

- Because Toyota had a limited number of stamping presses, they were challenged to **manufacture a wide variety of vehicles using less equipment than their competitors.**

Shigeo Shingo

- In 1950, Shigeo Shingo studied mold changeovers at Mazda and later he was hired as a consultant at Toyota as well.

- His work led to:
  - Eliminating bottlenecks
  - By 1970, Shingo and Toyota managed to reduce changeover times on 1,000 ton stamping presses from 4 hours to 3 minutes.
  - **Today, these changes are performed in 30 seconds.**

What is SMED/Quick Setups?

- **SMED (Single Minute Exchange of Die)** is a Lean method used to reduce waste in any type of process. The phrase **"single minute"**, referring to single digits, suggests that all setups should take **less than 10 minutes.**

- **Quick setups** employs this principle of quickly preparing processes (e.g., service, manufacturing, logistics, administrative, etc.) in order to maximize the ability to deliver products or services on time.

Quick Setups (Changeovers) are similar to when race cars make pit stops to change tires, refuel, make inspections, perform cleaning, etc.

What is a SMED event?

- A **SMED or Quick Setup Event** is an improvement event that is performed by a cross-functional team to substantially reduce product or service setup times.

- The goal is to produce **a high variety of products or services in the shortest time, using fewer resources.**

- It is based on the principle that it is better to dedicate more time to effective processing and less time to setup.

Quick Setup example

Production mix =   8733   8206   8783   8827   8816

Day 1	▪ 8733
Day 2	▪ 8206
Day 3	▪ 8783
Day 4	▪ 8827
Day 5	▪ 8816

Change

Day 1	8733	8206	8783	8827	8816
Day 2	8733	8206	8783	8827	8816
Day 3	8733	8206	8783	8827	8816
Day 4	8733	8206	8783	8827	8816
Day 5	8733	8206	8783	8827	8816

More setups with less waste!

Setup Time	Machine Time	Lot Size	Number of unique parts produced
2 h	6 h	512	1
1 h	6 h	256	2
30 min	6 h	128	4
15 min	6 h	64	8
7.5 min	6 h	32	16
3.75 min	6 h	16	32
113 s	6 h	8	64
56 s	6 h	4	128
28 s	6 h	2	256
14 s	6 h	1	512

The table shows how machine flexibility increases when setup time is reduced from 2 hours to 14 seconds.

- The goal of **quick setups** is to substantially **reduce the time** it takes to deliver an order once it has been submitted by a customer.

- **Minimizing setup times**, provides companies with opportunities to produce a large variety of products or services using the same resources.

Significant reduction in:

- Delivery time
- Defects
- Work-in-Process inventory
- Finished product inventory
- Waiting
- Investment in inventory

Significant increase in:

- Flexibility to respond to customer demands
- Inventory rotation
- Productivity
- Capacity

Important definitions

- **Setup Time (manufacturing process):** Time required to prepare equipment or a system to change from producing the last good item from run "A" to the first good item from the next run "B".

- **Setup Time (service or office process):** Time it takes after finishing one task to prepare and complete the next task correctly.

- **Internal Setup Time:** Time spent on the setup when the machine or process is stopped.

- **External Setup Time:** Time spent on the setup when the machine or process is running.

Prerequisites for Quick Setups

- Commitment from management

- Initial training for all participants

- Knowledge on how to conduct Kaizen events

- Creation of the necessary documentation

- 5S Housekeeping implementation is a requirement

- In-depth knowledge of setup processes and procedures

Before the event

1. Draw a value stream map of the service or manufacturing process.
2. Evaluate the impact of the planned Kaizen event.
3. Determine which process you will focus on according to the bottleneck from the VSM.
4. Establish a cross-functional team.
5. Schedule the Kaizen event.
6. Create an agenda for the Kaizen event and share it with the team.
7. Record the changeover on video.
8. Train the team members on Quick Setups.

During the event

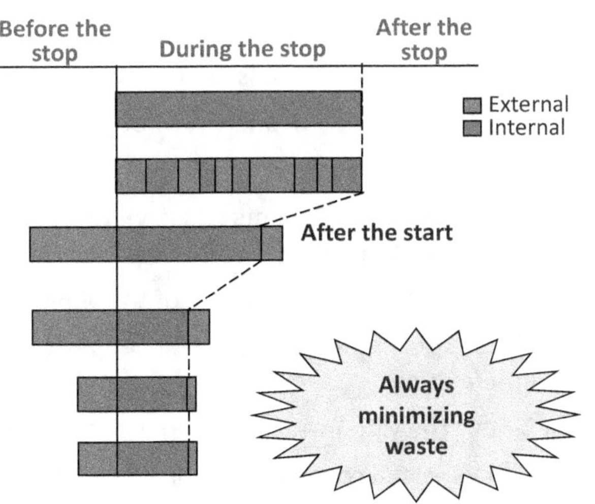

1. Observe and measure total setup time.
2. Differentiate internal activities from external activities.
3. Convert internal activities to external activities and then practice them outside the stop.
4. Eliminate waste from internal activities.
5. Eliminate waste from external activities.
6. Standardize and maintain the new procedure.

1. Observe and measure total setup time

Record the entire setup including all personnel movements associated with the setup. The rest of the team will look for improvement opportunities.

Note: Activate the time display on the video

Video recording guidelines

- Identify everyone who is involved in the setup
- Be respectful if someone does not want to be filmed
- Record a panoramic view of the entire process
- Record hand movements (closely), tool handling, and interactions with other processes
- Document the time and date of the video
- Record personnel comments since they often provide valuable information
- Watch the video with the people involved soon after the event
- Schedule and conduct meetings to review the video during the Kaizen event

2. Differentiate internal from external activities

- When analyzing the video, review every activity and complete the "Setup Analysis" form.

- Classify all activities:

  - **External activities** are those that can be performed while the process is still running.

  - **Internal activities** are those that can only be performed when the process is stopped.

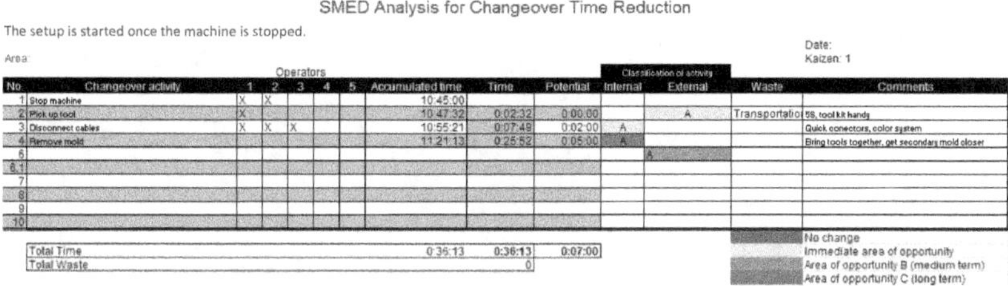

SMED Analysis for Changeover Time Reduction

The setup is started once the machine is stopped.

Area:

Date:
Kaizen: 1

No.	Changeover activity	1	2	3	4	5	Accumulated time	Time	Potential	Internal	External	Waste	Comments
1	Stop machine	X	X				10:45:00						
2	Pick up tool	X					10:47:32	0:02:32	0:00:00		A	Transportation	5S, tool kit handy
3	Disconnect cables	X	X	X			10:55:21	0:07:49	0:02:00	A			Quick conectors, color system
4	Remove mold						11:21:13	0:25:52	0:05:00	A			Bring tools together, get secondary mold closer
5											A		
6.1													
7													
8													
9													
10													
Total Time								0:36:13	0:36:13	0:07:00			
Total Waste									0				

No change
Immediate area of opportunity
Area of opportunity B (medium term)
Area of opportunity C (long term)

3. Convert internal activities to external

In this step, activities performed during the stop will be analyzed, simplified and/or improved. To do this, consider the following activities.

Common external activities during a setup:

- Find and retrieve the tools needed for the setup.
- Communicate the need for a setup.
- Communication between people who are involved.
- Inspections and paperwork related to the setup.
- Schedule or contact the personnel ahead of time who will perform the setup when production has stopped.

Suggested activities for this step:

- Keep tools close by or in a designated setup cart.
- Implement an Andon System used to communicate when setups will take place.
- Standardize roles for every team member.
- Wait until process is running before doing the paperwork.
- Have a setup plan and follow it.

4. Eliminate waste from internal activities

- Use quick-setup tools to reduce setup times

- Use teamwork to eliminate or reduce walking and transportation

- Design standardized parts and tools to simplify the setup

- Relocate parts and materials to an easy-to-find location to reduce time spent walking and searching

5. Eliminate waste from external activities

- Reduce required paperwork

- Relocate related storage areas to reduce travel and transportation time

- Use a checklist to improve efficiency

  The list should include elements such as:

  - Tools, specifications, the number of required workers, etc.

  - Correct operating conditions for each process

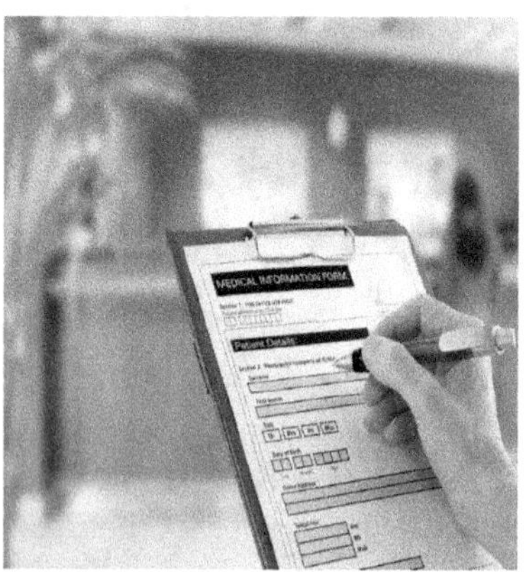

LSSI
LEAN SIX SIGMA INSTITUTE

6. Standardize and maintain the new procedure

- Document improved setup procedures.
- Share the new procedures with all involved employees.
- Train everyone involved in the setup.
- Post standardized work instructions in the workplace.
- Establish goals for the setups.
- Measure, publish, and keep track of setup times.

Before	Now
6 hours	4 hours

Rules and considerations for Quick Setups

1. For setup initiatives to be successful, it is important that **Total Productive Maintenance** is working correctly.

2. Keep in mind that **changes are gradual** and it will require multiple events to achieve your setup time improvement goals.

3. It is required to implement **5s Housekeeping**. Good housekeeping will result in having setup items in their correct places when needed.

Reduction in loading time for a bottling company

What prompted our changes?

Business case: As a company, our **loading times** for the logistics, finance, commercial and warehousing areas are not meeting our 30 minute goal. As a result, we are not meeting our customer satisfaction goals and we are losing sales and customers.

Takt time: 720 min / 45 Loads = **16 min** per loading.

Cost per transaction: **$ 44.00** per load.

Entry	Uploading	Loading	Exit	Total
6	11	42	24	**1:18**
10	11	29	16	**1:08**
6	10	25	25	**1:09**
8	13	9	30	**1:02**
7	6	42	23	**1:17**
		Minutes		Hours/Minutes

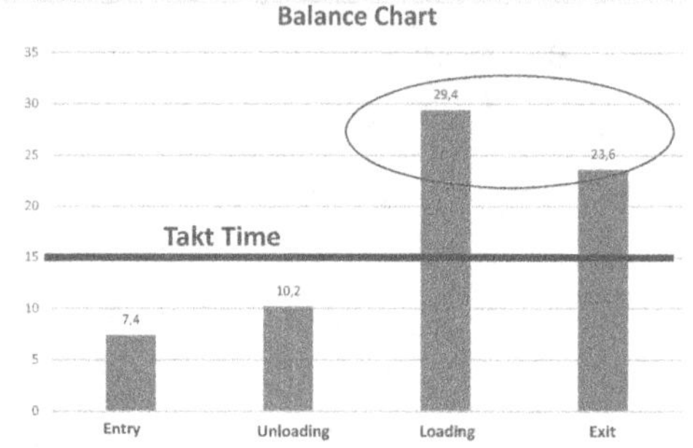

Transformation phase

What actions did we take?

1. Team Training on Quick Setups
2. Conducted an analysis to identify process improvement opportunities

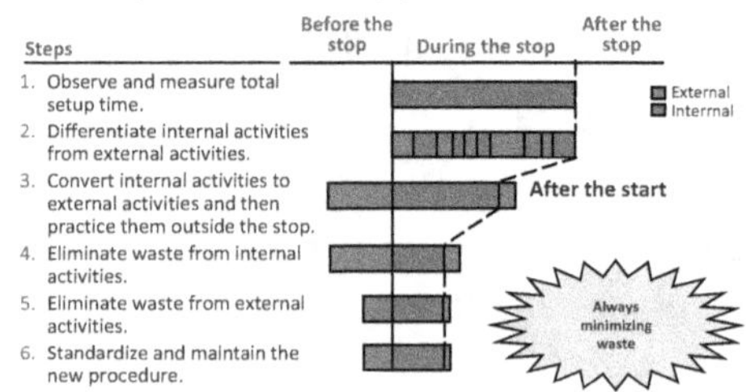

Entry: Unscheduled truck loadings

Unloading: Lack of coordination by loading personnel. Excess movement of forklift operators.

Loading: Loading areas are not defined. In this area, unnecessary movements of people and resources. The area is unsafe, there are unattended vehicles, rework is constantly being performed, paperwork processing is slow, and there is inefficient inventory control.

Exit: Long wait times due to slow truck releases.

What we did?

ENTRY 1 – 2 min
- Arrival notice by WhatsApp message
- Pallet arrangement is standardized

UNLOADING 5 – 8 min
- Unload and load area is assigned (bottle unloading in the same area)
- Two forklifts are assigned

LOADING 7 - 10 min
- Previous count is performed by finance and logistics
- Checkout receipt is printed in advance
- Product is loaded in both sides of the truck
- Two forklifts are assigned

EXIT 1 – 2 min
- Check out information is ready

What we achieved

ACTUAL TIMES

Entry	Unloading	Loading	Exit	Total
6	11	42	24	**1:18**
10	11	29	16	**1:08**
6	10	25	25	**1:09**
8	13	9	30	**1:02**
7	6	42	23	**1:17**
7.4	**10.2**	**29.4**	**23.6**	

FUTURE TIMES

Entry	Unloading	Loading	Exit	Total
2	9	7	5	**23**
0.5	4	23	1	**29**
1	9	9.5	1	**20**
2	4	4	0.5	**11**
1.375	**6.5**	**10.875**	**1.875**	

Balance Chart

Future Balance Chart

Quick Setups help reduce inventory

- Achieving quick setups helps **reduce inventory** because the company only replenishes items according to customer demand.

- Using forecasts typically results in an **excessive accumulation** of inventory.

Hospital operating room

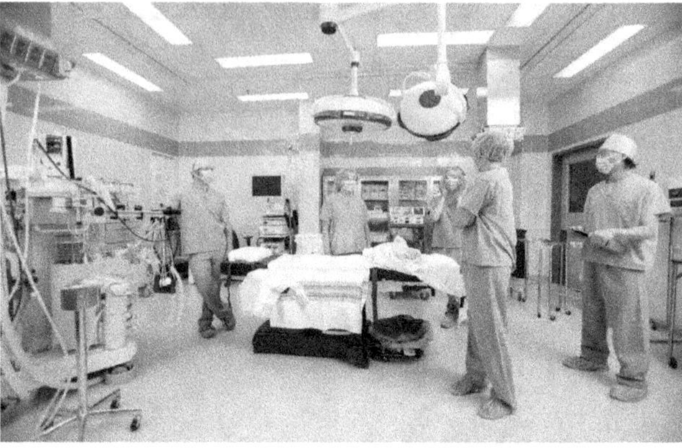

As a result of implementing quick setups, preparation times decreased from 30 minutes to less than 10 minutes.

SMED applications in different industries

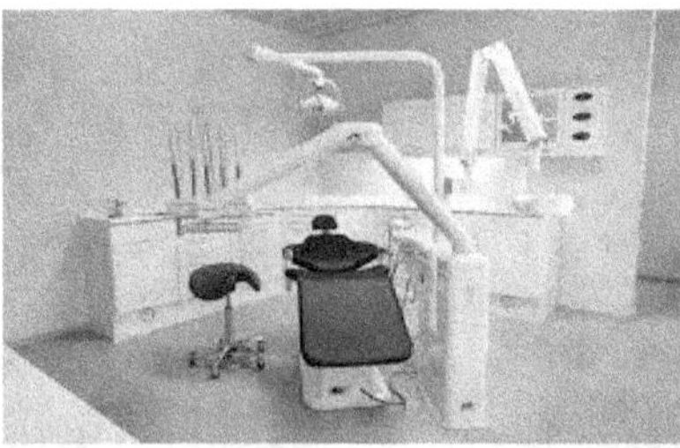

21

Total Productive Maintenance (TPM)

Learning objectives

1. Understand the importance of having proper maintenance at any organization.
2. Understand the key elements of Total Productive Maintenance (TPM).
3. Learn the procedure to implement TPM.

Content

> Background
> What is TPM?
> Benefits
> Types of Maintenance
> Pillars of TPM
> Procedure

Background

- Maintenance is required by service and manufacturing companies.

- In our life, maintenance is also an important activity.

Has this happened to you before?

- Frequent stops due to repairs.

- Failure to meet customers specifications.

- High risks related with equipment.

- Frequent challenges getting tasks done on time.

Origins of TPM

- **Total Productive Maintenance** has its origins in the United States where manufacturing companies applied practices to prevent untimely equipment failures.

- In the post-war period, Japanese business executives and engineers visited U.S. manufacturing plants to gain knowledge and apply what they learned at their own companies back in Japan.

- The concept of all company employees (not just maintenance staff) performing maintenance duties was first introduced by **Nippondenso**, one of Toyota's auto parts suppliers at the time.

Maintenance costs

- Maintenance costs typically account for about 15% to 40% of a company's total operating costs.

- Emergency repairs tend to be more than three times as expensive as planned repairs.

- Typically, about 58% of maintenance costs are due to the improper operation of equipment.

- About 17% of maintenance costs are due to poor equipment lubrication.

Defect triangle

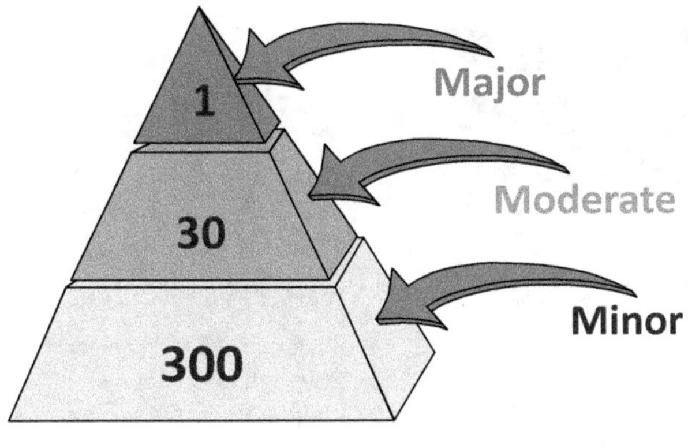

From statistical analyses of the root causes of problems, findings suggest that a certain proportion of minor and moderate issues must first occur before a major problem occurs.

What is TPM?

Total Productive Maintenance (TPM) is a method to achieve optimal equipment effectiveness through the participation of all company employees.

Leaders + Users + Maintenance

Definition

TOTAL

- Refers to all departments, facilities and processes.
- All employees are involved.
- Aim is to eliminate all defects, breakdowns, accidents, etc.

PRODUCTIVE

- Maximization of the efficiency of production/service systems.
- Minimization of the productivity losses in any production or service process.

MAINTENANCE

- Establishes a complete system of preventive equipment maintenance.
- Refers to the entire lifecycle of production/service systems.

Benefits

- Improved total equipment effectiveness.

- Improved production quality.

- Longer equipment life expectancy.

- Reduced equipment lifecycle costs.

- Converts reactive activities into proactive activities.

- Increased job safety and process reliability.

Focus of autonomous maintenance

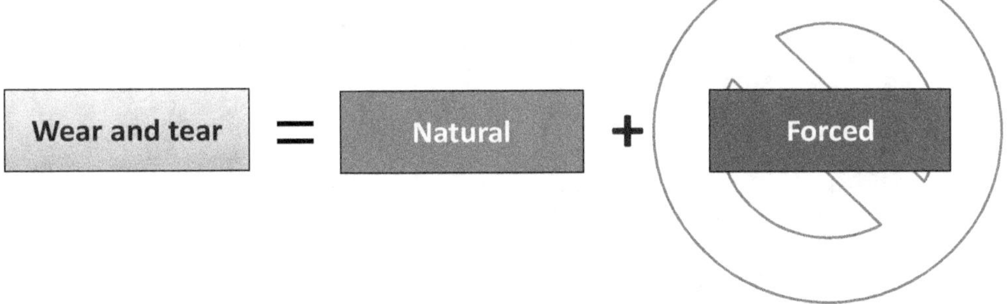

TPM helps eliminate forced wear and reduce natural wear.

Types of Maintenance

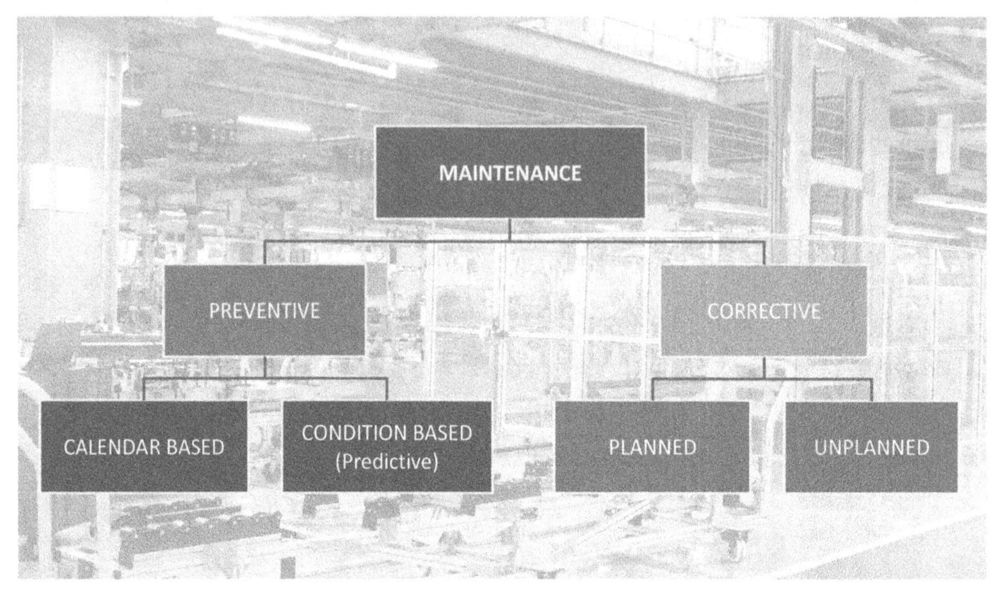

Pillars of TPM

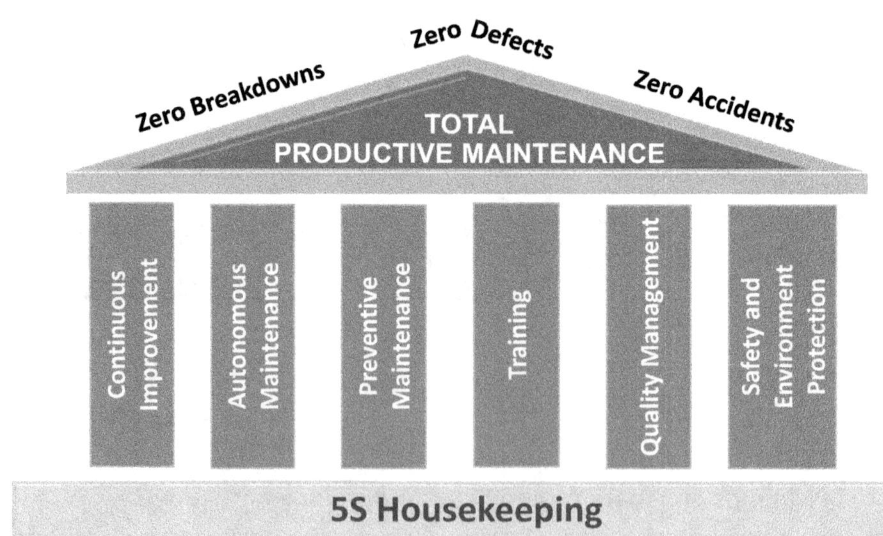

Procedure

BEFORE	DURING	AFTER
Sponsors, Leaders, Black Belts	100% Team Involvement	Sponsors, Leaders, Black Belts
Define the project 2 – 4 weeks	Monday Tuesday Wednesday Thursday Friday	Follow-Up 4 – 8 weeks
DEFINE	**MAI**	**CONTROL**

TPM Kaizen event agenda

Before the Event

- Define the project and team
- Implement 5S Housekeeping
- Select team members
- Perform TPM assessment
- Create Value Stream Map and Balance Chart
- Develop FMEA and Failure Matrix
- Schedule the event date with the logistics and production staff
- Make sure that the following items are complete and available:
  - Cleaning supplies for super-cleaning activity
  - Opportunity cards
  - Equipment manuals
  - Documentation of Preventive Maintenance routines
  - TPM training materials

OPPORTUNITY CARD	
Date:	Number:
Area:	
Opportunity detected: (Muda, Muri, Mura)	
Activity to be performed:	Classification
Equipment:	
Observations:	
Date:	Folio:
Area:	
Opportunity detected: (Muda, Muri, Mura)	
Activity to be performed:	Caissification:
Equipment:	

Apply 5S Housekeeping to maintenance

During the Event

Monday	Tuesday	Wednesday	Thursday	Friday

- Explain A3
- Basic Training
- Present VSM
- Calculate OEE
- Assessment
- Super Cleaning event to identify improvement opportunities

- Analyze Failure Matrix
- Develop FMEA Analysis

- Develop Planned Maintenance

- Develop One-Point Lessons
- Develop Troubleshooting Charts

- Deliver Training
- Kaizen Presentation

- Develop Autonomous Maintenance

- Implement "A" Opportunities

| Measure | Analyze | Improve | | Control |

TPM event launch - day one

Measure

- Explain A3 (Project Definition)
- Training (Approx. 1 hour)
  - What is TPM?
  - What is TPM for?
  - The 6 Pillars of TPM
  - Explain OEE and the 6 big losses
- Present VSM and Balance Chart
- Calculate OEE
- Present initial assessment

Conduct super-cleaning event

The team really knows about the equipment and conditions when they:

- Superficially clean the machines
- Clean the equipment's interiors
- Identify leaks, loose parts and equipment, etc.
- Enthusiastically work in teams
- Document potential improvements on opportunity cards
- Identify anomalies
- Ask experts about anomalies
- Identify unsafe working conditions
- Take pictures

Super-cleaning event

- Search for visible and hidden defects:
    - Heat
    - Vibration
    - Dirty Filters
    - Missing pieces
- Observe to determine ease-of-cleaning obstacles:
    - Improperly positioned lubrication points
    - Covers that are difficult to remove
    - Parts that are difficult to clean
- Ensure that all measuring instruments are working well.
- Investigate leaks/product spills (e.g., steam, water, oil, compressed air).
- Look for hidden problems such as corrosion and obstructions.

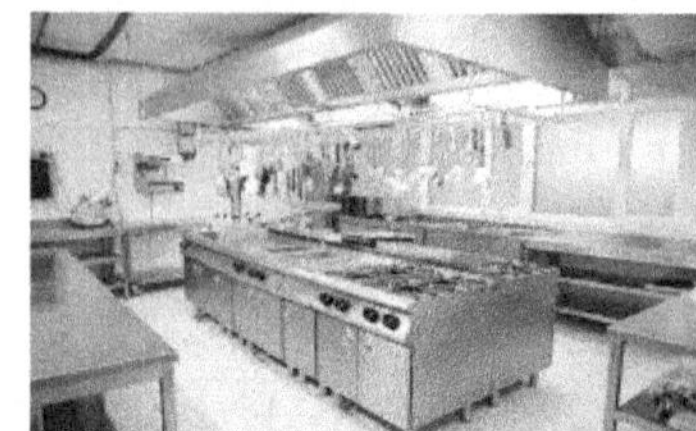

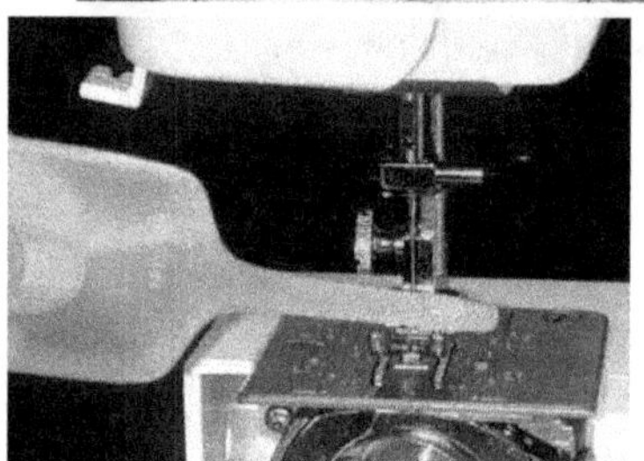

Day two

Analyze

- Continue working on opportunity cards.
- Analyze opportunities found.
- Analyze Failure Matrix.
- Develop Failure Mode and Effect Analysis (FMEA).
- Conduct a cause and effect analysis (equipment-quality).
- Establish an action plan.
- Develop Autonomous Maintenance Activities.

LSSI
LEAN SIX SIGMA INSTITUTE

Day three

Improve

- Develop autonomous maintenance records
- Develop autonomous maintenance instructions
- Develop planned maintenance calendar
- Develop planned maintenance instructions
- Move forward with "A" opportunities

Autonomous maintenance records

Autonomous Maintenance Records		Month	
Machine			

		1	2	3	4	5	6	7	8	9	10	11	12	13	14	15	16	17	18	19	20	21	22	23	24	25	26	27	28	29	30	31
BEFORE																																
1	Check level of lubricant in table guides																															
2	Check cutting oil level																															
3	Check hydraulic oil level																															
4	Check hydraulic pump pressure																															
DURING																																
1	Verify rough edges. Do not clog the extractor																															
2	Identify abnormal sounds																															
3	Go over safety guidelines																															
4	Clean the floor and coolant lines																															
5	Keep workspace clean																															
AT THE END OF THE SHIFT																																
1	Lubricate daily points																															
2	Clean the machine and workspace																															
3	Clean accumulation of burr																															

Supervised by:

Comments:

Autonomous maintenance instructions

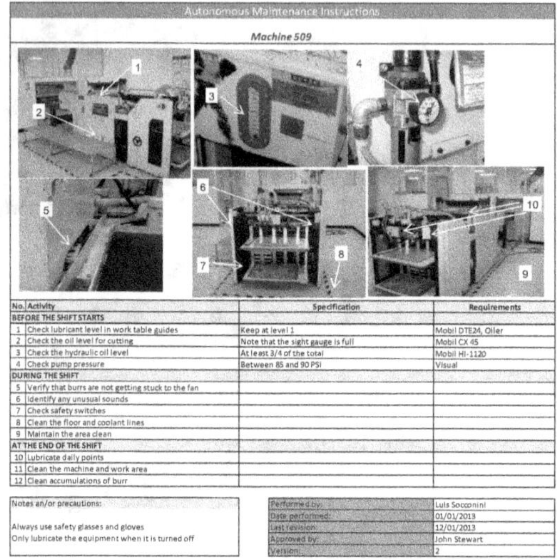

No.	Activity	Specification	Requirements
	BEFORE THE SHIFT STARTS		
1	Check lubricant level in work table guides	Keep at level 1	Mobil DTE24, Oiler
2	Check the oil level for cutting	Note that the sight gauge is full	Mobil CX 45
3	Check the hydraulic oil level	At least 3/4 of the total	Mobil HI-1120
4	Check pump pressure	Between 85 and 90 PSI	Visual
	DURING THE SHIFT		
5	Verify that burrs are not getting stuck to the fan		
6	Identify any unusual sounds		
7	Check safety switches		
8	Clean the floor and coolant lines		
9	Maintain the area clean		
	AT THE END OF THE SHIFT		
10	Lubricate daily points		
11	Clean the machine and work area		
12	Clean accumulations of burr		

Notes an/or precautions:		Performed by:	Luis Socconini
		Date performed:	01/01/2013
Always use safety glasses and gloves		Last revision:	12/01/2013
Only lubricate the equipment when it is turned off		Approved by:	John Stewart
		Version:	2

Planned maintenance: preventive and predictive

Preventive and Predictive Maintenance Plan   Month [ ]

Machine [ ]

		1	2	3	4	5	6	7	8	9	10	11	12	13	14	15	16	17	18	19	20	21	22	23	24	25	26	27	28	29	30	31
WEEKLY																																
1	Lubricate maintenance unit filters					X							X							X							X					
2	Grease cylinder vacuum					X							X							X							X					
3	Grease sliding base frame					X							X							X							X					
MONTHLY																																
4	Verify that burrs don't get stuck to the fan												X																			
5	Identify unusual sounds												X																			
6	Check safety switches													X																		
7	Clean the floor and coolant lines													X																		
8	Keep the work area clean													X																		
BI-ANNUALLY																																
9	Check bearings	X																														
10	Change oil																															
ANNUALLY																																
11	Check connections									X																						
12	Retightening of bolts																															
13	Change filters																															
14	Deep cleaning of the machine																															

Supervised by:

Comments:

Day Four

Control

- Develop one-point lessons (OPL).
- Develop troubleshooting charts.
- Finish "A" opportunities.

One-Point lessons (OPL)

- Focused training
- 10 minutes
- Theory
- Practice
- Everyone participates
- Based on instructions

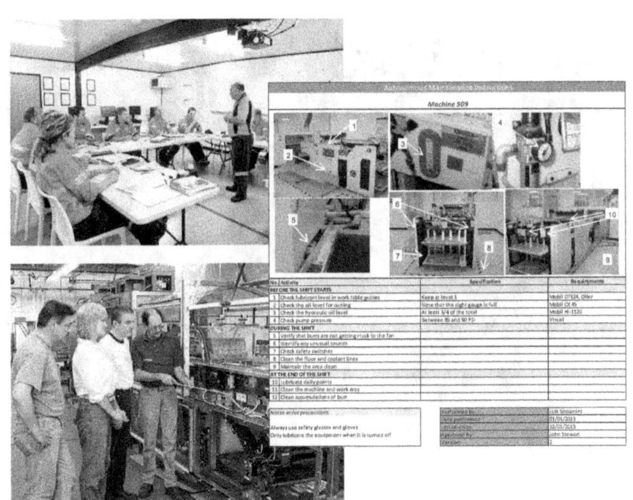

Day five

Control

- Deliver Training on:
    - Correct use of equipment
    - Autonomous maintenance
    - Planned maintenance
    - Equipment safety
- Present results (Kaizen picture)
    - Introduce the team
    - What was our initial situation?
    - What did we do?
    - What did we accomplish?
    - What's next?

Follow-up agenda

After the event

- Conduct daily or weekly analysis meetings.
- Visit the equipment to analyze progress.
- Continue working on "B" and "C" improvement opportunities.
- Analyze OEE progress through daily or weekly box score.
- Review activities at the Gemba according to TPM instructions.
- Apply acquired knowledge to improve other equipment.

LSSI
LEAN SIX SIGMA INSTITUTE

Sustain TPM

- Management teams walk the process (Gemba Walk)

- Employ qualified personnel

- Active guidance to implement TPM

- Celebrate successes

- Show appreciation

- Continuous improvement of Overall Equipment Effectiveness (OEE)

- Expand and implement to all processes that require the use of equipment (service and manufacturing)

22

Kanban

Learning objectives

1. Understand the basic concepts of Kanban.
2. Understand the different types of Kanban.
3. Know how to calculate Kanban sizes.
4. Know the procedure to implement a Kanban system.

Content

> Background
> What is Kanban?
> Benefits
> Types of Kanban
> When is it used?
> Procedure
> Examples

Kanban

- Japanese executives visited manufacturing plants in the United States to learn about their **inventory control systems**.

- Taiichi Ohno and his colleagues visited multiple vehicle assembly plants in search of a system that prevents **excess inventory**. They didn´t find what they were looking for.

- However, after visiting a few supermarkets, they became interested in the way products were restocked after customers took them from the shelves.

- The customers' payments acted as signals to the supplier (store employee) that he/she needed to restock the products that the customer had just purchased (pulled).

Supermarket

Demand orientation

The **Kanban system** was inspired by the way that U.S. supermarkets restocked their shelves. Kanban cards symbolize the dollar bills that served as a signal to the suppliers (employees).

Key features:
- Kanban provides a *visual display* of what is needed in the work area.
- It quickly identifies the *minimum* and *maximum* stock required.
- It *drives* the time for when inventory items must be replenished.
- It ensures a FIFO (first-in, first-out) inventory sequence.
- It helps *synchronize* the elements of the supply chain.

What is Kanban?

A **Pull System (Kanban)** is a communication system that enables the control of operations, synchronizes manufacturing or service processes with customer demand, and supports production scheduling.

A Kanban is a card that:

- Identifies the items.
- Controls the flow of the items.
- Documents the results.

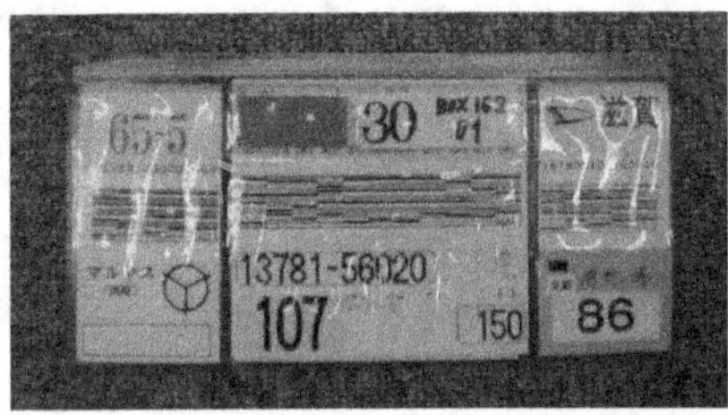

Original Kanban used for
purchasing at Toyota

Information contained on a Kanban card

- Part number
- Container type and size
- Container capacity
- Location
- Part destination
- Delivery time and place
- Part drawing or picture
- Process where it is used

**Information that facilitates *effective material flow*
while eliminating delays and time losses.**

Benefits

Some of the applications and benefits of Kanban are:

- Prevents overproduction.
- Supports the ability to work with low inventory levels.
- Ensures that customers will receive their products or services on time.
- Allow us to produce only what the customers need.
- It is a visual system that enable us to compare what is produced with what the customers want.
- Eliminates complications that arise from production planning.
- Provides a common system for moving materials through the facility.

Types of Kanban

- ***Withdrawal Kanban***

  Indicates the type and quantity of products that a process should withdraw from the previous process.

- ***Production Kanban***

  Indicates the type and quantity of products that a process should produce.

Withdrawal Kanban

Indicates the type and quantity of products that a process should withdraw from the previous process.

Storage Rack #	F26-18	Part Code	A5-34	Previous process
Part #	56690-321			**STAMP B-2**
Part Name	MOTOR SUPPORT			Next process
Type of vehicle	SX50BC			**MECHANIZATION**
Box capacity	20	Type of box	B	

Production Kanban

Indicates the type and quantity of products that a process should produce

Storage rack #	F26-18	Part Code	A5-34	Process
Part #	56690-321			**MECHANIZATION**
Name of the part	MOTOR SUPPORT			
Quantity to produce	200			

Example

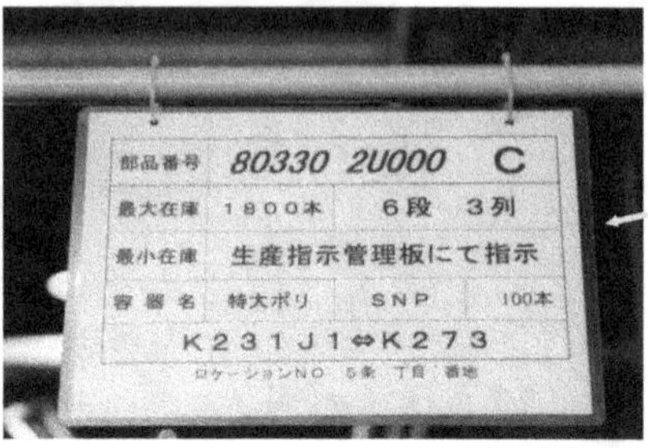

Part number	80330	2U000	C
Maximum stock	1,800 pcs.	6 rows 3 columns	
Minimum stock	As showed in production indication control board		
Name of container	Super big "poly" (polyurethane	SNP	100 pcs.
	K231J1	K273	
	Location No.	*A factory address*	

When is it used?

- When the material and production control systems need to be reorganized for high-mix/low-volume production.

- After other core Lean Tools such as 5S Housekeeping, Quick Setups, TPM, and Continuous Flow have been implemented.

Procedure

1. Determine items to include in the Kanban.

2. Calculate the number of items in the Kanban.

3. Select the type of signal and container.

4. Calculate the number of containers.

5. Monitor the WIP-to-SWIP indicator (work in process / standard work in process).

1. Determine items to include in the Kanban

- Select items for the Kanban system:
  - Parts to produce products
  - Materials to perform a service
  - Finished goods
  - Etc.

- It is important to select items that are already involved in other Lean methods such as Continuous Flow, Quick Changes, TPM, etc.

2. Calculate the number of items in the Kanban

Formula for the number of parts: = **D x LT x L x (1 +** % VD **)**

Where:

- **D = Weekly demand** (refer to the box score).

- **LT = Internal or external supplier lead time** (in weeks)), which includes:

    - **For purchased products:** Time to generate the order + supplier lead time + transportation time + receiving, inspection, and stocking time.

    - **For manufactured produtcs:** Time to generate the order + total processing time + receiving, inspection, and stocking time.

- **L = Number of locations.** When first implementing Kanban, it is recommended to have 2 full locations, one for the supplier and another for the customer. It is possible that later we will be able to use one single location, but at the beginning with this we ensure continuity in the supply process.

- % VD = Demand variability coefficient, is the standard deviation of demand for a specific time period, divided by the average demand for that same period.

Example

1. Determine items to include in the Kanban.

No. 2214 Motor support.

2. Calculate the number of items.

Weekly Demand = 270,408 / 52 = 5,200 items.

D = 5,200 parts.

LT = 1 week.

L = 2 locations.

% VD = Standard deviation of demand during a specific time period/average demand during that same period

% VD = 5,608 / 22,534 = 25 %.

Kanban size = 5,200 $\times$ 1 $\times$ 2 $\times$ 1.25 = 13,000 items

Part #	2214	Description	Motor Support

January	22350
February	28570
March	35514
April	25468
May	24515
June	20667
July	18422
August	14304
September	17209
October	19129
November	22345
December	21916

Average	22,534
Std. Dev.	5,608
Variance	25%

3. Select the type of signal and container

- In order to apply visual control by part type, it is important that the containers are easy to identify and handle, and are of the same color for a specific Kanban.

- Ideally, select a container and its capacity based on the workers' carrying load limit.

- The container can be a box, stand, cart, tray, pallet, etc.

4. Calculate the number of containers

$$\text{Number of containers} = \frac{\text{Number of items in the Kanban}}{\text{Container capacity}}.$$

If the container's capacity is 100 items, then the number of containers needed is 130, calculated as follows:

Number of containers = 13,000 / 100 = 130 containers.

5. Monitor the WIP to SWIP indicator

- *WIP* to *SWIP* is calculated by dividing the inventory in process (WIP) by the minimum necessary in-process inventory to maintain standard work (SWIP):

$$\text{Formula: } \frac{\textbf{WIP (Work-in-process)}}{\textbf{SWIP (Standard-Work-In-Process)}}.$$

- The ideal ratio is **1**, which means that WIP is equal to SWIP.
- If the result is **greater than 1**, there is an excess of inventory in process.
- If the result is **less than 1**, there is insufficient inventory in process and might be at risk of being short in materials or products.

Kanban rules

1. Do not transfer defective items to the next processes.
2. A *Kanban card* is withdrawn when a process withdraws items from the previous process.
3. Earlier processes produce items according to the quantity specified by the withdrawn *Kanban card* (the *Kanban* makes a production order).
4. Nothing is produced or moved without a *Kanban card*.
5. The *Kanban card* acts as an attached production order to all items.
6. The number of *Kanban cards* should be decreasing over time.

Production Kanban

The Kanban indicates what needs to be done, at what time, and in what quantity.

Kanban supply in an operating room

The surgery personnel withdraws what they need from the storage area. All of the utilized items are later replenished so they are available for future surgeries.

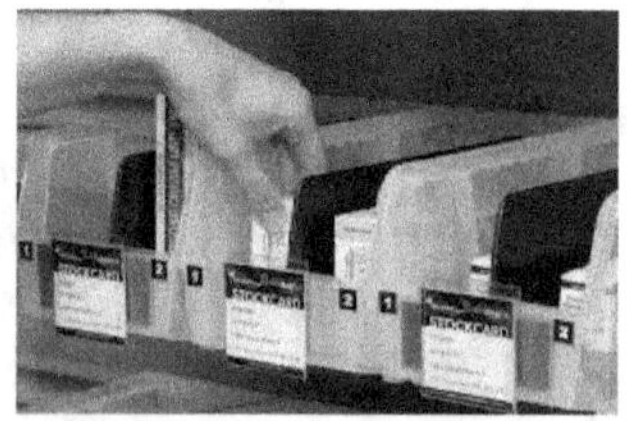

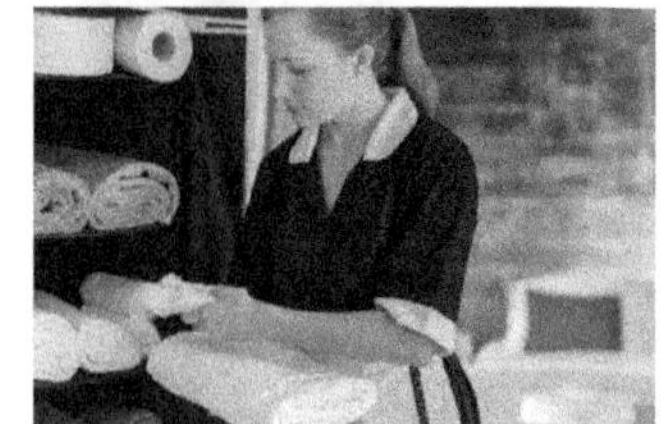

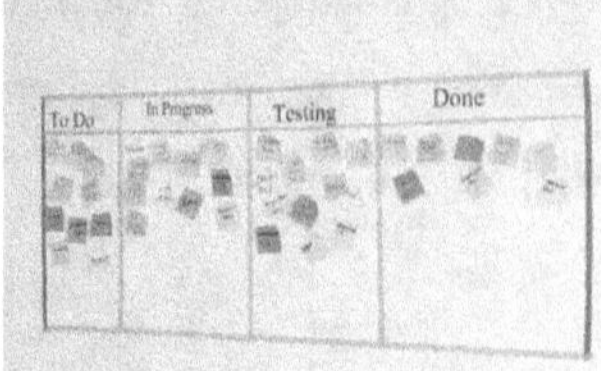

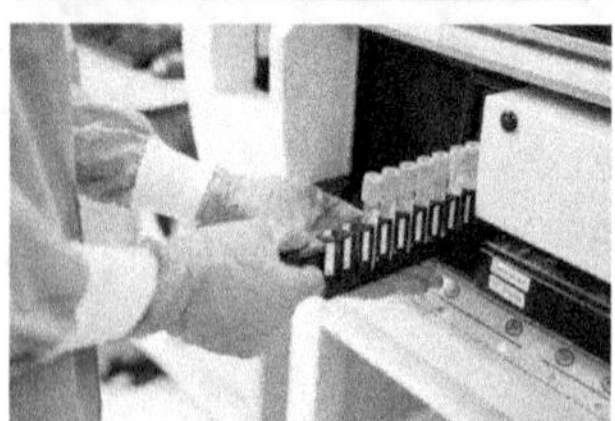

Future State Value Stream Map

Learning objectives

1. Identify critical areas of opportunity and bottlenecks that need Lean improvement actions.
2. Learn how to develop a future state map of the value stream, that minimizes cycle times.
3. Know how to develop a continuous improvement action plan aimed at transforming the value stream.

Content

> What is a Future VSM?
> Benefits
> When is it used?
> Procedure

Future State Value Stream Map (VSM)

- A **Future State Value Stream Map** represents the short-term improved solution that we want to incorporate into the production or service system.

- Provides a starting point to develop a new work strategy.

Benefits

- Improved process flow

- Optimized resource utilization

- Improved customer satisfaction

- Improved quality and reduced costs

- Allows us to see things differently than we do initially

- Reduced cycle times

When is it used?

- It is used when the **bottleneck** has been analyzed, and the following elements have been identified:
  - Root cause of the main problems
  - Any type of waste
  - Variation
  - Overburden

"We could not build a house without a plan."

Value stream mapping process stages

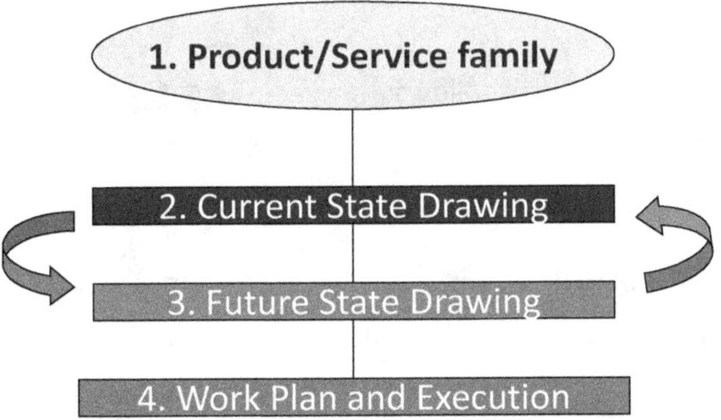

Develop Value Stream Maps for each of your product/service families.

Procedure

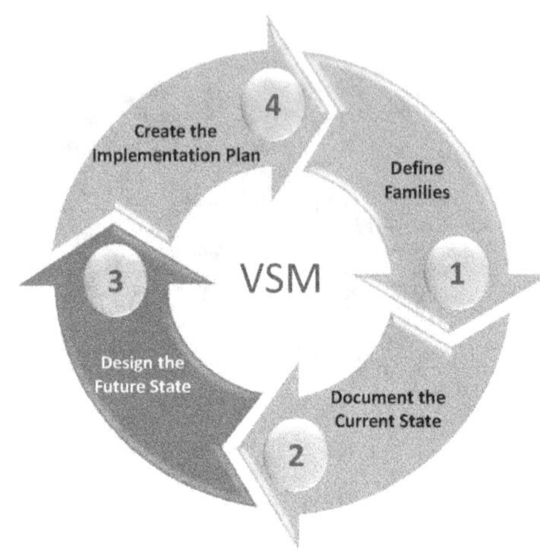

3.1. Determine the system's capacity and identify the bottleneck

3.2. Develop continuous flow wherever operations can be performed next to each other

3.3. Whenever operations cannot be performed or placed next to each other, introduce supermarkets to bring discontinuous flows as close as possible

3.4. Propose *kaizen* events to implement improvements with the use of Lean tools

3.5. Draw the Future State VSM

3.6. Quantify the Future State

3.1. Determine the system's capacity

Process capacity is calculated as follows:

- Available Working Time
- The Longest Cycle Time

$$\text{Capacity} = \frac{\textbf{Available Working Time}}{\textbf{Longest Cycle Time}}$$

$$\text{Capacity} = \frac{27{,}000 \text{ sec}}{134 \text{ sec}} = 201.49 \text{ units}$$

Refer to the Balance Chart in the next slide.

Initial data:
Total time = 8 hr. = 480 min
Break time = 30 min
Available time = 450 min * 60 sec / min = 27,000 sec
Monthly demand = 7,510 units
Workdays= 22 days
Daily demand= 7510 units / 22 = 341 units

Identify the bottleneck

The bottleneck determines the capacity of the system. The bottleneck can be either:

Internal: **If Demand > Capacity**

Or

External: **If Capacity > Demand**

For **LeanShop**, the bottleneck is the Final Assembly & Testing operation, and it is internal because **demand** is greater than the **system's capacity**.

Internal: **341 units > 201 units**

Operation Number	Operation Code	Description	Time	Takt Time
1	A	Cutting	22	79
2	B	Painting	45	79
3	C	Drilling	19	79
4	D	Electronic Assembly	63	79
5	E	Upload Software	22	79
6	F	Control Module Assembly	32	79
7	G	Final Assembly & Testing	134	79
8	H	Packaging & Shipping	49	79
		Total Cycle Time	386	79

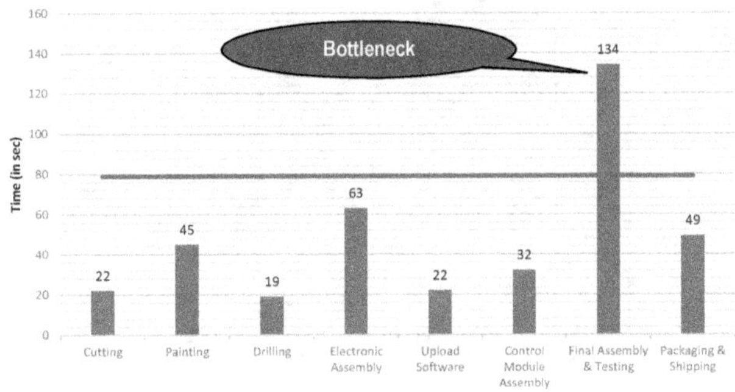

3.2. Develop a continuous flow

To illustrate this example, we will first arrange all operations in such a way that allows us to establish a continuous flow and create work cells. In other words, the objective is to move material from one workstation to the next in a single flow with as few interruptions as possible. We will represent this in the Future State VSM.

Number of operators = Total cycle time / Takt time

= 386 / 79 = **4.88 = 5 operators**

Operator	Time	Operations
1	67	A + B
2	82	C + D
3	77	E + F + Part of G
4	77	Part of G
5	83	Part of G + H

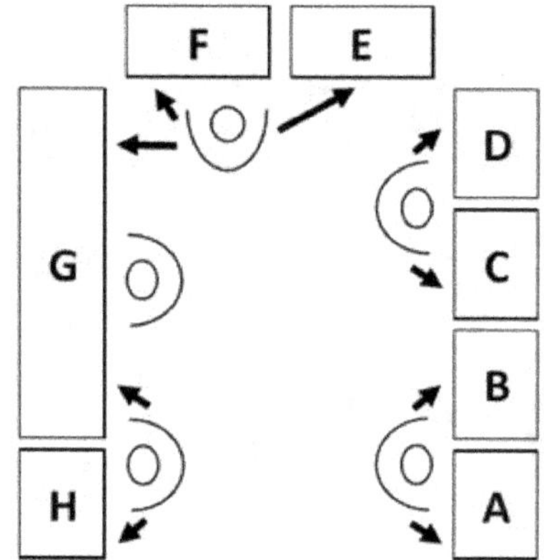

3.3. Develop supermarkets

Given that we were able to group all operations without any constraints, we will then proceed to establish supermarkets: one for raw materials and the other one for finished goods.

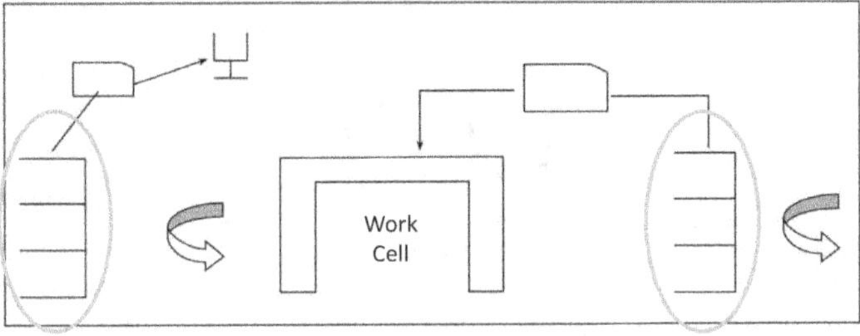

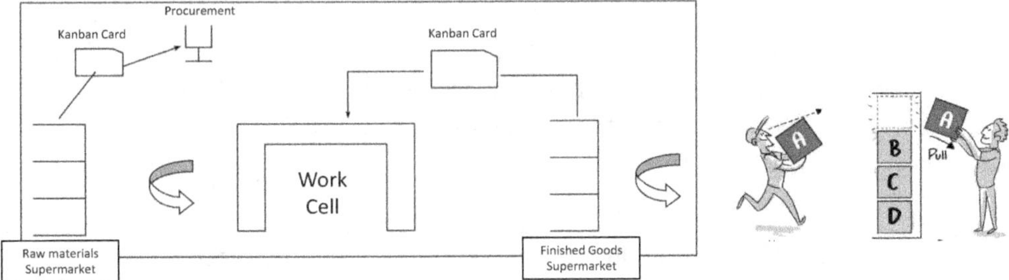

- In this arrangement, we can observe that when a product is withdrawn from the Finished Goods Supermarket, a *kanban* card is withdrawn from that good and sent to the work cell to indicate that it must produce another unit to replace the one the customer has 'pulled.'

- Since work cells require material in order to produce goods, they withdraw this material from the supermarket and simply send the card to the Procurement (or Purchasing) department so they can request additional material from the corresponding supplier(s).

3.4. Perform improvements via kaizen events

Lightning flash symbols on the Future State VSM indicate that improvement events are being performed and processes are being modified.

- The order in which *Kaizen* events are performed is determined by the priorities identified in the analysis of the Future State VSM. It is helpful to use a prioritization matrix.

- The starting point is usually continuous flow or cell manufacturing. If the process involves machinery or equipment, then Total Productive Maintenance (TPM), quick preparations (SMED), and *poka yoke* are implemented. It is important to note that this order or sequence varies depending on the priorities of each organization.

- In order to implement what has been drawn on the Future State VSM, we must first ask ourselves whether the company will implement *kanban* for its finished goods and send the product directly to the customer – without storing it.

Kaizen events

In the **Lean Shop** case, we initially implemented the work cell and made improvements to reduce the cycle times of operators 2 to 5 in order to adapt to a maximum time of 70 seconds. The result was the following:

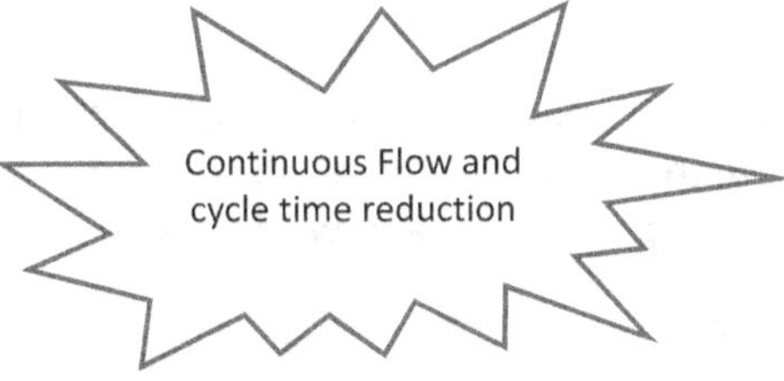

Operator	Time	Operations
1	67	A + B
2	70	C + D
3	70	E + F + Part of G
4	70	Part of G
5	70	Part of G + H
Total Cycle Time	347	

$$\text{Balance Efficiency} = \frac{\text{Total Cycle Time}}{\text{Slowest Cycle Time} * \text{Number of operations}}$$

$$= \frac{347}{70 * 5} = 0.99 \quad \text{(originally it was 0.36)}$$

- Implement Total Productive Maintenance (TPM) to improve the availability of equipment – especially of the cutting machine – but without forgetting that daily maintenance plans should also be implemented for *all* equipment.

- Implement quick preparations (SMED) in order to make several models on the same day and to have greater flexibility when facing changes in demand.

- Finally, implement a four-day finished goods supermarket to start and subsequently calculate the correct *kanban* size as teams adapt to the system and continuous flow between work cell operations is achieved.

- The Future State VSM allows us to see that, even though customer input and demand is still the key trigger in the production process, the flow has now been shifted to a **pull** system – as opposed to a **push** system.

- Now, when the customer purchases a unit, a *kanban* card immediately notifies the previous process. In other words, the work cell is "informed" that the customer ***pulled*** a unit that must now be replaced with a new one.

- Suppliers must also replenish the material the work cells used in order to keep supermarkets stocked and prevent any interruptions in the production process.

3.5. Draw the Future State VSM

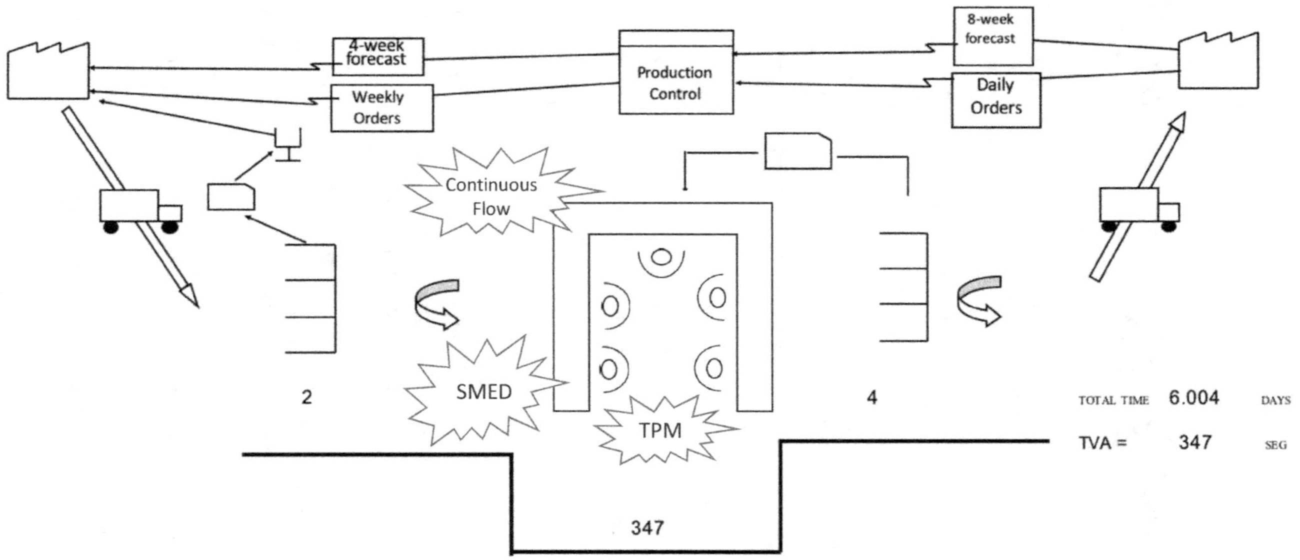

We can see how production planning and material control are now completely dependent on the *kanban* system. They now manage production according to real-time data and demand.

3.6. Quantify future state

Metric	Current State	Future State (Goal)	Improvement
Space required (sq. ft.)	13,500	6,900	6,600
Number of employees	10	7	3
Distance traveled (ft.)	607	302	305
Lead time (days)	14.4	6.0	8.4
Raw materials inventory (days)	3	2	1
WIP Inventory (days)	7.1	0	7.1
Finished Goods Inventory (days)	4.3	4	0.3
Inventory Turnover	18.3	44	25.7

Conclusions

- These results reflect significant achievements in a very short period of time and, above all, show how a company can become more flexible in the face of ever-changing markets and ever-increasing customer requirements.

- It is very important to draw the current and future state VSMs *before* implementing improvements, since adopting changes without first understanding the system can result in poor impact, wasted effort, and failure to adequately implement and benefit from *Lean*.

- Drawing value stream maps using a piece of paper and a pencil helps us fully understand how processes take place and how they are interrelated – something a computer cannot help us grasp as deeply. Once we have manually drawn the maps and understand where value and waste are found, we can then use software, spreadsheets and symbols to develop the computerized maps.

Standardized Work

10

Learning objectives

1. Understand the essential elements of standardized work to ensure optimal performance.
1. Know the procedure for achieving standardization in any process.

Content

> Background
> What is Standardized Work?
> Key Elements
> Benefits
> Procedure
> Exercise

Background

Stability

- Stability is the ability to produce consistent results over time.

- Instability is the effect of variability on a process.

- The first step towards **Lean** implementation is reaching a maximum level of **process stability**.

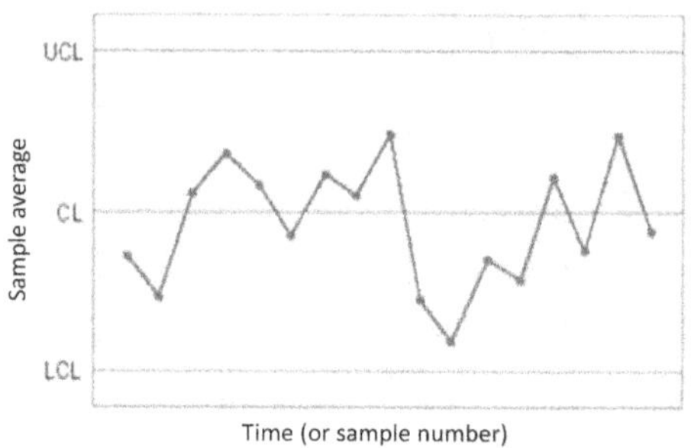

Standardization

- **What is standardization?**
  The safest, easiest, and most effective way to perform any job.

- **What is a standard?**
  A clear picture of a desired condition (something that serves as a basis or a model).

- **Why are standards important in a Lean system?**
  Standards allow us to immediately identify anomalies and as a result implement corrective actions.

- **Characteristics of an effective standard**
  Simple, clear, and visual.

Stability and standardization

Symptoms of instability and lack of standards:

- High variation in performance indicators
- Inconsistent work methods
- Accumulation of WIP (work-in-process)
- Sequential operations working independently

What is Standardized Work?

- A tool used to guarantee **maximum performance and minimal waste.**

- A set of documents that help **us understand how our work meets** customer requirements.

- A **methodology** used to examine the workplace.

- A **systematic** approach to identify improvement opportunities.

White Belt

Number	SEQUENCE OF OPERATIONS	KEY POINTS		ILLUSTRATIONS
1	Pick up the material	**Job Instructions**		
2	Affix the material to the work table	Use clamps	2	
3	Place tips towards the edges	Make sure the piece is properly balanced		
4	Cut the piece to the desired length		3	
5	Place cut pieces on the next table		4	

CHANGES					SAFETY CONSIDERATIONS	SIGNATURES			
Date	Rev	Description of change	Elim.	Approved		Date	Shift	Supervisor	Operator
					Safety gear must be worn at all times.				

Note: This format was taught in the basic tools.

Yellow Belt

Process			**Time Study Data Collection Sheet**							Process #	
										Observer	
No.	Work elements						12	13	14	15	Lowest repeated time
Cycle Time											

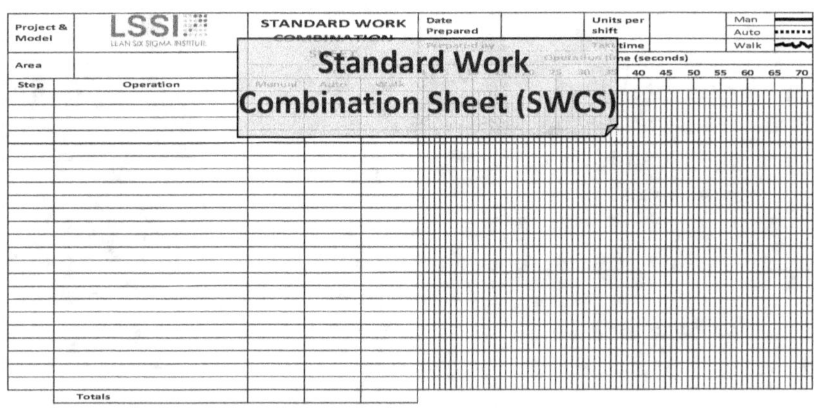

Standard Work
Combination Sheet (SWCS)

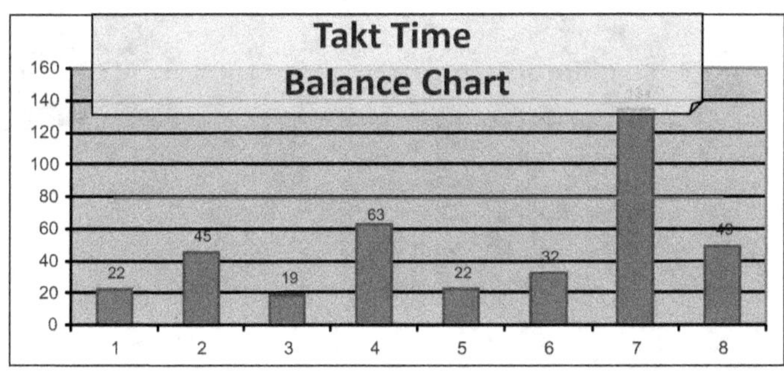

Takt Time
Balance Chart
22
45
19
63
22
32
49
1 2 3 4 5 6 7 8

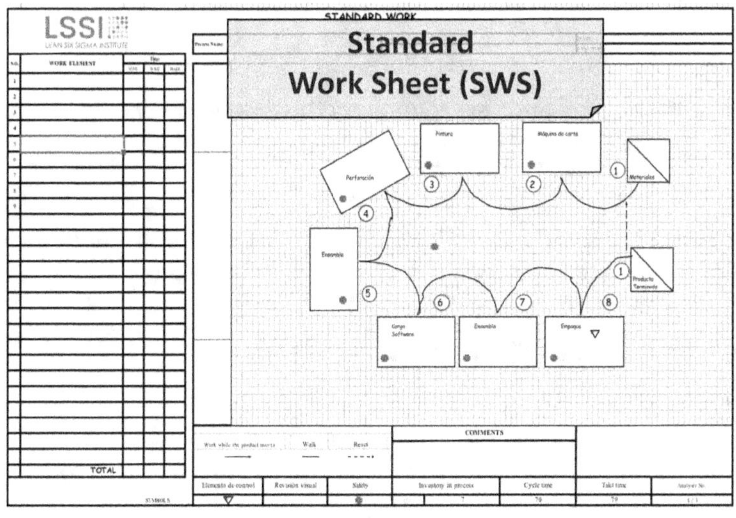

Standard
Work Sheet (SWS)

Benefits

- Achieve **process stability**
  - Standardization ensures that work is always performed identically to meet quality and speed standards.

- It is a tool that initiates **improvement actions**

- Establishes a **baseline** to evaluate and manage processes and assess their performance

- Ensures **safer** and more **effective** operations

- Extraordinary source of **information**

Procedure

1. Select a specific process or operation within a process
2. Conduct a time study and record data on the "Time study data collection sheet"
3. Calculate process or operation capacity
4. If necessary, balance the operation using the Balance Chart and design or document the capacity's optimal sequence on the "Standard Work Combination Sheet" (SWCS)
5. Draw the process in the "Standard Work Sheet"
6. Document work instructions

How to implement standarized work?

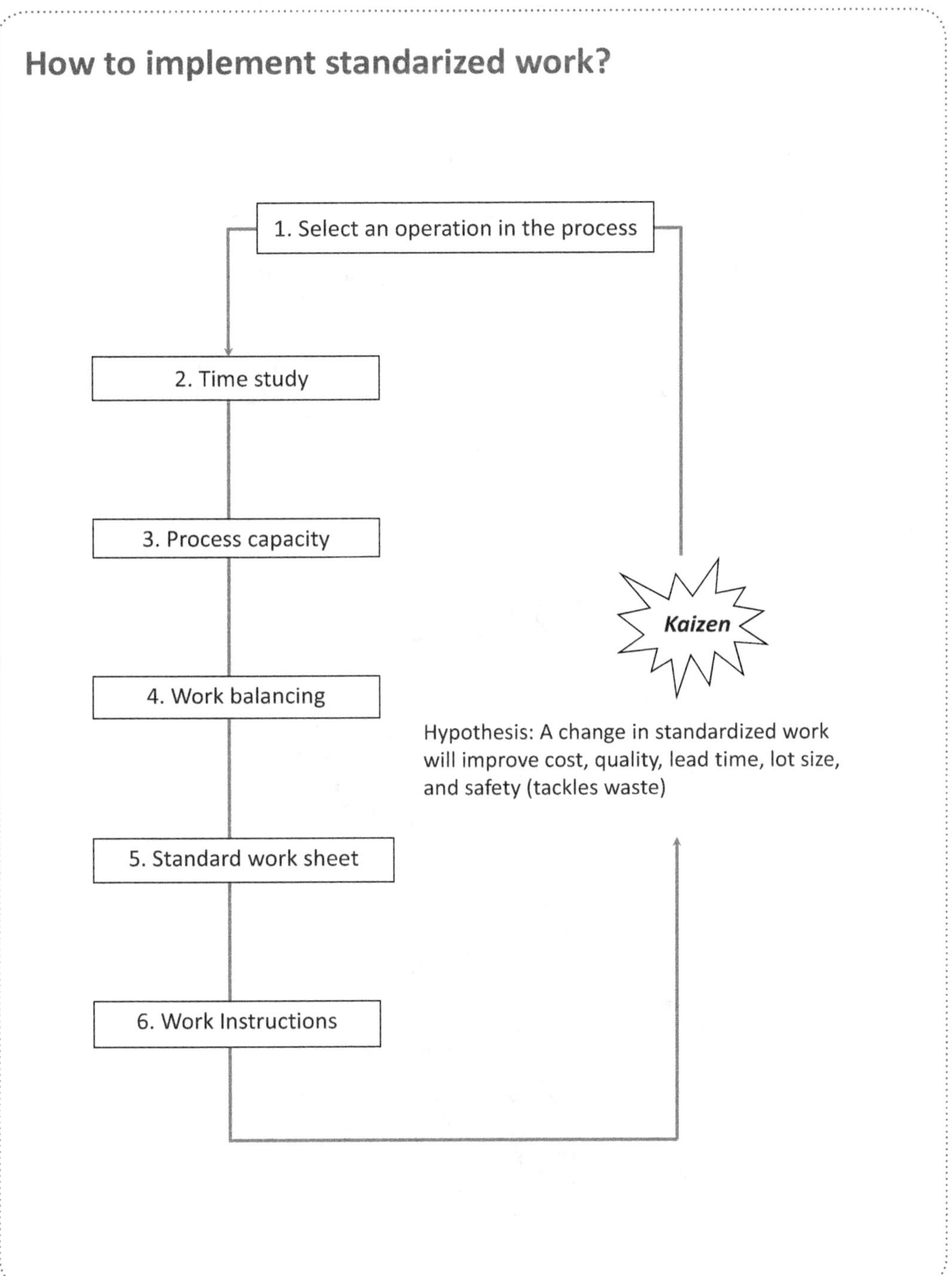

1. Select an operation in the process

- A process is composed of operations.

- An operation is composed of elements.

- It is recommended to begin by selecting the operation **bottleneck** found in the Value Stream Map or some critical operation.

- It is important to observe the selected operation for a given time in order to identify how information, material, and people interact.

- Understand every step in the operation and why it is performed.

2. Conduct a time study

The Time Study Data Collection Sheet includes work element start and end times. Each work element is measured and standard times are established for each operation in the process.

Process		TIME STUDY DATA COLLECTION SHEET		Date			Process #	
				Time			Observer	

No.	LSSI LEAN SIX SIGMA INSTITUTE	Measure point	1	2	3	4	5	6	7	8	9	10	11	12	13	14	15	Lowest repeated time
1	Cutting	Cutting Station	21	20	22	22	25	22	23	21	22	22	20	27	22	22	21	22
			22	22	23	22	22	21	22	22	20	25	22	23	22	22	22	
2	Painting	Painting Station	47	45	45	43	47	45	45	45	43	49	45	45	43	45	45	45
			45	47	45	43	45	45	45	40	45	45	43	45	45	43	41	
3	Drilling	Drilling station	19	17	21	19	19	21	19	19	20	21	19	19	25	19	21	19
			23	19	19	19	21	20	19	19	21	19	19	21	20	19	19	
4	Electronic Assembly	Assembly Station 1	65	65	63	63	67	63	63	63	61	63	65	63	67	63	67	63
			63	63	65	63	63	67	65	63	63	63	61	62	63	65	63	
5	Upload Software	Upload software ta	22	23	23	22	22	22	21	22	25	23	22	22	23	25	22	22
			21	22	23	22	21	23	22	23	22	22	25	22	22	22	22	
6	Control Modul Assembly	Assembly Station 2	33	32	35	32	32	35	33	32	32	32	35	32	32	35	32	32
			35	32	32	35	32	32	35	32	33	32	32	32	35	32	33	
7	Final Assembly & Testing	Assembly Station 2	134	137	135	139	130	131	134	134	133	135	134	137	131	134	129	134
			134	137	134	131	130	130	134	134	133	134	134	137	134	133	134	
8	Packaging & Shipping	Packaging Station	51	49	49	47	51	49	49	50	51	49	49	50	53	49	49	49
			45	50	49	49	47	49	49	51	49	53	49	49	51	49	49	
Cycle Time																		386

3. Process capacity analysis

The **capacity** of any process is determined by the slowest step.

Operation	Code	Description	Time	Takt time
1	A	Cutting	22	79
2	B	Painting	45	79
3	C	Drilling	19	79
4	D	Electronic Assembly	63	79
5	E	Upload Software	22	79
6	F	Control Module Assembly	32	79
7	G	Final Assembly & Testing	134	79
8	H	Packaging & Shipping	49	79

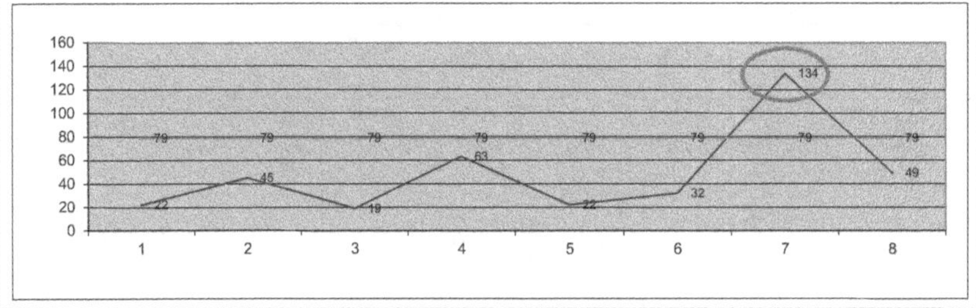

Capacity = Available time / Longest time

= (27,000 s/shift) / (134 s/piece)

= **201 units/shift**

Note: Document in the Current Standard Work Combination Sheet and Standard Work Sheet

4. Work balancing

The **standard work combination sheet** allows us to graphically see the **sequence** of the process in order to evaluate it and optimize the capacity. It is also useful for balancing operation workload in relation to takt time.

Project & Model	LSSI LEAN SIX SIGMA INSTITUTE	STANDARD WORK COMBINATION SHEET	Date prepared		2/1/20	Units per shift		201	Man	
			Prepared by		John Bruce	Takt time		79 secs	Auto	
									Walk	

Operation	Cutting		Time			Tiempo de Operación (en segundos)
Step	Operation	Manual	Auto	Walk		1 5 10 15 20 25 30 35 40 45 50 55 60 65 70 75 80
1	Pick up the material	3				
2	Affix the material to the work table	4				
3	Place tips towards the edges	10				
4	Cut the piece to the desired length	2				
5	Place cut pieces on the next table	3				
	Total	22				

5. Standard work sheet

- The Standard Work Sheet includes a design of the process (layout) including the operator or service provider and material flow to determine the **most efficient movements.**

- The operations are analyzed as a group to give a clear view of the sequence and flow.

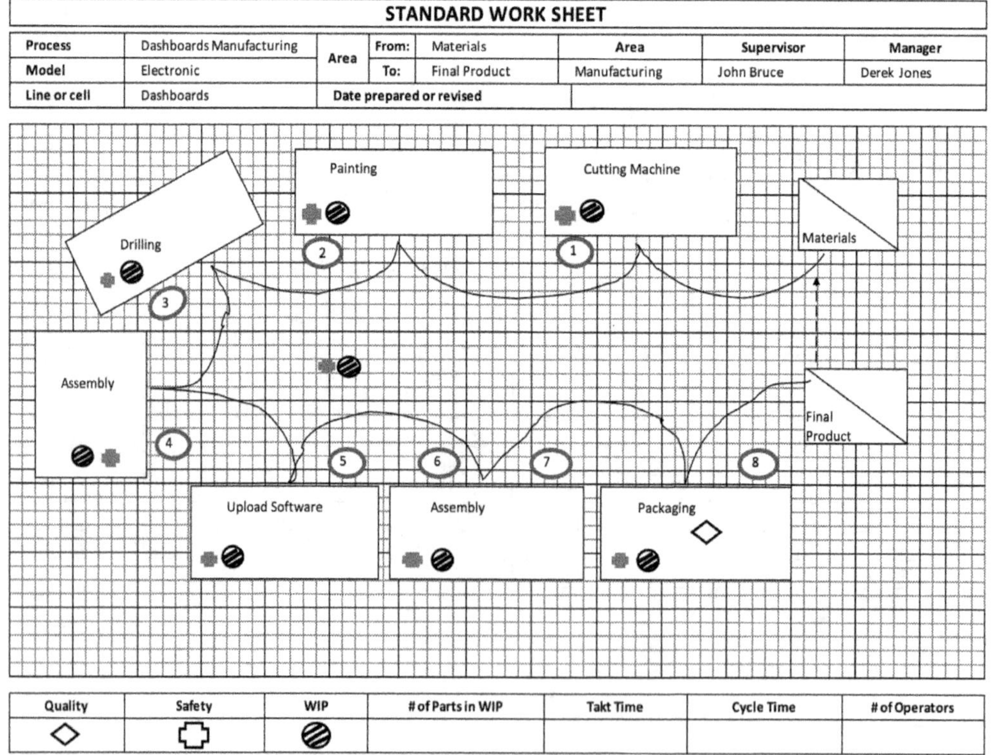

STANDARD WORK SHEET

Process	Dashboards Manufacturing	Area	From:	Materials	Area	Supervisor	Manager
Model	Electronic		To:	Final Product	Manufacturing	John Bruce	Derek Jones
Line or cell	Dashboards		Date prepared or revised				

Quality	Safety	WIP	# of Parts in WIP	Takt Time	Cycle Time	# of Operators

6. Document the work instructions

Describe how activities should be performed on the workstation:

- Provides a clear description of the activities.

- Shows the key points related to the operation.

- Defines the elements of the job.

- Identify the critical points of safety and quality.

Note: They are not necessary for very simple operations.

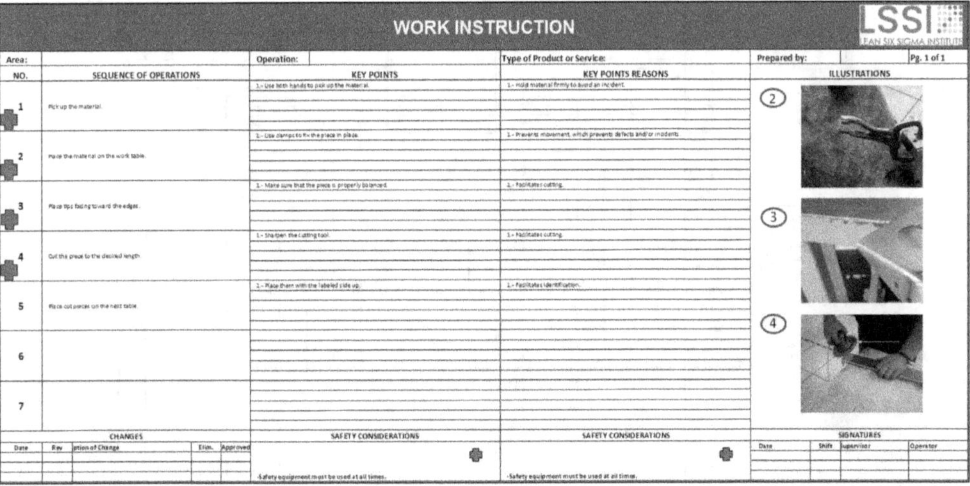

It is recommended that operators, service providers, engineers, quality personnel, and HR staff all participate in the creation of work instructions to ensure all aspects are included.

Filling out the Standard Work Combination Sheet

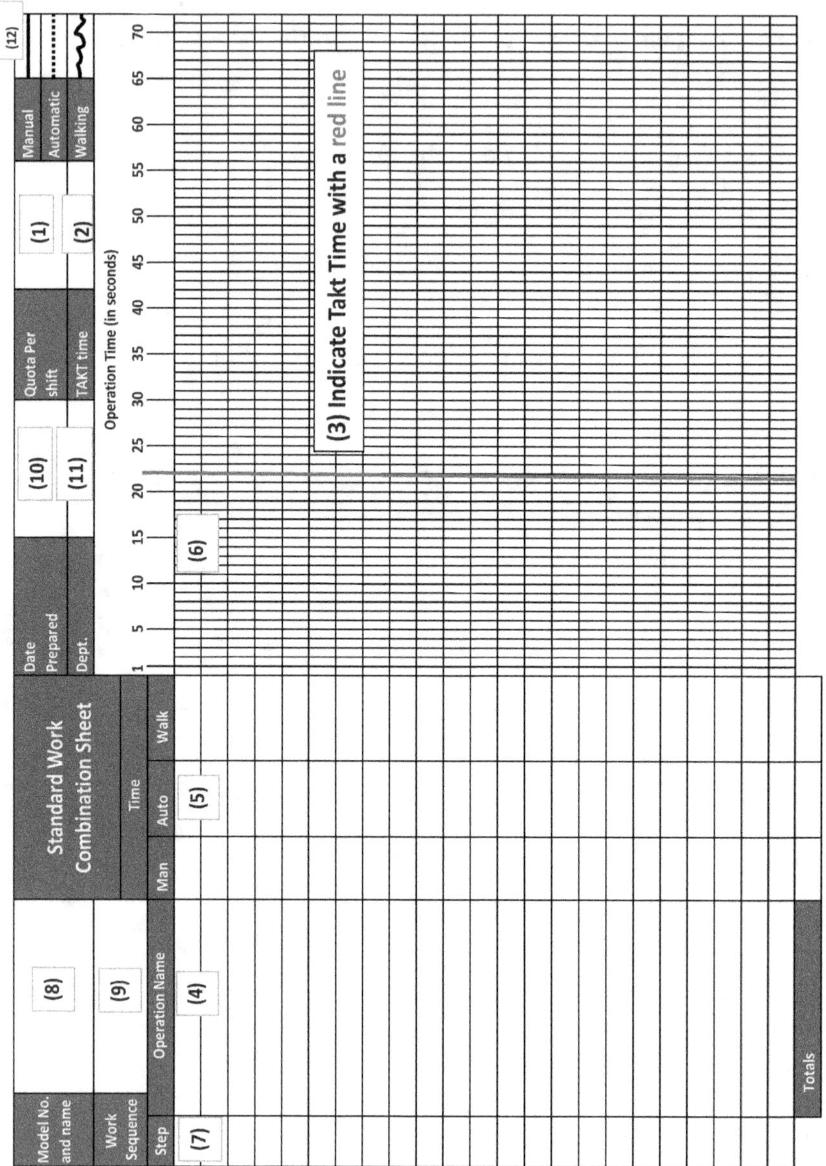

| (1) Quota per shift | Obtain the required production volume or services to-be-provided per day or shift. |

(2) Takt Time

$$\frac{\text{Available time}}{\text{Demand}}$$

* Round decimals to nearest whole number.

(3) Red line *(takt time)* — Corresponds to Takt Time of the operation, comparing it to total operating time (Manual work time + Machine work time).

(4) Operation name/description — Determine the scope of each operator's work. Prepare a Standard Work Combination Sheet for each operator. Be sure to include walking and/or transportation times.

Describe the details of the tasks performed by each operator.

Use expressions that combine present-tense verbs (for example: Press button, assemble part, grab tool).

Record machine times and numbers, if applicable.

(5) Time

Manual work time — Record the time for human tasks.

Automatic machine time — Record the time for machine tasks.

Walking time — Record the time it takes to move/walk to the next workstation to pick up or put down parts/tools. Leave the space blank if there is no walking time.

TOTAL — Record totals times for manual work, machine, and walking at the bottom of the sheet. Record total wait times as well.

(6) Graph times using different lines

Indicate manual work time using a solid line.

(———————)

Indicate automatic machine time using a dotted line.

(- - - - - - - - - - - - -)

Indicate walking time using a wavy line.

(∿∿∿∿∿∿)

Indicate waiting time using a double line.

(◄——————►)

(7) Work sequence — Enter numbers to indicate the frequency in which the operator performs the operations/tasks.

(8) Model name and number — Enter the model/part name and number.

(9) Process name — Enter the name of the process, line, or cell.

(10) Date prepared or revised — Enter the date when the Sheet was prepared or revised.

(11) Department/Area — Enter the department/area that prepared the Sheet.

(12) Operator number — There should be one Standard Work Combination Sheet per operator.

Filling out the Standard Work Sheet

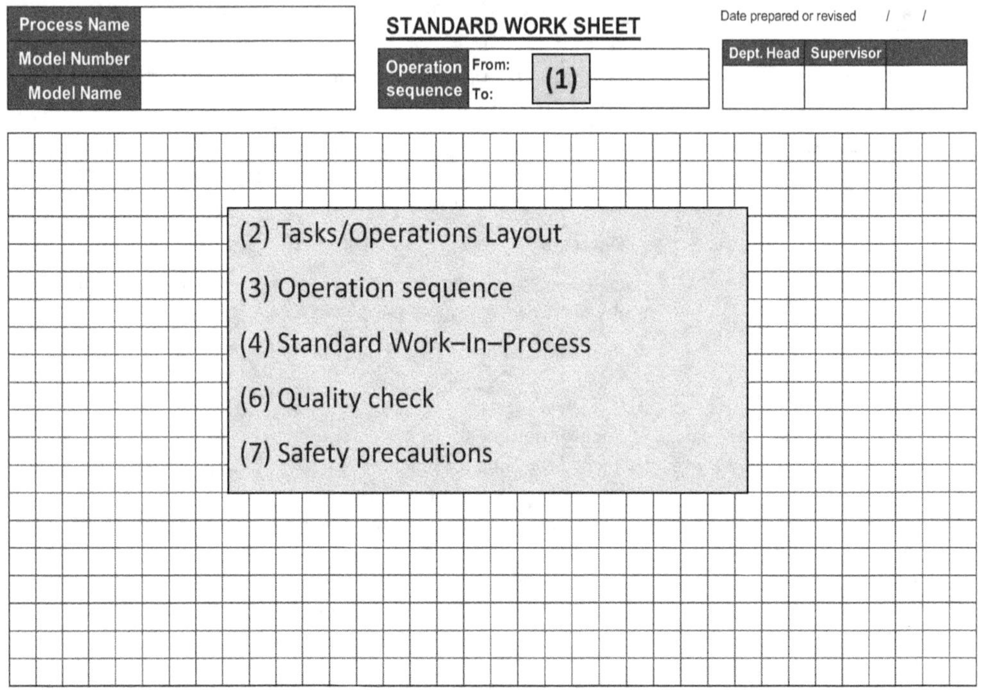

This format clarifies the scope of the tasks/operations and adds three important components: Quality checks, Safety precaution symbol, and Standard WIP.

(1) Scope of operations: Has the same number of operations as the Standard Work Combination Sheet.
(2) Draw a layout of the tasks/operations performed by the operator.
     Team layouts: While drawing team cells, use an approximate scale in order to reduce space between teams and workstations.

(3) Operation sequence: The number of operations for the task or workstation should be the same as for the Standard Work Combination Sheet and should be connected by solid lines. Show the point between the last operation back to the first operation using a dotted line.

(4) Standard Work-In-Process: Only the WIP required to maintain and facilitate flow. Must be indicated for each machine and/or workstation. Do not include raw material, nor finished goods. Draw a (⊘) to indicate standard WIP.

(5) Indicate the total Standard WIP per cell in each box.

(6) Quality checks: Draw a (◇) for each machine or process that requires a quality inspection.

(7) Safety precautions: Draw a (✛) next to each machine or workstation that requires specific safety measures.

(8) Takt Time: Located at the bottom of the Sheet; would be the same that was previously calculated for the Standard Work Combination Sheet.

(9) Cycle Time: Enter the cycle time according to the tasks assigned to each operator.

(10) Draw symbols in the appropriate locations.

Cake factory

- Form teams.

- Complete the Standard Work documentation for the cake baking cell.

- Fill out the Standard Work Combination Sheet with the current and future states, generating ideas that will balance the operations and achieve a time no greater than 55 seconds (Takt time = 55 s).

Poka Yoke

Learning objectives

1. Understand the importance of implementing Error-Proofing (Poka-Yoke) mechanisms.
2. Learn the basic principles for implementing Poka-Yoke mechanisms.
3. Understand the classification of Poka-Yoke mechanisms.

Content

> Background
> What is Poka Yoke?
> Benefits
> Classification
> Procedure

Background

- In the 1960s, quality control was only about **inspection activities**.

- However, no matter how rigorous the inspections were, **Shigeo Shingo**, an industrial engineer and consultant for many companies, realized that the goal of having **zero defects** could not be met.

- After concluding that most defects are due to **human error**, he realized that the best way to ensure quality was to integrate simple mechanisms to detect errors before they became defects.

- Shingo called them "**Poka-Yoke** mechanisms" (mistake proofing).

The error

- Many things can go wrong in a work environment.

- Every day, there are opportunities to make mistakes which can result in defective products or services.

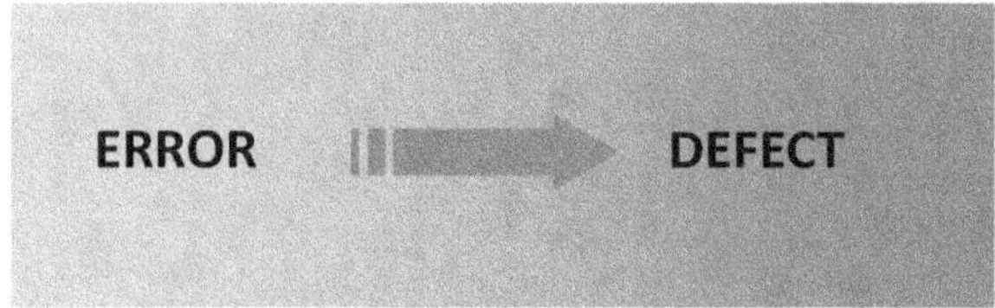

The key to success is **eliminating the error**.

There are two essential attitudes towards human error

Traditional thinking

Errors are inevitable!
We are humans!

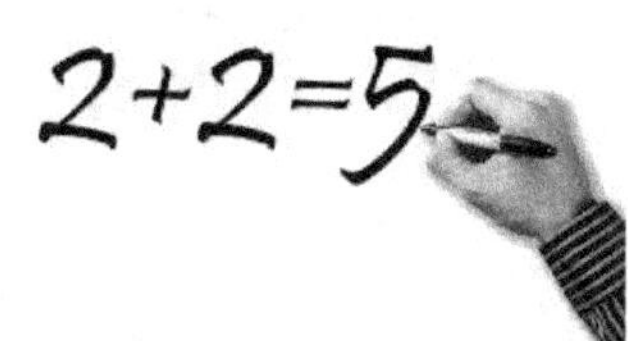

Lean thinking

Errors can be avoided!
If we develop a way to
eliminate the cause.

Source of defects

Materials	Manual Labor	Methods	Machines	Measurements	Environment
• Damaged • Incorrect • Out-of-specifications	• Improper training • Inadvertent errors • Mistakes • Negligence • Incorrect operation of equipment	• Incomplete • Lack of documentation • Obsolete • Incomprehensible or complex	• Improper maintenance • Incorrect adjustments • Inadequate changeovers • Dirt and contaminants affecting products • Inadequate installations	Improper calibration Incorrect Sampling	• Humidity • Excessive heat • Cold

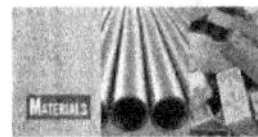

What is Poka Yoke?

Poka-Yoke is a mechanism that anticipates, prevents, and detects the error before it becomes a defect.

The term **Poka-Yoke** comes from Japanese:

"Poka" = inadvertent mistake   **"Yokeru"** = prevent

Basic principles

- Errors and defects can be avoided.

- We need to detect the error before it turns into a defect.

- The best tool to prevent a defect is the one that most effectively isolates the **source of the problem.**

Benefits

Some of the applications and benefits of implementing Poka-Yoke are that it:

- Eliminates or reduces the possibility of errors

- Prevents accidents caused by human distraction

- Eliminates actions that depend on memory and inspection

- Ensures quality at every workstation

- Is inexpensive to implement and simple to use

Example: Poka-Yoke and Andon

Poka-Yoke was born from *simplicity* and can be either really *inexpensive* and *simple* or very expensive and complex.

- Poka-yoke combined with Andon **to prevent train accidents.**

Level 1:
Only visual.

Level 1:
Visual and Audible.

Level 2:
Visual, audible and restrictive.

Level 3:
Mistake Proof.

Poka-Yoke effectiveness

A. Detects the defect after it has already occurred.

B. Detects the error as soon as it occurs and before it turns into a defect.

C. Eliminates or prevents human error before it occurs.

Classification

Richard Chase and Douglas Stewart have defined 4 basic types of Poka-Yoke:

1. Physical

2. Sequential

3. Counting and Grouping

4. Information

LSSI
LEAN SIX SIGMA INSTITUTE

1. Physical Poka-Yoke

A **physical Poka-Yoke** is intended to guarantee the characteristics of a **product** or **process**.

- **Product characteristics:** *Weight, dimensions, volume, depth, color, etc.*
    - A. Guide
    - B. Template
    - C. Scale
    - D. Gauge
- **Process characteristics:** *Temperature, time, torque, pressure, etc.*
    - E. Critical condition indicators
    - F. Sensors
    - G. Dispensers

A. Guide

Type of error: Orientation or positioning

- The shape of the device prevents it from being inserted incorrectly

Type of error: Space

B. Template

Type of error: Positioning, presence, absence, polarity, color, and alignment

C. Scale

Type of error: Quantity

- Process: Packaging of screws

- Problem: Some screws missing

- Solution: Weigh the screws

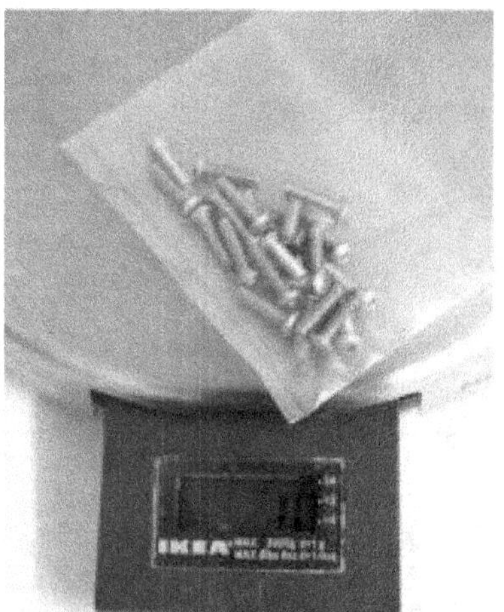

D. Gauge

Type of error: Dimensions

Product: Electric motor

Gauge helps to measure:
- Diameter
- Distance
- Depth
- Alignment
- Presence of holes

E. Critical conditions indicator

Typo of error: temperature, time, pressure, etc.

- Manometer
- Thermometer
- Etc.

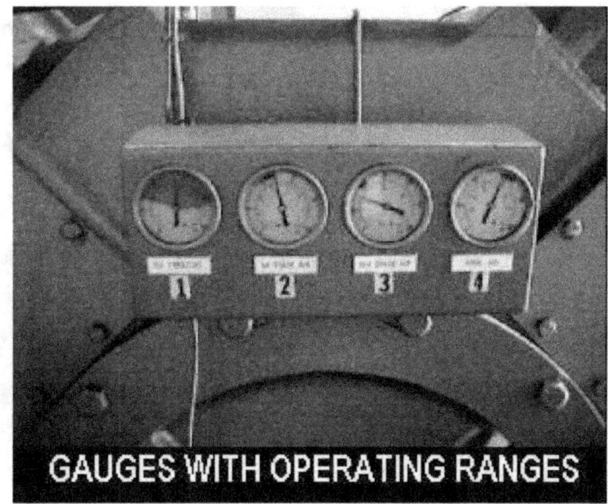

F. Sensor

Type of error: Incorrect positioning

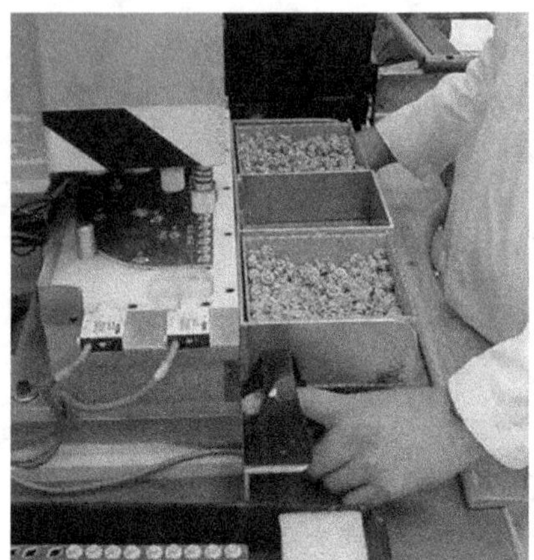

G. Dispenser

Type of error: Quantity and / or positioning

Example:
Chemical dispenser at a specific location and dispensing in just the right quantity

2. Sequential Poka-Yoke

- When order or sequence is important, any change or omission in the order can result in errors.

- Therefore, ways to restrict incorrect sequencing have been developed so that only a predetermined order is followed.

Sequence is frequently a key factor for packaging, preparation, assembly, and inspection.

Example of sequential Poka Yoke

Type of error: Incorrect sequence

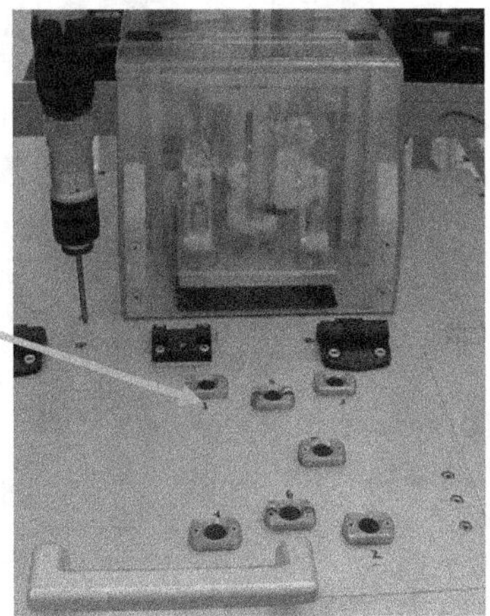

1. Open
2. Keep near by
3. Close

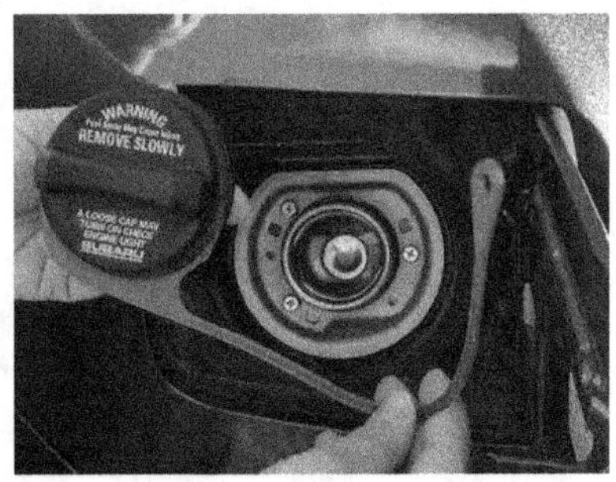

Numbering is provided to indicate the steps you should follow

Example of sequential Poka Yoke: Healthcare

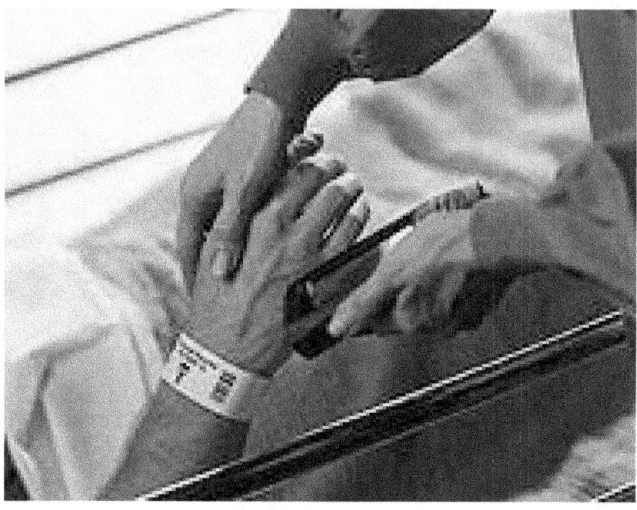

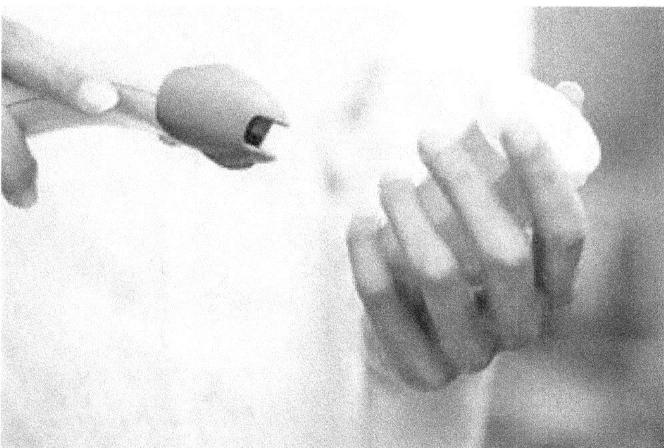

- The bracelet is scanned to ensure the correct patient.
- The medicine is scanned to ensure that it belongs to the right patient and it is given at the right time.

3. Counting and Grouping Poka-Yoke

A. ***Counting Poka-Yoke :*** A counter keeps track of parts, cycles, exits, etc., for a particular machine or operation. A counter can be mechanical or electrical and can be combined with machines or equipment such as sensors.

B. ***Grouping - kits:*** Is subdivided as follows:

- Kit

      Kit example

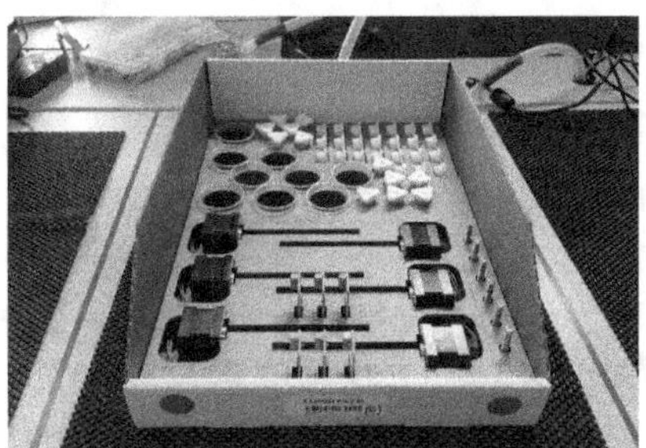

- Spare Parts

     Type of error : Missing items

     Nothing should be left behind when the fire officer leaves the station

4. Information Poka-Yoke

Alert method: Usually the device is a visible or audible alarm, or a combination of both, which notifies the person in charge that an error has occurred and there is a need to resolve the issue.

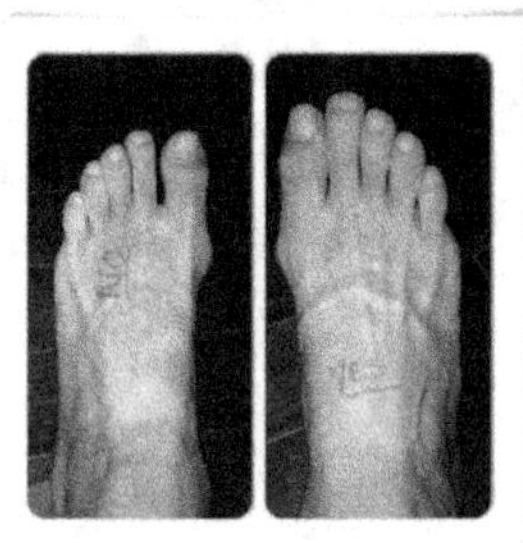

Example of information poka yoke

A simple mark is used to identify which foot should be operated on.

1. **Identify the stages of the process:** The step-by-step stages of each process are identified to know the sequence of operations.

2. **Identify the type of Poka-Yoke that can be used:** When we establish controls or mechanisms to test errors in the critical inputs of the processes, we are applying **preventive mechanisms**. When we establish controls for the outputs, we are applying **reactive mechanisms**.

3. **Characterize the inputs and outputs:** el objetivo es identificar las entradas y salidas de cada operación que puedan convertirse en fallos o errores.

Note: When defining the process for which the Poka-Yoke will be used, be sure to identify places where the risk of failure is high due to the severity of the process, level of occurrence, and degree of detection by the system. Use FMEA (Failure Mode and Effect Analysis) if possible.

Kata

Learning objectives

1. Understand the concepts of a powerful methodology to develop leaders.
2. How to use Toyota Kata to solve problems and improve specific situations in the workplace.

Content

> Background
> What is Kata?
> What is it for?
> Key elements
> Who participates?
> When is it used?
> Procedure
> How long does it take?
> Example: Toyota Kata

Imagine a management system that:

- Generates initiative among employees to adapt to changing business conditions.

- Keeps the organization moving (improving).

- Is easy for everyone to understand, even though Kata is different.

This is the goal of Toyota Kata.

Organizations typically have a sense of frustration due to the difference between expected and actual results.

Recurring problems

Most companies are led and operated by hardworking people who want their colleagues and organization to succeed.

Conclusion: The problem is not the people!

It is the Management System.

Definition of management

The systematic search of target conditions by using human capabilities in the most effective way.

Because we cannot predict the future,

an effective management system will make the organization able to adjust to:

- Unpredictable events
- Dynamic business conditions
- Changes in customer requirements

Toyota makes mistakes too

But no other company seems to adapt and improve every day as Toyota does.

Implementing Lean Company

does not mean there will be no problems, but that we will be able to solve them more quickly and effectively.

Kata is the way Toyota manages continuous improvement and adaptability to changing business conditions.

Research on Toyota Kata

2004 - 2009
Mike Rother

How to apply the management system in companies different from Toyota:
1. What are the invisible thinking and management routines behind Toyota's success in relation to its improvement and constant adaptation system?
2. How can other companies develop similar routines and thinking processes?

"If we study Toyota's management system long enough, a common thinking and acting pattern will emerge and become evident in every level within the company."

Mike Rother

Improvement based on waste reduction

Kata

What is Kata?

Katas are routine practices that help us adopt new ways of acting and thinking.

Kata

What is improvement Kata?

It is a pattern of scientific thought that is combined with **practical routines** which help us adopt **new ways of thinking and acting**.

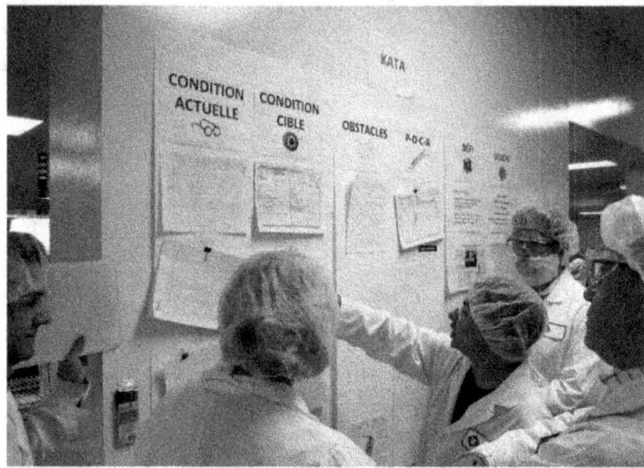

What is it for?

It helps us achieve the goal we seek in a process, without generating unfocused ideas, but with a focused model of improvements based on well-founded hypotheses, experiments, and frequent monitoring.

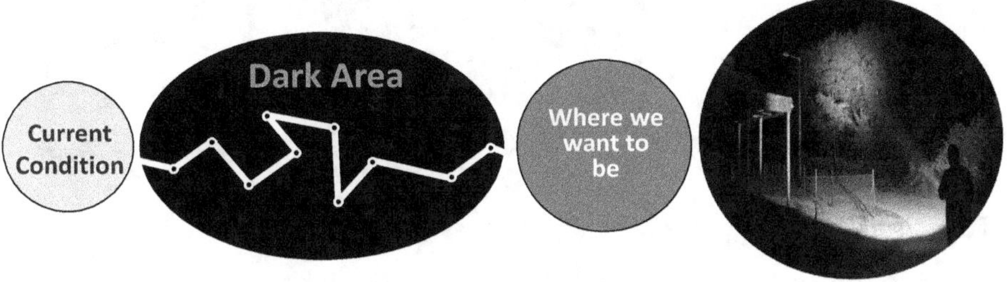

Principles

To develop new habits, you must practice new routines and experience the sense of progress once you have mastered them.

The following ingredients will help us re-wire our brains to acquire new skills and a new mentality.

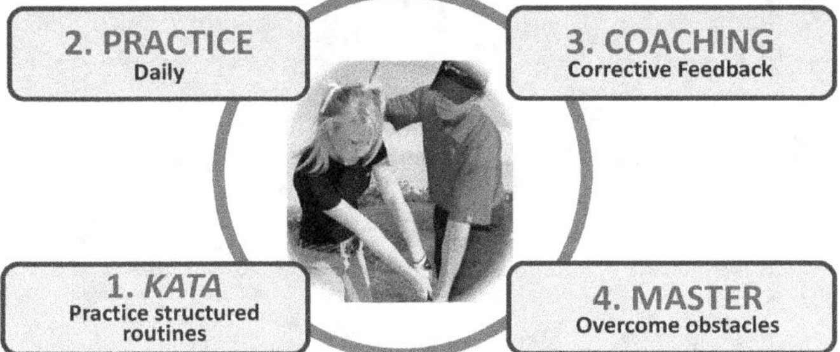

1. Kata: structured routines

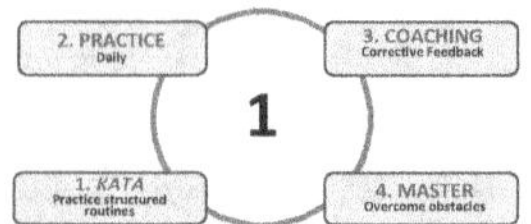

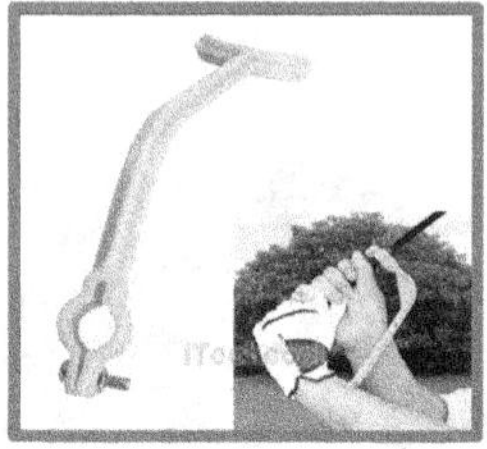

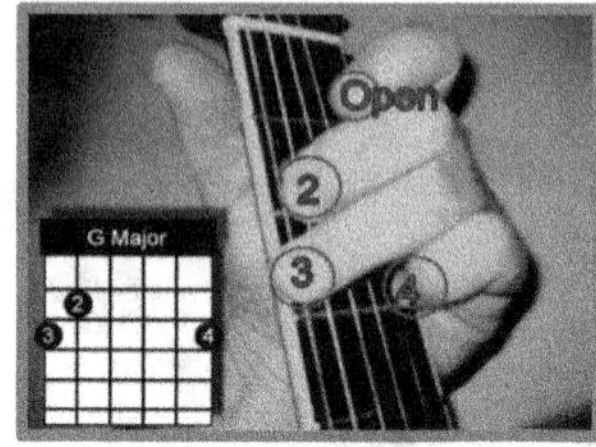

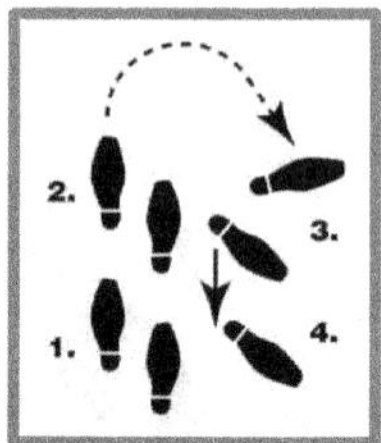

- The foundation to build a learning process.
- A way to transfer and develop skills and share a thinking method among the organization.

2. Daily practice

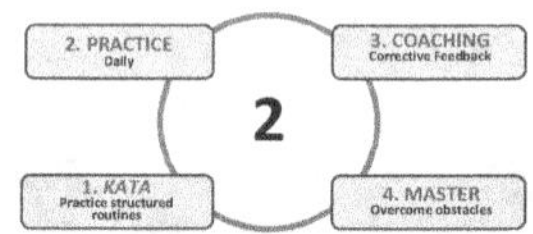

If we occasionally practice improvement events (Kaizen) – and the rest of the time it is "business as usual" - then, according to neuroscience, what we are really teaching is "the usual."

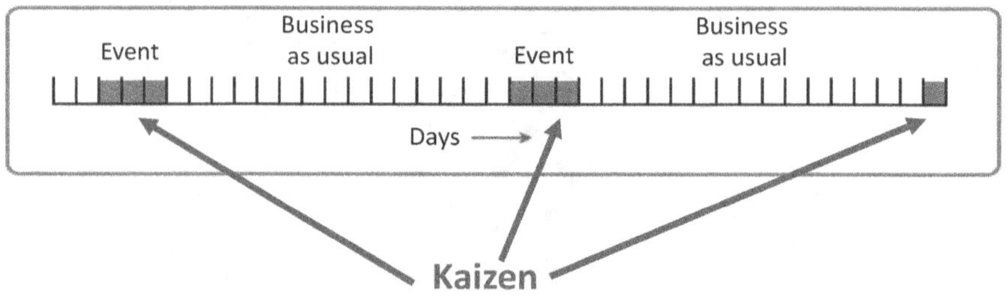

3. Coaching: corrective feedback

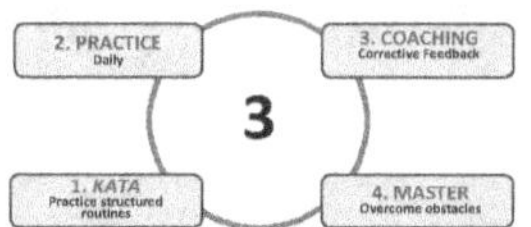

If we leave our trainees alone, they will practice existing habits.

The coach (manager) provides **corrective methods** to ensure the student practices the new routine in the right way.

The **coach's** job is not to provide solutions, but to develop and improve their **students' skills.**

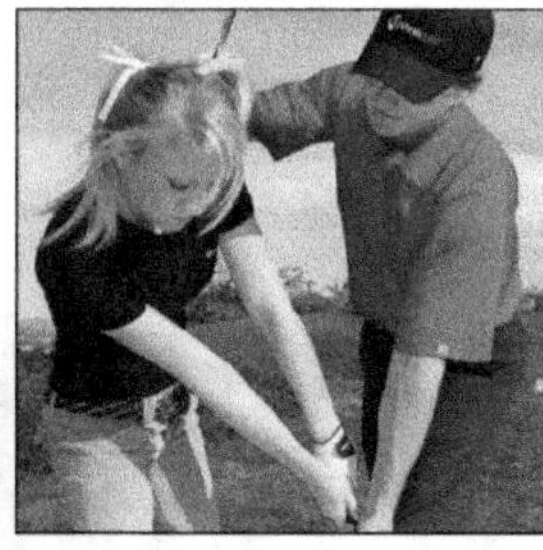

Kata training is a set of practice routines where leaders teach improvement methods (Kata) through **daily training cycles.**

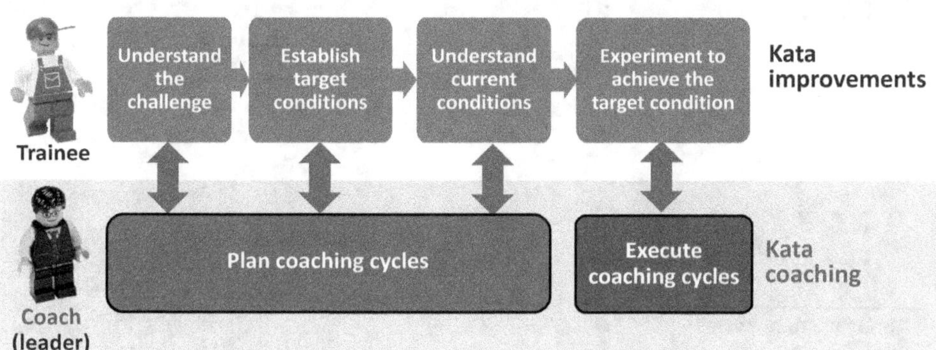

4. Master: overcome obstacles

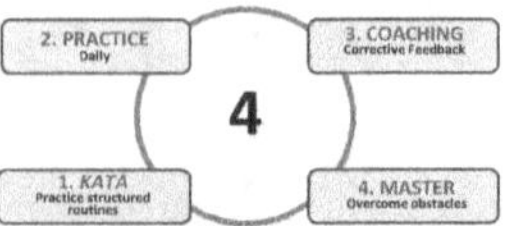

To learn new skills and a new mentality, the student must practice in a learning zone beyond their comfort zone to feel they are making progress.
This is a responsibility of the coach.

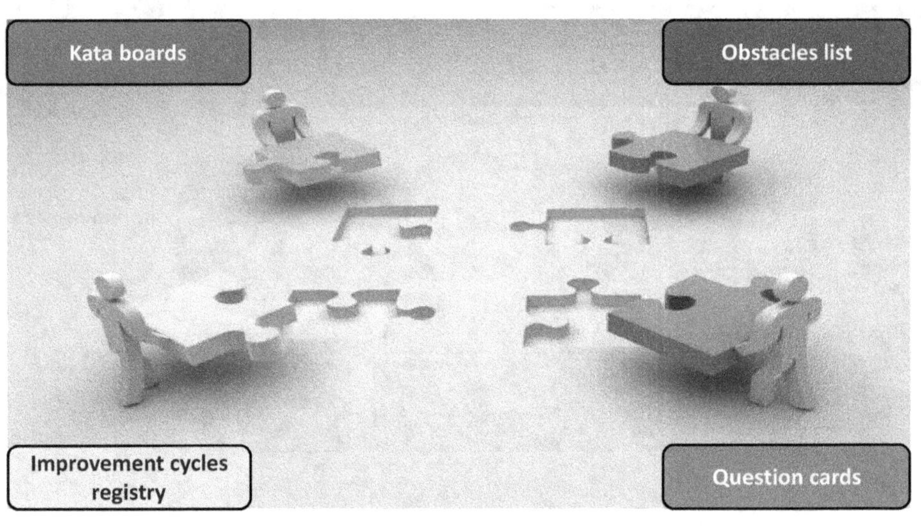

LSSI
LEAN SIX SIGMA INSTITUTE

Kata board (storyboard)

The **Kata board** should be located in the workplace.

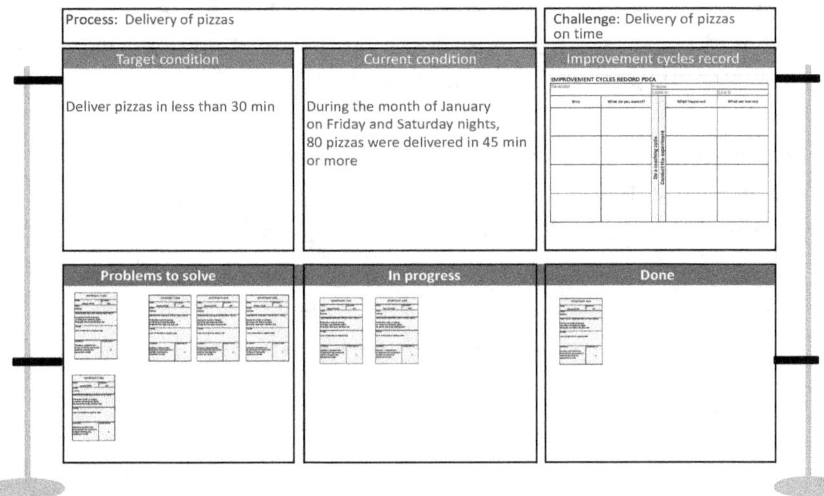

Question cards

- Kata is made by a sequence of questions and answers.
- Question cards contain the questions to be asked by the leader or coach.
- Usually the coach has authority over the learner.
- Cards can be carried along with a company nametag.

	The five questions
Coaching Kata	1. What is the **target condition**?
	2. What is the **Actual condition** now?
	3 What **obstacle** are preventing you from reaching the target condition? Which *one* are you addressing now?
	4 What is your **next step** (next experiment)? What do you expect?
	5. When can we see what we **have learned** from taking that step?
	* You'll often work on the same obstacle for several PDCA cycles.

List of obstacles

All the problems, opportunities, or obstacles that prevent reaching the target condition are listed, or at least the most important ones, using the opportunity cards seen in the White Belt training.

- Each problem (opportunity) is recorded on a card to make it visible and is shared with the team.
- Opportunity cards are placed on the *Kata boards*.

<table>
<tr><td colspan="2" align="center">OPPORTUNITY CARD</td></tr>
<tr><td>Date:

January-10-20</td><td>Number:

001</td></tr>
<tr><td colspan="2">Area:
Delivery</td></tr>
<tr><td colspan="2">Opportunity detected: (Muda, Muri, Mura)

During the month of January
on Friday and Saturday nights
80 pizzas have been delivered late</td></tr>
<tr><td colspan="2">Cause

Lack of standard to capture data</td></tr>
<tr><td>Solution

Develop a standard form to document the customer's address including the apartment number</td><td>Clasification

A</td></tr>
</table>

Classification
A = 1 – 5 days.
B = 1 – 2 weeks.
C = 1 – 2 months.

LSSI
LEAN SIX SIGMA INSTITUTE

Record of improvement cycles

Used by the student to document experiments (steps),
expectations, results, and what was learned.

IMPROVEMENT CYCLES REDORD PDCA (every line = one experiment)

Obstacle:		Process:	
		Learner:	Coach:
Step	**What do you expect?**	**What happened**	**What we learned**

Do a coaching cycle / Conduct the experiment

Card and improvement record

The 5 questions card and the improvement record
are used together in every Kata.

Coaching Kata — The five questions

1. What is the **target condition**?
2. What is the **Actual condition** now?
3. What **obstacle** are preventing you from reaching the target condition?
   Which *one* are you addressing now?
4. What is your **next step** (next experiment)? What do you expect?
5. When can we see what we **have learned** from taking that step?

* You'll often work on the same obstacle for several PDCA cycles.

Coach

IMPROVEMENT CYCLES REDORD PDCA (every line = one experiment)

Obstacle:		Process:	
		Learner:	Coach:
Step	What do you expect?	What happened	What we learned

Do a coaching cycle / Conduct the experiment

Student

Who participates?

All leaders at all levels perform **Katas** with their collaborators.

When is it used?

Every time we need to achieve an objective in terms of:

- Quality
- Sales
- Safety
- Delivery
- Inventory
- Cost
- Etc.

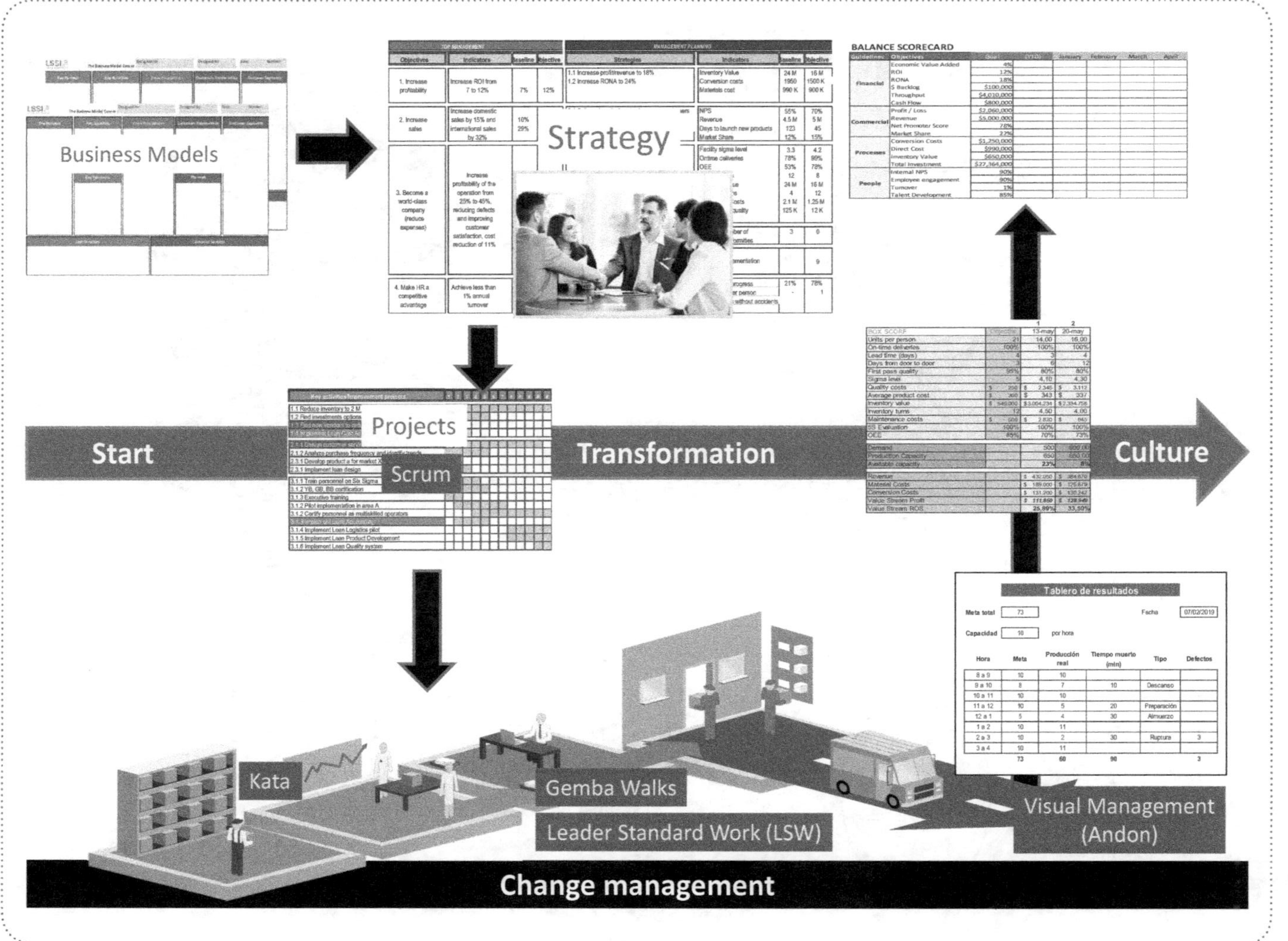

Business Models
Strategy
BALANCE SCORECARD
Start
Projects
Scrum
Transformation
Culture
Kata
Gemba Walks
Leader Standard Work (LSW)
Visual Management (Andon)
Change management
Tablero de resultados

Improvement Kata

Practice the scientific method to achieve improvements.

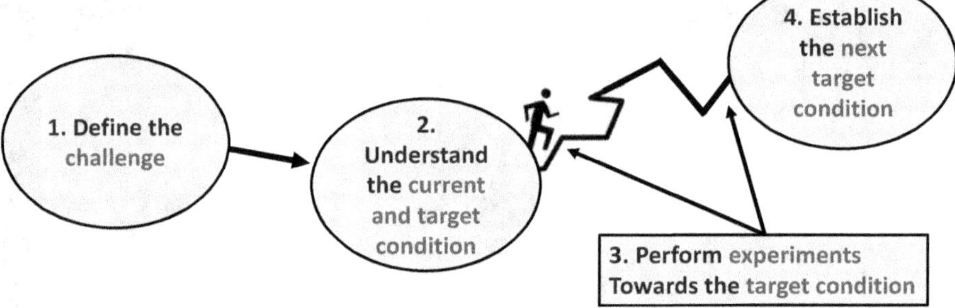

How long does it take?

- Average Kata = **10 - 15 minutes.**

- It is a simple process, but the fact of doing it continuously **solves big problems**, in **small amounts of time.**

LSSI
LEAN SIX SIGMA INSTITUTE

COACH	**TRAINEE**
• Good morning, Peter! Nice to see you. How are you?	• Good morning, John.. I'm doing well.
• I'm very interested in the **challenge** that you and your team have in the electrical components production process.	• The challenge we face in our value stream is to **increase our production capacity.**

Kata coaching example

1
- What is the target condition?
  - Increase our production capacity per shift to **600 pieces** with the current staff.

2
- What is the current condition?
  - Our current production capacity per shift is **500 pieces.**

- When do you plan on reaching it?
  - By the end of year, which means **4 months** from today.

3
- What obstacles are preventing you from reaching the target condition?
  - We have identified 4 main obstacles:
    - Material deliveries come in lots.
    - Production stops due to a lack of materials (purchasing or incoming inspection).
    - Occasional high defect rates.
    - No cross training.

- Which obstacle are you addressing now?
  - **Production stops** due to a lack of materials (purchasing or incoming inspection).

4
- What is your next step? (Experiment) and
- What do you expect?
  - To assign people dedicated to receiving materials only.
  - To find out in what we need to focus on in order to improve.

5
- What happened?
  - They don't have a sampling plan.
  - They don't know how to do sampling.
- What did you learn?
  - We learned that receiving inspectors need additional information and training.

4
- What is your next step? (Experiment) and
  - Learn about sampling.
- What do you expect?
  - Develop an optimal sampling plan.

Process: Electronic components		Challenge: Increase capacity

Target condition	Current condition	Improvement cycles record
600 pieces per shift with the current staff by the end of year (4 months).	500 pieces per shift with the current staff.	

Problems to solve	In progress	Done

PDCA CYCLES RECORD

Obstacle:			Process:	
			Learner:	Coach:
Step	**What do you expect?**	Do a coaching cycle / Conduct the experiment	**What happened**	**What we learned**
Assign people solely dedicated to receiving Materials.	To find out what we need to focus on to improve.		They don't have a sampling plan and they don't know how to interpret sampling Levels.	Receiving inspectors need additional information and Training.
Study the information and develop a sampling plan.	Learn about sampling needs and develop an optimal sampling plan.			

Conclusions

Leaders are teachers.

> With everyday words and actions, leaders teach their staff about the proper mentality and focus, which has a significant effect on creating problem solving capacity and culture.

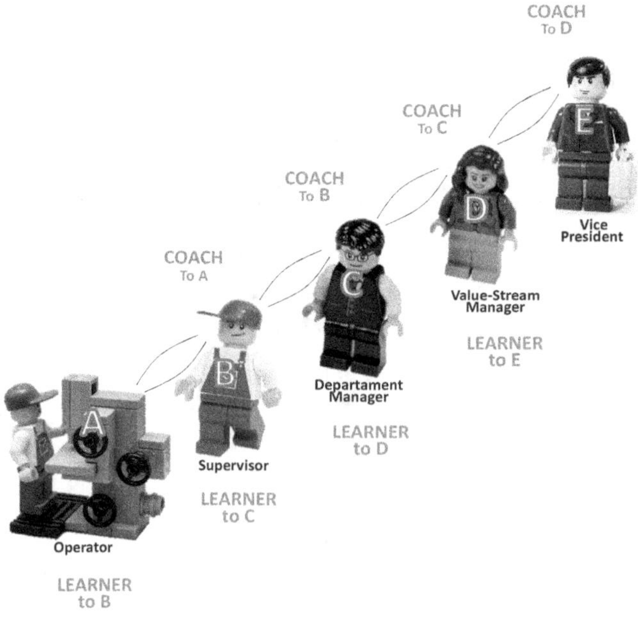

**Sales and operations
planning.
S&OP in 14 steps**
Cristina Peña Andrés

**Lean Manufacturing.
Step by step**
Luis Socconini

**Practical guide to the
Incoterms 2020 rules**
David Soler

**Shipping & Commercial
Case Law**
Albert Badia

Lean Six Sigma.
Management System
for Leaders
Luis Socconini, Carlo Reato

Lean Services.
Certification Manual
Luis Socconini

Lean Six Sigma Yellow Belt.
Certification Manual
Luis Socconini

Lean Six Sigma Green Belt.
Certification Manual
Luis Socconini

València, 558 – 08026 Barcelona – Tel. +34-931 429 486 – marge@margebooks.com – www.margebooks.com